PRAISE FOR
HOW TO TRAIN YOUR DOG
WITH LOVE + SCIENCE

"This is the perfect book for people who want to learn positive dog training methods. The science is explained in an easy-to-understand way."

—Temple Grandin, *New York Times* bestselling author of *Animals Make Us Human*

"From Darwin to Pavlov and beyond, this is the best dog training book I've ever read—in fact, if I wrote a dog training book, I'd want it to be this one."

—Seth Godin, *New York Times* bestselling author of *This Is Marketing* and *Purple Cow*

"Using the latest science and wonderful stories, Annie Grossman shows us how to allow dogs to express as much of their dogness as possible and have satisfying dog-appropriate lives without forcing them to do things they'd rather not do. When dogs feel safe and trust us, it's a win-win for all—what could be better?"

—Marc Bekoff, Ph.D., author of *Dogs Demystified* and *The Emotional Lives of Animals*

"Annie and School For The Dogs taught my dogs, but mostly taught me. The school is really School For The Dogs And The People Who Love Them, and it is always the most cheerful place to go. Annie is an astonishingly good trainer who leads with compassion, and this book breaks down how that compassion and understanding unlocks behavior modification. You see dogs and people in sync, learning. You can palpably feel the love and see the physical results. If dogs play a significant role in your life, you need this book."

—Maureen Johnson, #1 *New York Times* bestselling author, human companion of School For The Dogs alumna Zelda and Dexy

"Both entertaining and educational, Annie Grossman's *How to Train Your Dog with Love + Science* rises to the top of the pack as an extremely well-written dog training book based on the science of operant conditioning. Full of fascinating stories about the scientists who were behavioral giants, Grossman's book covers sound dog training practices, and she's not afraid to call out misguided notions and methods. *How to Train Your Dog with Love + Science* is here to make the world a better place for dogs and their people."

—Mary R. Burch, PhD, author of *How Dogs Learn*

"Every rescue and shelter should be giving away copies of this book. The easy-to-consume information about the science of learning is combined with relatable and interesting examples from Annie's own experience living with dogs. It's a dog training book, yes, but it is also a book that shines a light on the evolution of our own consciousness and how it reinvents the world we live in—a world where our success and strength are rooted in our compassion and our knowledge."

—Debbie Jacobs, CPDT-KA, RBT, author of *A Guide to Living With & Training a Fearful Dog* and *Does My Dog Need Prozac?*

"Dog training has undergone significant changes in the recent past. After many decades of resistance, a large part of the training community has learned about and has accepted the long-established scientific principles of learning as well as the training techniques based on them. This happened in the interest of dog welfare and the human-dog relationship.

However, outdated and often cruel techniques still have their defenders and are made popular by 'experts' in books and especially on television. Fortunately, there are knowledgeable and eloquent authors like Annie Grossman, who can explain the science and effective, humane procedures understandably and convincingly to any dog lover. This is a very worthwhile read for anybody having to do with dogs."

—Andrew Luescher, DVM, PhD, DACVB, Prof. emeritus, Purdue University, Department of Veterinary Clinical Sciences

"A thrilling read! I love the way Annie addresses her readers with straight-talk: delivering practical, no-nonsense information in a way that everyone can understand and use. There is a humor and a realness in her writing that I interpret as coming from her many years of running School For The Dogs in a place like New York City. This book will hold a unique place in my library."

—Ken Ramirez, Executive VP Karen Pryor Clicker Training, author of *The Eye of The Trainer: Animal Training, Transformation, and Trust*

"In this fun and fascinating book, Annie Grossman unpacks the mysteries of dog training in a loving, compassionate approach that will leave you and your dog with bounces in your steps and smiles on your faces."

—Clive Wynne, PhD, director of Arizona State University's Canine Science Collaboratory, author of *Dog is Love: Why and How Your Dog Loves You and Do Animals Think?*

"This book takes its people—dogs and humans—into worlds of deep connection and wise education with each other. Love and Science, indeed. Use this book!"

—Donna Haraway, author of *The Companion Species Manifesto* and *When Species Meet*

"An entertaining and down-to-earth, easy-to-follow explanation of the science of behavior change and how we can harness this knowledge to make dog training effective and kind. This is a very useful book with lessons you can do at home! If you have been seduced by celebrity dog trainers on TV, you need to read this book. In fact, Cesar Millan should read this book."

—Lili Chin, author of *Doggie Language: A Dog Lover's Guide to Understanding Your Best Friend*

"I've brought my dogs to more classes and individual trainers than I can count. They became AKC Canine Good Citizens, but one in particular, who was quite fearful, tended to struggle. The usual lessons didn't always compute for her. It sometimes took us quite a few trainers to find one who could help me understand the world from that dog's point of view, so we could succeed. Author Annie Grossman sounds exactly like those standout trainers in her book *How to Train Your Dog with Love + Science*. Many of her suggestions are things that I paid a pretty penny to learn from top trainers. I'll be keeping my copy handy for when the next puppy comes along, for sure. "

—Kim Kavin, author of *Little Boy Blue* and *The Dog Merchants*

"In *How to Train Your Dog with Love + Science*, the guardian wins and the dog wins. Just as in the title, in real life there need be no dichotomy, no conflict. It turns out that positive reinforcement makes for a joyful bond as well as successful training. This book is a gem."

—Eileen Anderson, MM, MS, blogger at eileenanddogs.com and author of *Remember Me? Loving and Caring for a Dog with Canine Cognitive Dysfunction*

"What makes this book particularly invaluable is its foundation in the latest scientific research, presented in a manner that is both accessible and engaging. Grossman demystifies the science of behavior and learning, offering practical advice that empowers dog owners to apply these insights in a loving, effective manner. This is crucial, as it bridges the gap between academic research and everyday practice, making the science of animal behavior accessible to all."

—Katherine Compitus, DSW, LCSW-R, C-AAIS, NYU assistant professor and author of *The Human-Animal Bond in Clinical Social Work Practice* and *Animal House: A Clinician's Guide to Animal Hoarding*

"Annie Grossman doesn't just teach us how to train our dogs; she brings us into her world with personal stories that touch the heart and illuminate the mind. She leads us on a three-part journey, starting with our historical mistakes in dog training, then covering foundational theories guiding modern methods, and concluding with specific instructions for at-home training. This book should be on the reading list of every new pet guardian. Both dogs and their people will benefit tremendously from it."

—Andre Yeu, CPDT-KA, KPA CTP, Founder of When Hounds Fly and Karen Pryor Academy Faculty

"Brave and bold, humbling and transparent, critical yet empowering enlightenment on the science of animal behavior—all this and more, packed in this book by The School for the Dogs' Annie Grossman. Annie contends we all are responsible as stewards of dogs to learn the best we can about dog training/teaching, and it is imperative we realize there is the science of behavior to use as guideposts. We should forgive ourselves for our transgressions from what we thought was the right way to do things, open ourselves to the science and the LOVE of positive training, and give our dogs this gift. Annie has knocked it out of the park."

—Cherrie Mahon, owner of River Valley Doodles, Professor, Rochester Institute of Technology

"Combining concise guidance with evidence-based methods, *How to Train Your Dog with Love + Science* offers a comprehensive approach to positive reinforcement training. This book not only delves into the evolution of dog training but also provides practical instructions, empowering readers to deepen their understanding of canine behavior while cultivating a strong bond with their dogs."

—Bradley Phifer, CPDT-KSA, Executive Director, Certification Council for Professional Dog Trainers

"How to Train Your Dog With Love + Science is one of the most refreshing books on dog behavior and training that I have read in a long time. Annie has a talent for weaving stories of her journey in with practical, easily digestible information about how to train your dog in the most loving way using the most up-to-date humane methods. Her clever analogies help the reader understand things from a dog's perspective. It may seem funny to say about a dog training book, and I am admittedly a dog training nerd, but you will not want to put it down. I want to get this book for every person I know who has a dog! This is a must read for anyone who has a dog, knows someone with a dog, or is thinking of bringing a dog into their family."

—Jenni Pfafman, KPA CTP, CPDT-KA, CSAT, CBATI-KSA, owner of Elevated Dog Training

"Walk away from power struggles and fall more in love with your dog with renowned dog trainer Annie Grossman's *How to Train Your Dog with Love + Science*. This engaging guide debunks dangerous myths, explores the history of dog training, and details practical strategies you can start today. Strengthen your bond with your furry friend through understanding, kindness, and positive reinforcement. Read this book. Learn something new. Try it at home. Transform your relationship with your dog. Change the world, one wag at a time!"

—Dr. E'Lise Christensen, DVM, DACVB,
chief medical officer of Behavior Vets

"I have referred patients to Annie for many years. Her methods are so simple that a five-year-old can train her fearful rescue dog and her parents can glean the value of positive reinforcement in parenting both dog and child. Annie's book teaches us to raise a happy dog with kindness and love. Her systematic study of animal training and human behavior analysis has informed her principles of conduct that reject unkindness and fear. Not all my patients have dogs, but I will refer this book even to those who don't, as it's essentially a manual for how to be a good parent."

—Dr. Barbara Landreth, pediatrician

"I was lucky enough to enroll my pup at The School for the Dogs under Annie Grossman's tutelage and learned so much. This is THE book for every dog owner: a thorough and friendly manual that will help you and your dog thrive in any setting, with empathy and confidence. Like a good dog, it's got your back."

—Cathy Erway, author of *The Food of Taiwan* and *The Art of Eating In*, human belonging to SFTD alum Doug

How to TRAIN YOUR DOG With LOVE + SCIENCE

How to TRAIN YOUR DOG With LOVE + SCIENCE

A DOG LOVER'S GUIDE
to Animal Behavior and
Positive Reinforcement Training

ANNIE GROSSMAN

sourcebooks

Published by Sourcebooks
P.O. Box 4410, Naperville, Illinois 60567-4410
(630) 961-3900
sourcebooks.com

Cataloging-in-Publication Data is on file with the Library of Congress.

Printed and bound in the United States of America.
KP 10 9 8 7 6 5 4 3 2 1

For my dad, and Amos

CONTENTS

PART FOUR: GOOD GOING FORWARD

Eat Your Homework

"I think at some level of my teenage consciousness I truly believed that the whole point of going to school was to learn how to focus attention on subject matter that was of no consequence to me."

—JOHN CLEESE

WHEN I WAS growing up, school was the last place I ever wanted to be. My education started out okay, but everything kind of devolved once I entered classrooms where there were no finger paints.

The intended missions were accomplished: I learned to read, write, and do some math. I can tell you a handful of things about history, although which of those things I learned in class and which I learned from listening to the *Hamilton* soundtrack is something I cannot say.

School never felt like a place where I was choosing to be. There was so much being told what to do. I complained endlessly to my parents, but they too were being controlled by the threat of punishment in the form of truancy laws. I remember my dad patting me on the back as he dropped me off one morning. "You only have to get through eleven more years," he said.

For years, I slouched through an educational system whose

parameters were carefully constructed to prescribe certain behaviors and hinder others. There was literally a guard at the door making sure I stayed in the building. As I matured, my behavior was molded by a growing knowledge of consequences.

Even when I succeeded, I often felt the sting of failure. The world around me seemed to shine the brightest lights on exception and talent, not on okay-ness. You could get more than half the answers right on a test and it'd still be considered a fail. If I had difficulty understanding a concept or expressing something in the right way, I considered myself at fault. I was lacking something. I tried to not cause trouble, since I feared the consequences of veering off the narrow path I seemed to be allowed to walk. (In discussing this once with a friend, she told me that her mother often warned her that poor behavior would result in "consequences." She thought "consequences" was an illness.)

What did I think the "consequences" were going to be if I didn't do well at school? I had cartoonlike ideas of cascading disasters that would result. I was stressed out about my future. And I wasn't even old enough to cross the street alone.

Socializing at school was not always easy either. When other kids weren't particularly nice, or anyone was socially uncomfortable for any reason, there was the mandate that we all needed to learn to "work it out." It was as if school were a microcosm of what the adult world was going to hand us. Like, in the class seating chart of life, you may find yourself perpetually next to the school bully, and you're going to have to learn to deal. There's no easy way out, kid!

In the pie chart of my youth, school and homework took up a Pac-Man–shaped portion of time. The rest of the time, I was too exhausted to do much of anything at all. I napped a lot. I was put on medication.

This is life, I thought. I would grow up and be spit out into some expanded version of this—nothing to look forward to. Each September, I counted the months until I would be out of school and swore I'd never be a teacher. *How cruel*, I thought, *to have to be in school forever!*

Well, I didn't become a teacher. I started my own school. And every day, I'm thrilled to go to work.

At my school, public displays of affection are not discouraged. In fact, a lot of the teachers and the students are actually in love with each other. There are no grades, no arguments, and no aging out of nap time. Recesses are sprinkled throughout the day, and if there's a social interaction that isn't ideal, future meetings of those individuals will not be forced. At my school, success is a moving target—it moves closer when necessary, to ensure a certain amount of success whenever possible. If a student gets something wrong, we ask ourselves how we can be better teachers. Also: The students love the food. In fact, we let them eat their homework.

WELCOME TO SCHOOL FOR THE DOGS.

Aliens Among Us

"If you see two life forms, one of them's making a poop, the other one's carrying it for him, who would you assume was in charge?"

—JERRY SEINFELD

IF YOU LOVE your dog, there's a good chance you're confused.

Both of you.

You're not confused about your love for each other, to be sure. But have you ever considered what a strange relationship you're in?

As modern dog owners, we are asking our Yorkipoos to live in a world they didn't choose—a world that isn't so simple. We bring these well-intentioned creatures into our homes and often don't do them the favor of explaining how arbitrary rules can be or what our expectations are. We expect dogs to be polite and compliant, despite not knowing our language; calm, confident, and collected, although they're a fraction of our size and easily stepped on. Food should only be eaten if it's on the floor in a bowl, but not if it's on the floor and it's not in a bowl. And not from a bowl if the bowl is on the counter. Don't chew a slipper, unless it's a chew toy that happens to be in the exact shape of a slipper.

It's okay to pee on the Astroturf at the dog park but not on the door-mat that feels nearly identical under one's paws. It's almost like dogs are alien visitors trying to figure it all out. Except that they didn't choose to be here, and there is no UFO waiting to take them back home.

Things aren't so easy for you either! The consensus about how to teach a dog to be the companion you want is… There is no consensus. Dog training is a largely unregulated industry, and misinformation is rampant. No wonder so many people *and* dogs are confused. Should there be an even balance of carrot and stick? Must you be a domineering "alpha"? If so, what does that even mean? Will you spoil a dog by giving treats? What about sleeping on the bed? Should you feed your dog raw beef out of your hand or serve kibble in a crate?

People do their best to figure it out, and that's fine, right? Most of the time, perhaps. But some of the time—I would say too often—dogs trained with baseless theories and crude techniques will end up stressed, which can end up stressing out their people. This can result in ruined relationships, maimed people, and euthanized dogs.

We're All Animals

We humans may think of ourselves as a reasonable bunch, but we sure do nutty things when it comes to dogs. I grew up surrounded by smart, gentle people who seemed to know things about dogs. I didn't doubt them. They were adults, after all. My parents would whack our dogs on the nose with two fingers when they were "bad." My uncle, the first person I ever saw let a dog lick him all over his mouth, recently greeted my dog by getting down on all fours. He then attempted to feed her a treat from his mouth. Somehow, dogs put up with us. And even forgive us. Hey, our intentions are good! They keep coming back to us. But that might be only because we don't let them have the car keys.

Here's the good news: You may be confused, but you know more than you think you do about dogs and dog training. When you begin to piece together the basics of the science that informs what we know about animal behavior, you can often take a shortcut by considering how *you* behave in the world. Don't forget, you are an animal too.

Dogs (and their people) are everywhere and always learning, not just at dog school and not just when they're young. Be it accidentally or intentionally, we are learning how to exist in the environment we're in all the time. Truly, the whole world is our school. You can't escape—conditioning—aka learning. When we start seeing how learning happens, we can try to set up our dogs for success in any environment and make learning so enjoyable for them (and us) that they (and we) will keep coming back. With this book, you can become your dog's favorite teacher. Your world—wherever you are—will be your classroom, and your dog will be your favorite student. Spoiler alert: You can get to that halcyon homeroom without attempting to tap into some mysterious internal power or asserting your will.

You're about to learn how the science behind learning has evolved over the last century, paving the way to make it possible to train without punishment and coercion. We have developed technologies of behavioral science to help learners learn effectively with little to no error—to keep them happy and engaged. School could be a place not just for filling minds with information but also for keeping the learners happy.

In the decade and change since Kate Senisi and I founded School For The Dogs, a two-story storefront in Manhattan's East Village, we have worked with some ten thousand dog owners locally and around the world virtually. We specialize in helping dogs who have behavior issues stemming from the stresses and confines of urban living. We have worked with countless breeds at every stage of their lives. In addition to teaching clients privately—in their homes, online, and at our school—we also offer a variety of group classes, from Puppy Kindergarten, which focuses on socialization and teaching basic behaviors, to Sidewalk Psychos, which helps dogs learn to coexist on leash with other dogs in close proximity.

It's a neat place. When I work the front desk, I see an awesome thing that happens all the time: The dog students play what I call "reverse-hooky," standing at our front door, begging to come in even when we are closed. At the end of the school day, they often try to stay, their owners sometimes having to literally scoop them up and carry them out.

Our goal with School For The Dogs was to create a good school in that we would offer good dog training for people who want their dogs to be good. As in, *Who's a good boy?!* Often, we say that rhetorically—we are talking to a dog, after all—but it's a really good question: What do we mean by *good*? What is good training, and what is a good dog?

Good Dog

"No Bad Dogs!" is a popular refrain among some dog trainers. I agree there are no bad dogs. But I'm also not sure there are "good" ones.

"Good" is a label whose definition may be one thing to one person and another to someone else. It also is going to change based on context. A dog's behavior seems good or bad according to our human expectations about what we think the dog should or shouldn't do in a given environment, in a given situation. Humans have wanted dogs to chase and round up livestock, flush game from bushes or dispatch rats from ships, bark to alarm us of trespassers, attack strangers, pull sleds, and so on. We bred them for these tendencies and called them good dogs! Today, my clients often want their dogs to do the opposite or very different things.

They want them not to chase things, or pull, or bark every time the guy in unit 17A takes out his trash. We want them to relax with us on the couch at night even if they haven't been outside all day pulling sleds or herding sheep.

Dogs can get into trouble for behavior that may be praised under different circumstances.

Not only are many of our modern human expectations unnatural for dogs, but we also make their lives even more confusing by shifting our expectations in different situations. I once heard one of my training idols, Kathy Sdao, imagine aloud that a dog's daily life must be like when you're going through airport security and you get reprimanded for holding up the line because you're untying your shoes, which is what you thought you were supposed to do, but today they're not doing that. And the TSA guy is looking at you like you're trying to cause a problem when really you're just trying to do the right thing and have it be done with. No one is applauding good intentions in a crazy, ever-shifting environment.

Often, when our dogs don't do what we want, it's easier to blame the dog than it is to change the setting or our expectations. It's easier, but it's often not conducive to behavior change. If we want to free ourselves from this fruitless blame game, we can start to reframe how we think about behaviors we don't like. Much "bad" dog behavior is, in a different light, a dog being really good at being a dog. Their behavior may only be a problem because the human world is an unnatural environment for them—no more so than in a noisy, crowded, paved, car-swarming, leash-requiring city. We can get away from labels by focusing on how we can be better at effectively getting dogs to willingly engage in behaviors we want. We can also build our ability to better understand them when they're letting us know about their needs. I wrote this book to help you start to better teach your dog, "read" your dog, think about what behaviors you want from your dog, and then get those behaviors to happen more often.

There are countless things any person might want their dog to be or do, but in the broadest sense, there is one single thing that I think makes a dog "good": you.

Now, that doesn't mean that your dog is "good" because you are. In chapter 2, you'll see why I do not adhere to the common school of thought that our dogs' issues are simply a reflection of our issues. I don't think they're little blank slates either. But I do think we can help them be as "good" as they can be in the world we're asking them to live in by working to be good guardians of them. We can do this by:

+ Working to understand how to encourage behaviors we want without using force or coercion
+ Assessing what behaviors we can teach that will help them live as comfortably and healthfully as possible in the human realm
+ Learning how they communicate when they are uncomfortable before they feel the need to flee or become aggressive

✦ Creating learning environments that give them parameters within which they're bound to succeed

✦ Approaching training as a game where both sides feel like they are winning

I believe that anyone who is looking to help their dog—whether they're trying to start out right with a new puppy or are facing some challenges with a dog that's already in the home—has good intentions. They're good *humans*, if you will. I'm lucky to have been able to steer so many of these kinds of humans toward a way of seeing their dogs, communicating with them cooperatively, and learning about the science of behavior on the way. I bet you are one of these good humans—good humans who don't just have *good* dogs. They have the *best* ones. I mean, isn't yours the best?

Good Dog Training

The work we do at School For The Dogs can truly be transformational for the humans as well as their dogs. When I first got into dog training, I wasn't shopping around for a shift in worldview. I didn't think it would lead me to discussions with ex-cons about using dog training to help people see how it's possible to get out of the loop of using punishment or with the Libertarian candidate for president on how operant conditioning works. I didn't think I'd have long conversations with people about "types" of dog training or what they were called.

What I now like to simply refer to as "good dog training" goes by many names, among them: science-based training, reward-based training, force-free training, and clicker training. Like many trainers, I use a small plastic box that makes a click-clunk sound, but you can "clicker train" without a clicker. I do it all the time.

Clicker training is a technique for what is frequently called "positive reinforcement training." I refer to myself as a "positive reinforcement trainer" as shorthand, but I think there are problems with this label. Positive reinforcement is at work all around us all the time. Anyone who attempts to train a dog is sometimes going to use positive reinforcement, on purpose or by accident.

Another problem I see with the "positive reinforcement" label is that it's easy to misinterpret the "positive" as having something to do with being smiley and nicey-nice. In fact, these qualities are not essential to a good dog trainer, and the "positive" in this context just refers to a consequence in the form of something added to the equation, as when we add peanut butter to a dog's mouth following a good behavior to increase the likelihood that a dog will do that behavior again. Positive reinforcement should also not be confused with "positive thinking"—thinking good thoughts about your dog may or may not solve your problems.

I have certainly called myself a "reward-based trainer" at times, but I worry it implies that we humans are just goody dispensers, when there's so much more to it than that.

I tend to like the term "science-based," because today's trainers are using and developing technologies that employ what we understand about science to develop ways of teaching and understanding the animals we are setting out to train. We're also, ideally, staying on top of the latest research and scholarship to inform our training. However, you could train using painful techniques, and that would be operating in the realm of science as well. There's plenty of evidence that animals learn from pain, but I think there's a lot of compelling evidence that it's smarter to avoid it—especially when avoiding it means you can stop having to do ethical gymnastics in order to justify cattle-prodding your best friend.

So, I've taken to just calling it "good" dog training. It's "good" in multidimensions. It's "good" in that it works, "good" in that it is kind, and also "good" in that both people and dogs tend to like doing it.

While its principles are timeless, good dog training is also new in the sense that it isn't what most people think of when they think of dog training. Good dog training doesn't require you to project a certain kind of energy or change your personality to be more alpha and become the leader of a pack. On the other hand, good dog training is more than teaching specific behaviors and practicing those behaviors over and over, more than using a specific handling technique. So much more. At School For The Dogs, we don't just teach dogs good behaviors and neat tricks; we help our human students learn to communicate with their dogs and in the process sometimes see the world anew.

Good dog training builds confidence, letting dogs make choices that are informed, rather than doing things because they're guessing. Don't we all feel better when we make choices based on knowledge? Lack of good communication on our end has helped dogs become a species that's good at hedging their bets. A well-educated dog is better at figuring us out—better at guessing right. And a well-educated dog *wants* to be in school, wherever in the world school is.

In the coming pages, my goal is to do four things. First, I want to talk about the recent history of dog training and help you start to reframe what the term even means. I'll walk you through my personal journey, how I went from thinking about dog training one way (if I thought about it at all) to wanting to sing from the hilltops about how excited I am to see a new wave of dog owners opening themselves up to the possibilities of good, science-based dog training. The science of behavior is the subject of the next part of the book. I'm not a scientist. I have no graduate degrees. I wasn't aware there was a science of behavior until I went to vocational school, but professional dog training left me wanting to read everything I could about the "laws" of learning (There are laws! Who knew?) and surround myself with people studying animal behavior in and out of labs. What I hope to offer you here is a foundational, middle-school-science-class-level breakdown of the basics to help create a better understanding of critical (and often loaded) terms like "punishment" and "positive reinforcement." From there, you'll start to see how you are already communicating with your dogs and shaping their behavior, and how you can do so more effectively.

Part three brings the discussion back to the dog in front of you. I'll give you a three-pronged approach that involves curating an environment conducive to learning and then using appropriate reinforcers delivered with thoughtful timing to get behaviors you want to happen in that environment.

Part four is about going forward with everything you've learned. I'll help you consider your next steps in training as a dog owner, whether you have hours or minutes in a day to do it. (I've lived both scenarios.) This last part is also a bit of a meditation on pet ownership and what it says about our existence in an ever-changing world. Because good dog training is nothing less than creating the conditions for a better—safer, kinder, and more encouraging—world for all animals, humans included.

If you detect an urban slant to this book, it's probably because I am a native New Yorker and for years my bread-and-butter has been working with people who have city dogs. However, even if you're not a city dweller this perspective can be helpful. A suburban—even pastoral—bias pervades traditional dog training, assuming everyone has, for example, access to wide open spaces for teaching recall or lives in a freestanding house where they can let a puppy "bark it out" without disturbing the neighbors. At School For The Dogs, we specialize not so much in working with tough dogs but in working with dogs in a tough situation: a big, crowded, noisy city. Urban dogs and their humans are under particular stress due to the literal confines of apartment life and tight sidewalks and condo boards. The non-urban dweller who uses our approach is swinging a weighted bat. It's like the song says: If you can make it there, you can make it anywhere... Start spreading the peanut butter!

PART ONE

How We've Been Getting It Wrong

People Are Weird with Dogs

"'We were making the future,'" he said, "and hardly any of us troubled to think what future we were making. And here it is!"

—H. G. WELLS, *THE SLEEPER AWAKES*

MY DAD WAS a bright guy. His favorite day of the week was Tuesday, which was when the *New York Times* published its Science section. He loved turning daily activities into experiments. Let's boil five eggs and remove them at thirty-second intervals to see which has the best consistency for eating! Let's see how many languages we can learn to count in, with our only teachers being cab drivers!

He was also unusually kind. He rarely said anything mean about anyone. And his generosity was epic. No matter how broke he was, dinner was always on him. When a blackout left people marooned in his Manhattan neighborhood during the summer of 2003, his girl-friend had to keep him from inviting random people on the street to sleep on the couch. He was also a bohemian par excellence, especially in his parenting style. Bedtime was never a thing, ice cream could be considered a meal, and showering was optional. There was a very long runway I could go down before he ever approached being angry with me.

And yet, his sweet curiosity and generosity did not always extend to the family pets.

In the days living on a farm before I was born, he kept male dogs away from his Doberman when she was in heat by shooting at them with a water gun filled with Tabasco sauce. When our dog Mabel was a puppy and her teeth grazed my arm, he told me to bite her ear "like a mother dog would do." I still remember the taste of furry ear. When she barked at sounds in the hall, he had a rolled-up newspaper at the ready. He was such a gentle person that it's hard for me to picture him hitting her. But he must have at some point, as I remember seeing her flinch if he just reached for it.

I don't doubt that his techniques "worked." Mabel followed him around the apartment slavishly—"master" *was* how he referred to himself in relation to her—and she would hang out the fourth-floor window looking for him when he went out. When something works, we're bound to do it again. And whatever he did worked, which is why I can still hear him saying to her—while patting her head as if he were dribbling a basketball—"Wwwwwwwwwhat a good girl…" His intonation was purposeful; he'd explained to me that the "w" sound was very meaningful to dogs, so it was important to draw it out. Indeed, the clear pronunciation of all consonants mattered in training, he said. That is also why he'd make a great effort to pronounce the "t" when he told Mabel to sit. "Sit-*TUH.*" She'd sit. Whether it was because of the "t" or because the rolled newspaper was in sight, I couldn't say.

The summer after my dad died, I was puttering around my kitchen with YouTube going in the background on my laptop. I don't remember what I had on, but it was something relating to dog training, and I was only half paying attention. It ended, and the algorithm chose something to play next. I had my back turned and was vaguely aware of an announcer with a stodgy British accent in the video, and then I heard something that made coffee come out of my nose.

"Sit-*TUH!*"

On the screen was a woman who looked like Mrs. Doubtfire dressed by the Church Lady. Stiff and white-haired, she had a lilting voice like the Dowager Countess from *Downton Abbey* but sounded like…my dad.

I couldn't look away.

Barbara Woodhouse was a celebrity dog trainer with her own show on the BBC.

What I was watching was actually from a British show that aired on PBS in the 1970s and 1980s.

"To make a dog sit, you have got to learn the right signal and the right tone of voice. Sit-*TUH*," the woman says, bending her arm toward her shoulder in a two-part motion—in rhythm with the syllables. Then there's a montage of everyone from 1980s talk show hosts to the Bee Gees either saying "Sit-*TUH*" or receiving the command.

And then we see the woman, Barbara Woodhouse, admonishing the owners who aren't pronouncing their t's clearly enough or aren't jerking the leashes with enough vim. But occasionally she'd soften, and when she did, it was a consonant on the other side of the interjection that got drawn out: *Wwwwwhat a good girl!*

Reader, I binged. I watched, incredulous, as she suggested to one woman that she leave her Alsatian tied to a retractable leash in the yard all day if she goes out, then showed a Scottie owner how to walk bent over in order to better be able to shake a plastic bag at the dog's behind to keep him from stopping during a walk. In one of the most memorable episodes, we meet a Doberman who chases bikes. To solve the problem, she enlists a bicyclist to ride past the dog and throw a mug of water in his face.

Bonkers

"Always remember: be nice!"

This is the plea of a ponytailed man in Buddy Holly glasses, seated at a desk with a pastel portrait of a blond toddler by his side. He smiles, then immediately cuts away to previously shot footage of himself talking to a small group inside a brown hotel conference room. He's there to tell them how to "bonk" a dog.

"You can never bonk a dog too early," he says. He's standing next to a nondescript young woman in ballet flats. In one hand, she's holding a cane; in the other, she's holding a leash attached to a Great Pyrenees, maybe seventy pounds. The dog is seated, panting, and looking at something off camera. "See that?" he says, pointing at the dog. "We can bonk right there." Then he takes a white towel, rolled up to be about the size of a wine bottle, raises it, and smacks the dog over the head. Hard.

I wish I could tell you that this was some kind of grainy archival video I dug up, but it's actually a clip from 2019 of a trainer who instructs people on how to bonk dogs and use electronic collars to tase them if they, say, approach a child too eagerly or bark when left alone. The clip has clocked more than a million views. The trainer isn't doing anything that unusual. Click on another video by someone else and you're just as likely to find some other form of what looks to me like abuse or torture. Swipe a bit or scan popular channels to find dog "experts" suggesting any number of new or old types of force and intimidation to get dogs to obey. Despite major scientific advances over the last century, not least in behavioral science, the techniques and tools of professional dog training have largely gone unchanged for generations.

Woman's Best Friend

The summer I was twenty-five, a guy I was in love with broke up with me. I'd like to tell you that I took it all in stride—to the left, to the left!—but the truth is that, like some Victorian caricature of female fragility, I took to bed. I couldn't think of anything that would ever make me feel okay again. Or even make me want to stand up. But then I had an idea: I could get a puppy. A puppy would help me want to continue existing. A puppy would help me get out of bed and structure my days.

So, one rainy Sunday, my mom and I went to Woodstock, New York, where we knew there was a little pet store on the main street. I walked out with a four-pound ball of black fluff they said was a Yorkipoo. I held him on my lap during the car ride home and stared at him. I chose him, I guess, but I also felt like we'd been sort of randomly assigned to each other. *I could have him until I'm forty*, I remember thinking. *What if we don't like each other?*

I named him Amos.

I wanted to do right by him, so I enrolled in a puppy training class at a dog daycare down the street. I remember having high hopes—the only thing that seemed more fun to me than having a puppy was being with other people and their puppies. But I mostly remember us standing around in a circle while the instructor periodically sprayed each dog with a water bottle. When the puppies were allowed to play together, a young German shepherd pounced on Amos and he squealed. "She thinks he's a squeaky toy!" said the trainer. Everyone laughed. I don't think it occurred to me that my dog might not enjoy being pounced upon, or that it might not be necessary to spray him in the face with water. These people were professionals. This was just what dog training was.

During one class, I asked one of the trainer's assistants what to do if Amos peed in the wrong place. She explained to me that dogs respond well to guilt trips. So I spent a few weeks investigating that approach whenever he went in the house. *"How could you do this! After all I've done for you!"* He eventually learned to go outside and, when he did, I patted myself on the back for giving really good guilt. When he barked at the doorbell, I said the word "No" as if I were "throwing a verbal rock" at him. This was what was recommended in a yellowed copy I had of the 1978 book *How to Be Your Dog's Best Friend*, which assured me that "all training methods use force to some degree." The book suggested I shut myself in a closet to practice developing my "No!"

The book also instructed me to do an "alpha-wolf" roll, which involved pushing Amos down to the ground by his neck, and rolling him to the side. This was to be "abrupt" and done with "great vigor" because "drama and surprise are essential to this technique."

Amos's eyes bugged out, then he hid all five pounds of himself under the couch. I had indeed stopped his barking. At least for the moment. He barked at the doorbell again the next day but just stood farther away from me. Was I really doing this right?

The doorbell barking continued, but after a couple of weeks I stopped trying to train him out of it. It wasn't because I lost interest in pretending to be a wolf bitch. Rather, it was because I realized that, living alone in New York City, it wasn't so bad to have such a reliable alarm system.

When Amos was a year old, I was walking around a bookstore with a guy I was dating when I saw a book on a carousel by the checkout.

The man on the cover smiled with his chin in his hand, surrounded by a couple of not-particularly-happy-looking adult dogs. "That's the Dog Whisperer!" my date told me. I'd never heard of him. He told me he'd been watching his TV show ever since it'd premiered on the National Geographic channel a few years earlier. "You HAVE to watch his show," he told me. "He's just incredible."

Let's Stop Whispering

"We live in a society exquisitely dependent on science and technology in which hardly anyone knows anything about science and technology."

—CARL SAGAN

IN LATE 2007 I was a busy freelance journalist, mostly writing about lifestyle topics like skin regimens and cultural trends and weddings. When my editor at the *New York Times* invited me for a lunch meeting, I went in prepared with two pages of story ideas, the last one being:

More people becoming dog trainers than ever before? As Plan B career, inspired by Dog Whisperer. Full disclosure: I maybe want to be a dog trainer :)

A statistic sold her on the story: the Bureau of Labor Statistics estimated the number of dog trainers in the United States had almost tripled since 2000.

I found enough people to support the hypothesis that dog training was an increasingly popular backup career choice. I interviewed a Long

Island bankruptcy attorney who had just left the law after spending years apprenticing trainers on weekends, a banker from New Hampshire who had quit a nearly $1-million-a-year job to try his hand at a new line of work, and an IT guy in Kentucky who had just bought a Bark Busters franchise after a few weeks of hands-on training. Everyone I spoke to cited the popularity of *The Dog Whisperer* as a reason for the surge in interest in professional dog training.

Part of my story was about dissension in the field, since no two self-labeled "professional dog trainers" seemed to agree on who should be allowed to call themselves a "professional dog trainer." Manicurists and barbers need licenses but not dog trainers? That fact struck me as worrisome: I didn't know much, but I knew dogs have teeth, and those teeth can lead to problems far worse than uneven sideburns.

Another divide I perceived in my research for the article was harder for me to flesh out. There seemed to be more than one idea about how to train a dog. This was news to me, but in sorting out what needed to be in this story, I wasn't sure that it really *mattered*. A trained dog is a trained dog, regardless of how you got there, right?

But a few people I interviewed mentioned they were not impressed with the Dog Whisperer. His training wasn't rooted "in science," they said. I was no expert, but I knew enough to train a sit: Put a treat over a dog's head. Their butts go down when they look up at it. It seemed a little much to call that science.

I was trying to be a levelheaded reporter, but I thought these people sounded like spoilsports—especially if they were putting down this guy. Clearly he was *incredible*. He was on *Oprah*!

While double-checking some parts of the article before publication, I sent an email to Parvene Farhoody, the then-president of the Certification Council for Professional Dog Training, an industry accreditation bureau. I wrote, "Would it be accurate to state that some trainers believe in behavior-modification theories that relate to broader ideas about the similarities in the ways humans and many other animals learn, while others favor pared-down methods about understanding the 'canine psyche' and communicating with a dog as a 'pack leader,'" and asked her to confirm.

She wrote back: "You are putting the legitimate field of behavior science on the same level as myth, misinformation, and marketing. What you're asking is similar to asking whether the statement 'some people think the Earth is round, but others take the view that it is flat' is accurate."

I forwarded the response to my editor with the subject: "Insider baseball."

Three years later, I would be in the dugout.

We live in a society where so much about you is defined by your job. After I graduated from the Karen Pryor Academy for Animal Training and Behavior, a six-month program designed to mint positive reinforcement dog trainers, people I met would inevitably ask what I did for a living and, just as inevitably, when I said, "I'm a dog trainer," they would respond with the same question. "Oh, like *The Dog Whisperer*?"

I didn't quite know how to answer. He defined himself as a dog trainer, as did I, so we had that in common. But I had never actually seen an episode. I didn't have much more information than that. So, I finally sat down to watch the show.

Please Don't Hail Cesar

"My dream is to share the knowledge that I was born with, with the rest of the world," Cesar Millan tells us during the opening credits of the first episode of his series, *The Dog Whisperer*, which first aired on National Geographic in 2004 and would go on for nine seasons, birthing multiple spin-offs, publications, and live tours. Episode one begins with a segment called "Demon Chihuahua" about tiny gray NuNu, who wants to bite everyone except Tina, the thirty-seven-year-old who rescued him two months earlier. Before Millan comes on screen, a narrator has declared that "Cesar's core philosophy is that people need to become assertive pack leaders to their dogs." Then there he is, the "dog whisperer" sitting on a couch next to Tina. She's weak, he explains, and the dog is exploiting that fact. "Giving him affection has nurtured that nervous state of mind, and from that point on he became the dominant one, so we have a dominant, nervous leader... If you represent a lovable figure, you're going to nurture his issues and develop new issues."

Millan tells Tina to place the dog in his lap. She does, and, as Millan starts to pet him, NuNu stiffens, ducks his head, and starts giving him side-eye. He growls. He shows his teeth. Millan doesn't change course. NuNu attacks. At first, Millan doesn't move, but then he grabs the tiny dog at his neck and holds him down, explaining that NuNu understands his hand to be the mouth of a larger, dominant dog, and his fingers, the dominant dog's teeth. He calls this move "Hand as Mouth." (In his book *Cesar's Rules,* he notes that this method can be seen in 57 percent of the show's first 140 episodes.) "But I'm not using *force*," he says. Tina has tears running down her face. She nods in agreement.

Millan further interprets, "The calm assertive energy is making him surrender and will get rid of this issue in a matter of no time. When he surrenders then you let him go... He's just pretending," he says. "It's a physical–psychological touch that is triggering his brain to be challenged by a human." Tina nods along eagerly. I have no idea what "physical–psychological touch" is, but she seems to.

When the dog finally escapes his grip and makes his way back to Tina's side, Millan reaches for him and grabs him again and pushes him into the couch anew. "This is *your* kingdom not his kingdom," Millan tells Tina. "If he comes to you, he becomes powerful again." The episode ends with Millan explaining that her energy has been too nervous, and that she needs to be more "calm assertive." He tells the camera: "She is going to have to take control of his life. And by her doing this, she is going to control *her own* life."

Tina shows nothing but appreciation for the schooling she has received. "Sometimes," she tells the camera, "you have to look inside yourself and change yourself in order to change the creatures around you."

The second dog in the episode is Kane, a Great Dane who, after an experience careening into a glass door after slipping on a linoleum floor, has developed a fear of walking on any type of shiny surface. Millan blames Kane's owner, Marina, a preschool teacher, for the dog's neurosis. In the seconds following the door-crashing incident, her fussing over the dog, Millan says, "nurtured his trauma." He explains that this might be okay when you're dealing with a human, but an animal "shouldn't receive affection while the mind is under stress."

Marina wants to bring Kane to her school to meet the young children she works with, but the dog won't walk on the linoleum in the lobby, and she claims that she's resisted just tugging him across the floor because that would be "negative." She attempts to solve the issue by rolling out a piece of carpet for him to walk on, but it's too short to extend the full expanse of the building's foyer. Millan claims to have the solution, and it doesn't involve a longer carpet. I watch as Millan drags and shoves and wrestles this massive dog across the floor.

After several minutes of being, Millan might say, "not forced" no matter how much he protests, Kane walks the floor with Millan, and then with the owner. The dog is hugging the wall and drooling buckets. But Millan is all smiles and raised thumbs. Marina sums up what she has learned: "You have to be the pack leader. You have to lead them with a positive and calm energy. I'm the boss," she says, adding that she is going to try these techniques with her schoolchildren.

The episode closes with Millan telling the camera, "It's a beautiful lesson. You don't have to be unstable your whole life. You can rehabilitate and let go of any kind of issue you have."

I had seen enough. Enough to recognize, to my horror, how dog training has come to be popularly understood in the twenty-first century, largely thanks-but-no-thanks to Cesar Millan. Approaches of this ilk could be found in a cursory review of the work of many others predating Millan's show by decades.

What Millan adds is a kind of New Age twist: an ineffable "calm assertive energy" that owners supposedly must attain in order to tame dogs, whose problems all seem to be due to their reflection of their human owners' deficient personalities.

This is, after all, reality TV, and the dogs are part of transmutations that could just as easily be about a living room renovation or a wardrobe makeover. The human is the problem, and the problem dog is merely doling out their due comeuppance. It seems to me that the people on the show are often anxious because they are trying to deal with a problematic dog, but in episode after episode, the script is flipped and the people's inevitable stress around their dogs is framed as the starting point of the issues, not the result.

In *The Republic*, Plato has an allegory about people chained to the wall of a cave all their lives, their backs turned toward the opening. All they know of the world is from the shadows projected on the wall they're facing. The shadows have become their reality. We all know shadows can be enticing, but they can also be manipulated and misleading. Twenty years after his show premiered, it seems that Millan is still casting shadows, and millions of people, including many of the next generations of dog trainers, have mistaken his reality TV for reality. But we don't have to stay in the cave.

In the opening credits of the show, Cesar Millan tells the audience he was born with a special knowledge about dogs. I wasn't. But I've learned a lot. It's led me to believe that anyone can be a good dog trainer. I not only believe this; I *know* this from the evidence and from my own experience. I've taught elderly people how to train dogs. I've taught small children how to train dogs. Some of the best trainers I know are both affectionate with their dogs and suffer from depression and anxiety. None of this impacts their dogs' abilities to learn. Do these trainers have good "energy"? Part of a "science-based" approach should be, in my opinion, to at least hesitate to speculate about something so subjective. It's possible, for instance, that a pilot's "good energy" is what helps them fly a plane, but there are more measurable criteria that have landed them in the cockpit. Similarly, there are basic principles of learning that apply to humans and dogs, with measurable effects when anyone applies them, no mysterious "energy" or "whispering" ability required. DO try this at home.

Before *The Dog Whisperer* went on TV, National Geographic sent the pilot episode to Dr. Andrew Luescher, a veterinary behaviorist, for comment. He replied to them that the show presented false explanations of dog behavior and suggested techniques that were tantamount to animal cruelty. "I very much hope

National Geographic will pull the plug on this program," he wrote. "My colleagues and I and innumerable leaders in the dog training community have worked now for decades to eliminate such cruel, ineffective (in terms of true cure), and inappropriate techniques. It would be a major blow for all our efforts if National Geographic portrayed these very techniques as the current standard in training and behavior modification."

Millan has had a new season of a show or a new book in store pretty much every year for twenty years. But I think the success of the Dog Whisperer brand depends on the wrong kind of magic: the magic of Millan's shaman-like charisma. Good animal training can feel magical too. Ken Ramirez, the chief training officer of Karen Pryor Clicker Training (which runs the Karen Pryor Academy), once trained several thousand butterflies to swarm on cue in choreography with a symphony orchestra in a London botanical garden; my friend Ilana Alderman trained her beta fish to dunk an underwater basketball and taught the neighborhood squirrels to ring her doorbell when they want acorns.

This is all done with an approach that can empower humans rather than blaming them, and that can feel pretty darn magical. Once, at a Super Bowl party, my husband completely wowed his high school friends by training one of their dogs to lie down during a commercial break. He did it from a La-Z-Boy. Thing is, it's not magic: It's simply smart applications of behavioral science that you can learn (and will, if you keep reading), whether your animal is a dolphin or a dog, a hamster or a human; you want your bichon to be a hospital therapy dog or want to get a Malinois to walk nicely on leash; or you just want to keep your puppy from getting into the bathroom garbage again.

3

Dog Training Science Deniers

"The amount of totally unnecessary interference in canine lives, the exercise of authority for its own sake, has to be seen to be believed."

—J. R. ACKERLEY, MY DOG TULIP

WHEN I TOOK a psychology survey class in college, it was mostly focused on concepts and ideas proposed by people like Freud, Piaget, and Jung. They each presented theories, not formulas. Science had to do with things that could be put in beakers and looked at under a microscope. Behavior, I thought, could only be understood in ways that could be discussed on couches.

Seeing it that way, it makes perfect sense that there would be one language for discussing human behavior and another, as Cesar Millan suggests, for canine behavior. Even very smart people readily accept that dog training is too enigmatic to learn from a textbook. Case in point: In 2006, one year after the writer Malcolm Gladwell was named one of the world's top "Scientists and Thinkers" by *Time*, he penned a nine-page profile in the *New Yorker* about Millan. Much of the article is devoted to discussing his idiosyncratic body language with dancers. The field of behavior science was not mentioned once in the piece.

Pay Attention to That Man Behind the Curtain

The fact that a science of behavior exists can be off-putting to some, especially because it can lead to uncomfortable questions about big stuff, like the concept of freedom. None of us are making choices in a vacuum, but the strings pulling us in one direction or another can be hard to see and acknowledge. Somehow, we've all developed ideas about what we want and which behaviors we can engage in to produce consequences that will bring us rewards or remove threats. Somehow.

If you suggest that that "somehow" has to do with a science of behavior, it can sort of feel like people are being reduced to mice, and it's an insulting comparison!

We're all special snowflakes, but we also all happen to shop on Amazon and look at our phones ten times a minute. Have we been…trained?

The more I learn about the science of behavior, the more I start to find myself asking these kinds of questions. Who knew there were really human life lessons to be found in puppy kindergarten.

Over the last century, huge strides have been made in understanding how learning works and how to teach effectively, no matter what the species. Decades of research have led to the resounding conclusion that it's never a good idea to drag a dog across scary linoleum.

Although behavioral science is an area of focus for those who work in organizational psychology (see the work of Aubrey Daniels), parenting (I've particularly enjoyed books by Glenn Latham on the subject), and special education (applied behavior analysis), I'm not sure that any group of people is as zealous about the discipline as dog trainers. This is probably because of the aforementioned positive reinforcement, which is codified within the science: When you train in such a way that your dog will want to engage in desirable behaviors again and again, you're going to want to train again and again, which is going to make your dog behave again and again...ad infinitum.

Unfortunately, however, most people who have attempted to train dogs (whether they've done so in a manner that is professional, amateur, or purely accidental) haven't benefited from any education in behavioral science, let alone considered the greater implications of animal training. In the next parts of this book, I hope to change that, because I want everyone—dogs and people—to experience this wonderful, virtuous circle of learning. And knowing even just a little bit about the science of behavior goes a long way.

Too Cute

In 2011, the show *Too Cute!* began airing on Animal Planet. More than a decade later, its seventy-plus episodes are still streaming and have clocked more than 100 million views on YouTube alone. Its popularity isn't particularly surprising. If, when I was six, you'd told me one day it would be possible to stream puppies playing in my living room all day, I'd have imagined never leaving the house when I grew up...unless I could also have the puppies on a screen in my pocket. Will wonders never cease?

Every hour-long episode of *Too Cute!* follows a litter of baby animals from birth through the age of ten or so weeks. The narrator tells us that Oscar the Chow Chow wants to take a bath in the water bowl and boss around his brother Tony; a family of Miniature Aussie puppies is trying to befriend a family of ducklings; a pit bull puppy wants to sneak into a kitchen cupboard to steal snacks. If I know these stories all too well, it isn't because I'm a fan of the show, it's because I helped write it. In 2012, I worked as an associate producer for the production company that was making *Too Cute!* I had no experience in the world of television, but I had a background in journalism, and, having recently graduated from dog training school, I had an expertise in dogs. This combination of abilities to research, write, and wrangle puppies made me something of a shoo-in for the job.

Back then, I was naive enough about reality TV that it surprised me to discover plotlines were written before the cameras were ever powered on. Prior to each shoot, I was one of the people helping the writers and editors who'd spend weeks devising the storylines that the film crew would try to capture. Which sphynx kitten would be the bully? Which Havanese would learn a valuable lesson? Which Mini Aussie would discover how special it is to have a big brother? On shoot days, I was one of the people who then tried to cajole a gray pit bull puppy to nose a cupboard door open so we could pretend he had discovered where the Milk-Bones were kept. At the time, these machinations for narrative's sake didn't bother me much. This was reality TV. Could be worse: The casting director who sat next to me was working on a show called *Douchebag.*

The kind of anthropomorphism that moved the plots of *Too Cute!* forward is so common that viewers hardly notice. We make sense of the world by projecting what we know about ourselves onto other creatures and sometimes inanimate objects. When she was two, I watched my older daughter befriend a drainpipe with two eyes painted on it, which made sense when I considered that every night I read her stories about dishes running away with spoons, pigs who are fearful of wolves who might blow down their houses, and poky puppies who feel sorry for themselves when they miss out on dessert. I grew up on these stories too, and I didn't turn into an adult who actually thinks some cats hate Mondays. No harm done, right?

It depends. This very human tendency to slap our own motivations onto other animals for the sake of a good story can lead us into some pretty foggy places.

It can be harmless, or even helpful, to attribute humanlike reasoning onto animals. However, my fellow dog trainers and I see how often it can blind us to more basic motivations that are key to good training.

I allow that good dog trainers will sometimes make broad guesses about what a dog likes or what their inner monologue might be, but those guesses are based on what can be observed. Assumptions about what a dog's thoughts and feelings are and how they may be driving behaviors are not always reliable. For instance, a dog who eats his dinner possibly is having mental machinations about liking the food, while the dog who doesn't eat the dinner may be feeling disappointed to be getting the dry food and not the wet tonight. But even those very broad and seemingly obvious and harmless assumptions don't hold up well. A dog might've gobbled food they didn't enjoy because they didn't want another dog to get it. Or passed on the dinner because they weren't feeling well, or they were scolded the last time they ate, or the food has been placed too close to the shelf that holds the blender, and the blender is scary.

As humans, we can talk about our emotions, but language only helps to a certain extent. You say you're angry, and that is why you punched the wall. I say I'm angry, and that is why I'm crying. So does my "anger" feel to me the way yours does to you? What's more, when you go looking for unobservable motivations, you quickly end up in a kind of loop that doesn't actually provide much useful information: How do I know you're angry? Because you punched the wall. But why did you punch the wall? Because you were angry.

Guessing the internal motivations of another being isn't only a crude measure—it's unnecessary. We can get great training results without ever knowing your dog's feelings. But that means considering emptying your vocabulary of some commonly heard—and terribly misleading—"dog training" words.

STUBBORNNESS

When we call a dog "stubborn," it implies that the dog really *knows* how to do something but is willfully choosing not to. Maybe! But how would we know, and what do we do with that anyway? This kind of thinking gets us into "bad dog" territory, maybe even makes us angry, when a simpler and more neutral assessment could be less emotional and more useful. A dog that isn't doing something a human wants her to do might not understand what you want her to do, in which case you can work on clearer communication. Or she may understand, but whatever you want her to do is simply not as rewarding as the thing she is doing.

"Stubbornness" usually boils down to your dog behaving in a way that lets you know that what you are offering just isn't as valuable to him as whatever he is doing.

Sniffing a lamppost might be worth a lot to her, while going in the direction you want to go is worth no more to her than the fact that it will relieve some pressure on her neck. In other words, the fragrant lamppost is worth her collar tugging. Coming inside for a bowl of kibble may not compare to the joy of chasing squirrels in the yard. My dog Amos knew how to roll over on a dime at home on the carpet, but if I asked him to do it in the dog park, he was unlikely to comply. I suspect this was because the cement on his back coupled with the thought of exposing his belly in front of lots of dogs he'd never met just wasn't worth the allure of freeze-dried lamb lung. I can understand that.

Stubbornness is also sometimes given as a "reason" why a dog is avoiding something, but again, I don't know how it would help to know that even if we could. Investigating the evidence instead of trying to mind-read, we often find the dog is avoiding something that was associated with punishment in the past. We inadvertently train our dogs *not* to do the thing we want, then blame their stubbornness! For instance, if, like the titular character in the classic book *Harry the Dirty Dog*, you have a dog who hates taking baths, you call him to you, and then you give him a bath, the behavior of coming probably was not reinforced; it's effectively being punished, and the chance that your dog will come in the future is reduced. Does he know "come"? Sure, he knows it means he's going to get a bath! Remember: Dogs aren't philanthropists. And even philanthropists have their reasons! The "stubborn" dog may just be one who has an idea about future consequences.

If I had to guess the most common reason a dog gets labeled "stubborn," it'd be when he doesn't have a clue what you want. Most dog owners should begin with the assumption that their dog has no idea what they're saying. Unless you've put in some effort teaching your dog the words or phrases you'd like her to know, your words probably sound like gobbledygook. And, even if you've taught her the meaning of some words or phrases, she may know what those sounds mean in the living room yet not realize they mean the same thing in the park. Dogs can learn to understand loads of things we say and do! But when they don't immediately get something, I think we should cut them some slack.

SPITEFULNESS

When your dog pees on your pillow after you left him alone for a long time or after you gave him a bath, it's easy to feel "spite" must be in play.

Spitefulness requires an ability to connect cause—pee on your pillow—and effect—inconvenience and annoyance for you, usually in the non-immediate future. Even in human interactions, spite is complicated. Plus, in cases involving pee and poop, spitefulness would only make sense if dogs didn't typically love their own pee and poop!

US: You peed on my bed!
DOG: Yes, I shared my urine with you!

Simpler reasons your dog may have peed on your bed:

✦ Dogs often like to pee on soft things.
✦ He happened to be on the bed when he had to go.
✦ Your pillow smelled like something that needed to be peed on.

But we point to spite when the urge to purge the bladder happened to occur after some other event that we assume was upsetting. Of course, the "spiteful" behavior happened after many *other* events too. There was a bath, but there was also dinner, a walk, a nap, and a game of tug. It's as if I accused my guests of leaving because I made dinner. Yes, I made dinner.

And some time after that, they left. Correlating events that happen to occur near to one another is often as inexact as it is useless.

DOMINANCE

A few years ago, a woman named Kara called me up, frantic because of what she referred to as a power struggle in her home. I went up to her apartment on the Upper East Side.

On one side of the couch was Marc, her affable guy, a thirtysomething wearing khakis. On the other side, Mickey, a Maltese, acting "dominant."

"I think he doesn't like that he's no longer the man of the house," Kara told me.

When Marc walks the dog, she elaborated, Mickey plants on the street every block or so, refusing to move. "He growls," she said. Mickey often growls when Marc puts on his leash, and recently he started to try to bite Marc too. "He's never like this with me," Kara told me, going on to explain that Marc had recently moved in, and she worries that Mickey feels he's losing his place in the pack. "It's totally a power thing," she said.

I looked over at Marc. I've met more men than women who like wandering down this trail of thinking, making lots of assumptions along the way about how a dog would behave in "nature." I was waiting for Marc to say something like, "He is trying to assert his dominance by attacking me and refusing to submit to being on a leash with me." But he didn't. Instead, he gently shook his head and said, "I think he's a great little dog. I want him to like me." I decided I wanted to see each of them walk Mickey. We all went out together and, after a turn around the block with Kara holding the leash—a thin leather tether with little daisies grommeted to it—I gave the leash to Marc. The dog was totally fine.

Marc compared the situation to bringing your stalling car to the mechanic and then suddenly it's working fine. Kara had a different view.

"It's probably because you're here—he knows *you're* the alpha," Kara said. I proposed we go upstairs, wait a beat, and then start the whole walk from the beginning.

Back upstairs, Kara unleashed Mickey, and we all sat. Had a coffee. Then I suggested Marc try to take him for a walk. He approached with a leash. Mickey retreated and started to growl. "You see," Kara said. "Isn't that dominance?"

His teeth were showing, but Marc picked him up anyway. I was torn between wanting him to put the dog down so as not to stress him out and wanting to be an unobtrusive observer. (Professional tip: If a dog growls when you pick him up, don't pick him up! Or else he may skip the growl and go straight to telling you what's what with his teeth. A growl is information to be heeded, not ignored.) In this instance, I opted to be an observer, as I wanted to see their routine. I watched as Marc fastened the leash to his collar and brought him out. I followed a few steps behind.

When they got out the front door, Marc put the little dog down. Mickey walked five feet and stopped. I saw the problem. Marc's leash was different than Kara's, with a sizable clasp at the end that I could see was hitting Mickey in the face. I ran upstairs for the daisy-emblazoned leash and brought it down to Marc, who swapped the leashes no problem. Mickey looked up at Marc on the other end of the daisies, shook off, and started trotting along like a champ.

Dog training, as it's been presented in popular culture, is often seen as a game with a winner and a loser. The idea that dogs are always jockeying for the top place in some kind of canine version of *Game of Thrones* largely stems from the observations of a single researcher, Rudolph Schenkel, who in the 1940s spent time watching wolves at a zoo in Switzerland. Studying assorted wolf individuals that had been plucked from their family units and were living in captivity would not be unlike making assumptions about human behavior based solely on watching *Survivor*. But it was more wolf-studying than anyone else had ever done. In describing the wolf captives' social machinations, Schenkel coined the term "alpha" wolf. His work was mentioned in the 1970 book *The Wolf: Ecology and Behavior of an Endangered Species*, written by Dr. L. David Mech, founder of the International Wolf Center, and the "alpha" idea took hold from there. My guess is that it resonated with the status hierarchies and power structures we humans live with, in a world of bosses and bullies who rule with fear and coercion. In so many areas of human life, someone is in charge and the rest of us fall in line either by force or out of fear of what will happen if we don't comply.

It's a sticky idea but, according to Dr. Mech, one that has led to a grand misunderstanding about canid behavior. He has spent decades begging the publishers of his book, still in print after more than fifty years, to pull it from shelves. His pleas have been ignored. On his website, he writes that "much is outdated. We have learned more about wolves in the last forty years than in all of previous history."

It's not hard to imagine how, removed from their families and put together with strangers in a strange place, those animals' fear and aggression would produce a more bellicose existence. But according to research, in wild and semidomestic situations, wolves tend to stay in small familial groups, with the elders parenting the young. And they tend to do so peacefully. Usually there's just one breeding pair and their offspring in the group. Bloodshed within the unit is as unlikely as, if you'll bear with a 1990s TV analogy, Uncle Jesse slaying Danny Tanner to be king of *Full House*. Indeed, wolves in the wild are rarely observed fighting—unless they are contained, they will first try to flee. What's more, scientists have observed that the leader of a group of wolves is not always the strongest and fiercest of a pack. Like hunting for food, fighting is a calorically expensive activity. If your next meal depends on whether you can kill a caribou, you are better off conserving your energy. The leaders in a pack are the ones who provide life's necessities and lead the group away from potential harm in an energy-efficient way.

This doesn't mean that dogs don't have social rules and hierarchies among themselves when, like wolves in captivity, they're put into unnatural, nonfamilial groups as might happen at, say, a dog park or a daycare. But I haven't seen that dissecting their dynamics in terms of "dominance" gets a dog owner very far. My dog Amos, for instance, was friendly with most groups of dogs but surly and vocal with puppies. Puppies move unpredictably and sometimes don't pick up on social cues, while Amos was relatively small and, I suspect, worried about getting hurt, so he'd growl and bark to keep them away. Was he trying to "assert his dominance"? That could be one way of describing the situation. I'd sooner say that he just didn't like puppies. I mean, is a crabby old man "dominant" when he shakes his cane at a group of kids? And is my dog controlling the puppies by making them go away, or are they controlling him by making him growl? In practice, dissecting intra- or inter-pack dynamics just isn't incredibly helpful in day-to-day training.

We dominate the pets in our homes if only because we control many things they need. If dogs are really in a power-struggle game with humans, then what would full domination on their part look like? What would it look like for them to "win"—killing the one who provides food at regular intervals?

Rather than viewing the dog/human relationship as a power struggle, we can think of it as more of a dance. We are leading, and we *want* our puppy-partner to get it right. Dancing, when we're in the swing, seems effortless on both sides.

DOMINANCE IN PLAY

Dog play can look a lot like fighting, and at the dog park I often hear people explaining that one dog is trying to dominate another The thing is, most dog play involves a lot of taking turns. The nearest equivalent would probably be kids swapping who is "it." So, even if we label the one who is physically on top as "dominant," chances are the positions will flip in a moment. What's more, play modes can vary depending on the environment. A dog may be the chief ball holder if he's with another dog in your home, but totally fine letting a stranger dog get the ball when at the park.

A New Type of Dog Owner

In the first year of the COVID-19 pandemic, the ASPCA reported that in the United States, more than twenty-three million dogs joined the households of people who realized working from home would make it possible for them to accommodate a *dog's needs*. A dog's needs! A dog's needs. Why did I type that three times? Because it's extraordinary! Think of all the generations of dogs that people used as tools to herd and hunt and protect themselves. For many dogs, for centuries, no one asked if being home alone was good or bad for the dog: Being home alone was the dog's *job*. Special are these new dog owners who only decided to bring a dog into their home when they felt they could devote resources and time into meeting that dog's needs.

So, what does a dog need? That is what the rest of this book is about. But before we move on to part two, let's remember what a dog does *not* need:

✦ A dog does not need to be pushed to the ground and growled at in order to understand that the bath mat is not a spot to pee on.

✧ A dog does not need to be yanked by the neck to walk in a straight line.

✧ A dog does not need to believe you're a dog or the leader of the pack to understand you and want to please you.

Good dog training is not a battle. Why would we choose war when we could choose love? Good dog training is also nonjudgmental of the human and the dog. We're all products of our environment: We're lucky if that environment includes teachers using instruction that is learner friendly. That isn't always the case for us in our lives. But it can be what your dog's world looks like.

Some people are already awake to what works and what doesn't, behaviorally. The rest of us have some studying to do. While the same teaching methods in this book will work on both dogs and people, dogs are much keener students. They are also greedy rascals who want things we can provide, and we can leverage that.

For their part, dogs are already genius animal trainers. Consider that they've essentially trained us to take care of everything they need in life. Talk about milking the system. Thing is, I'm totally okay with this setup! In fact, good dog training will make your pet think he's only gotten better at manipulating you. When you're a good trainer, you're like a con man whose mark thinks the con is on you.

PART TWO

The Better Way

What We Have in Common

"The difference in mind between man and the higher animals, great as it is, certainly is one of degree and not of kind."

—CHARLES DARWIN

BEFORE YOU EVEN opened this book, the following things were already true about you:

✧ You share billions of years of evolutionary history with your dog.
✧ You are innately familiar with the workings of animal behavior, since you too are an animal who is behaving all the time.
✧ Your canine partner-in-training is the product of natural selection that has most likely occurred due to an ability to coexist with you.

In other words, you know more than you think you do. We all do.

Dogs are not people. Can we put baseball caps on them with little cutouts for their ears? Sure. Do we pen their inner monologues in photo captions and give them names usually reserved for people, like Kevin? Absolutely. But we can all agree that a dog is never going to write his own will or perform open heart surgery or see the problem with eating chicken bones from the gutter. We humans have the knowledge of our own death, and know about things that happened millennia ago and about things that have happened light-years away. Big stuff! The enormity of these differences makes it not unlike comparing an ant to a whale. But ants and whales actually have a lot in common, and even more so humans and dogs. Just the fact that we're non-extinct mammals living in the same climate makes us pretty similar, and that's before we even consider the fact that many members of our two species are sharing beds.

When I set out to be a dog trainer, it didn't occur to me that I would spend so much time thinking about animals…or thinking about the fact that *I* am an animal. There can be an insult implied when people are compared to animals. But I'm suggesting we accept our animalness—and even learn from it—without a value judgment. I mean, "animal" is just a category, and if I'm not an animal, what am I, a vegetable? A mineral? A Muppet?

If you are reading this, you aren't just any kind of animal: You're part of a species that still *exists*. Dogs are too. It's an obvious but also incredible fact that is easy to overlook: Nearly 99 percent of all species who've ever existed are *extinct*. Dogs and humans are more than just not extinct. We're thriving.

Our success on this planet has a lot to do with our abilities to adapt to our environments, both physically and behaviorally, from one generation to the next but also within each individual's lifetime. Some of our success has had to do with luck, but most of it has to do with our species' killer ability to learn.

For these reasons, unlike some of the most popular dog trainers who preach how important it is *not* to compare dogs to humans, who would have us learn "dog psychology," I prefer to start with what we have in common.

Evolving to Learn from Humans

Humans and dogs are both good at adapting to our environments. This is what learning is all about. Learning can be facilitated by a good teacher or trainer, but it's an ability that comes baked in. Our two species' excellent learning ability has evolved to be what it is today. Natural selection favored those who did what worked and those who were good at figuring out what worked.

All animals want one thing, biologically speaking: to live long enough to procreate, and to do that requires keeping oneself safe and getting basic needs met. Humans learned to behave in ways that have paid off big time and so have dogs. The better a dog is at figuring out how to be safe and not go hungry, the fewer calories he has to expend, something dogs—and many humans—happen to know a lot about. The easier the work of obtaining calories, the more time and energy available for staying safe, and procreating, and watching Netflix.

In the developed world, at least, humans stumble along and make money and babies, affected by the laws of learning but not thinking too much about them. We tend to do the same thing with dogs. Rather than use behavioral science to our advantage, we muddle through with a mix of intuition, good intentions, and emotional reactions. But, for many of my clients, the challenges of trying to be a good dog owner with a good dog in a big city have forced them to wake up and take a more conscious, intentional approach. Fortunately, dogs are happy to comply with our efforts, no matter what methods we use. In fact, their willingness to be in close proximity to us, regardless of how we treat them, is a trait nature likely selected. But we shouldn't give ourselves too much credit for this.

Instead, we may want to pay our respects to a human tendency for which children are often scolded: not finishing our dinner.

Survival of the Fittest (Trash Eater)

One of my first memories of a dog is of my Uncle David's dog Elsa licking plates. We'd just had Chinese food, and she was doing the rinse cycle with her tongue. I vividly remember thinking *Elsa is so useful!* She was probably thinking the same thing about us.

In their 2001 book *Dog*, ethologists Ray and Lorna Coppinger argued that dogs evolved to be what they are largely thanks to the natural selection of certain behavioral traits, over a relatively short period of time, about twelve thousand years ago. Human selection, they posit, had little to do with it. When our Mesolithic forebears started settling in one place rather than roaming all the time, they accumulated piles of garbage. As we humans began to cultivate our own food rather than having to hunt and gather it, we were more likely to have some left over. And what dog doesn't like leftovers?

For a proto dog, scavenging our garbage was *way* less dangerous and labor intensive than hunting. That *really* worked. Those species members—the ones who were less spooked about being around humans—were more likely to procreate. While we're most familiar with the Cavapoos in our living rooms today, who may or may not benefit from the occasional doggie bag or learn how to get into the garbage can, the fact is that three-quarters of the estimated one billion dogs in the world today do not live in homes at all. They're still doing fine eating our garbage.

The dog's genius, if you ask me, is that they put up with us. They're willing to deal with a lot if it means reliable access to our surpluses. This is why I think many people can do no formal training with their dog, or use crude and possibly ineffective dog training, but still have dogs who are pretty well behaved.

Basic Instincts

When I was working at *Too Cute!*, I had an assignment that basically involved producing an adorable interspecies playdate. I was dispatched to a New Jersey petting zoo, where I had to pick up some ducklings. I then drove with my box of ducklings to a Connecticut home where they would encounter some Miniature Aussie shepherds. It was going to be, indeed, too cute.

When I arrived, I was put on the other side of a small footbridge from where the puppies were. I was told that, when I got the signal, I was to release the ducklings and have them cross the bridge. So, at the cue, I picked up each one and gently set it down. Then I ran ahead of them, hoping they'd follow. One did. And right behind it, the next and then the next, forming a perfect little line of baby ducks.

The producer was thrilled. "Annie got them to walk in a line!"

For months, I got accolades. In fact, I have, to this day, never trained a duck. Through a coincidence of timing, I happened to get credit for something that ducks just do.

No one teaches a baby to crawl, or a bird to build a nest, or a spider to build a web. Like preinstalled software on a new computer, some behaviors are coded into genes, along with the shape of your eyes or where your nose should go. A tendency to engage in certain behaviors has been selected for, based on an animal's environment, just like certain physical traits that have served the animal well.

Dogs come with behaviors preinstalled too. Some behaviors you may want, some you may not want, some you may think you want but then you realize you don't want, or vice versa. Innate behaviors are instinctive.

Baked into the pie. They aren't taught, or learned, but they also aren't random; they are triggered by stimuli in the environment. A sneeze is precipitated by something irritating your nose or by looking at the sun. Babies have a suckling reflex, but they usually need a nipple, or something nipplelike, to trigger it. Most reflexes are involuntary, and some can be triggered by stimuli in a way that may take you by surprise. I learned this when I began breastfeeding my daughter. Once, the sound of a baby crying on TV made my milk come down. Behaviors, observable or not, either have a purpose that is beneficial to survival or are vestigial behavioral leftovers from a time when they were beneficial. My mom's dog Sketch used to hide his chew toy in the couch, a tendency that probably helped his ancestors protect precious resources, and a few thousand generations later you have a Shih Tzu mix shoving bully sticks into the daybed.

CAN DOGS' INNATE BEHAVIORS BE CONTROLLED BY HUMANS?

The short answer is: yes. The rest of the book is largely about understanding that control and using it wisely. But over time and generations, we have also controlled for some innate behaviors through breeding dogs to do tasks that are important to us. Some behaviors that started out innate have been bred out of some dogs or altered. For instance, upon seeing a rabbit, the proto dog's natural tendency—which would've allowed him to survive in a world without kibble—would've been to hunt and eat it, specifically ORIENT > EYE > STALK > CHASE > GRAB-BITE > KILL-BITE > DISSECT > CONSUME. Those behaviors, in that order, came preloaded. But we humans have found it useful to have dogs who would do a certain part of this sequence, but not the rest. Terriers, for instance, were bred to see rats (EYE), go after them (STALK AND CHASE) and the rest, except *not* be constantly searching for them (ORIENT) and *not* dissect and consume (because that's gross). The first and last parts of the sequence were bred out of them, which is why Amos loved tennis balls but wouldn't go searching one out, like a pointer might when trying to find prey. He also never ate tennis balls (because that's also gross).

Descartes and the Water Machines

In the early seventeenth century, two Italian brothers built an exhibition of moving statues at the Saint-Germain-en-Laye gardens in Paris. In one grotto in the park, a dragon would pop out of a water feature and then Perseus would swoop in from above to slay it. The movement happened thanks to water-powered mechanisms below the surface, which propelled the stone beings into lifelike action.

Among those who went to see the delightful show was René Descartes. Descartes, a philosopher, mathematician, and scientist, had seen inside of dead animals. He knew that animals were filled with tubes and liquid. Maybe, he thought, animal actions are propelled by external forces, rather than solely by invisible internal machinations. Animals move when sensory input produces motor output, he theorized. "Animal spirits" travel through a series of internal tubes and pulleys to produce animation, just like water's voyage through tubes and pulleys caused the stone figures to move about in those Parisian gardens.

He was, of course, off base about the internal pulleys. He was also probably misguided to totally divorce human from nonhuman animal behavior. Other animals might be like water-operated windup toys, but *human* animals, he reasoned, couldn't be since we were made in God's image and can reason. By the same logic, he posited that mammals kept conscious during vivisections could not feel pain, for instance. While he may be poorly remembered by modern animal rights activists, we can credit him with being the first to consider the interplay of natural physical tendencies turned on and off by some mechanisms outside of our flesh, and not by some tiny homunculus driving our moves from inside, like Remy the rat controlling the young chef in *Ratatouille* by hiding in his hat and pulling his hair to steer him around.

Here is what Russian scientist Ivan Pavlov had to say about Descartes in 1927:

> Our starting point has been Descartes's idea of the nervous reflex. This is a genuine scientific conception, since it implies necessity. It may be summed up as follows: An external or internal stimulus falls on some one or other nervous receptor and gives rise to a nervous impulse; this nervous impulse is transmitted along nerve fibers to the central nervous system, and here, on account of existing nervous connections, it gives rise to a fresh impulse, which passes along outgoing nerve fibers to the active organ, where it excites a special activity of the cellular structures. Thus a stimulus appears to be connected of necessity with a definite response.

When Pavlov's work on dogs and their reflexes began circulating in America in the 1920s, it pollinated a new field of psychology. "Why don't we make what we can observe the real field of psychology?" wrote John B. Watson in his 1924 book *Behaviorism*. He labeled those who were studying psychology by looking at observable behavior as *behaviorists* and described their desire to "consign to the waste basket the work of his predecessors and to start the problem over again." His observation of adults in his lab at Johns Hopkins, where he chaired the psychology department, led him to assert that people display a wide group of reactions that belong under the general name of "emotions"—a radical departure from the orientations of Sigmund Freud and William James, considered the fathers of psychoanalysis and psychology. Watson wanted to shift the focus to looking at the reactions, not internal unobservable and nonobjective stuff.

"According to James," Watson elaborates in a chapter on emotions, "the best way to study emotions is to stand stock still while having one and begin to introspect… No verification of observations is possible."

I don't know if we should toss aside all of James and Freud. But, when we're working with animals who will never tell you their feelings about their parents' divorce, looking just at the observable stuff doesn't seem like such a bad idea.

In the century since Watson, we've come a long way to being able to observe "emotions" internally: We've learned a lot about neurotransmitters; we have fMRI machines that can look at brain activity. Still, as a starting point, the behaviorist idea of looking at the observable results of emotions makes a lot of sense to me, as a dog trainer. It's a good reason to learn about dog body language—it can help you make some educated guesses at your dog's comfort level, and watching your dog is more practical than neuroimaging! Roughly speaking, I'm going to categorize dogs' emotions into two categories: happy and unhappy feelings. How are we going to get more of the former than the latter, in tandem with behaviors we want? By considering their preinstalled tendencies and figuring out how they can be discouraged or encouraged. That's where good dog training starts.

Learning by Association

THIS EQUALS THAT

"That which I see in dogs, I immediately transfer to myself, since the basics are identical."

—IVAN PAVLOV

MABEL WAS THE daughter of my uncle's dog, Elsa, who had been found on the side of the Cross Bronx Expressway. She got lucky when my uncle found her. She then got lucky again (spaying and neutering weren't de rigueur in the 1980s). I literally got the pick of the litter, an all-black puppy with a perfect five-pointed white star on her chest. Mabel.

When I was ten, I inadvertently figured out how to get her to race up the stairs of our building on cue. Upon getting home from a walk, she would sit patiently just inside the front door as I took off her leash, then she'd bolt as soon as it came off. But, if I took off the leash stealthily, she'd hold still until I pulled back its metal clasp, held it near her ear, and made a little *clink* noise. Then she'd take off.

My dad had his own idiosyncratic method of getting Mabel to run, from her bed in the far room of our loft to the front door in a second, at the sound of a perforated check being torn out of a page of checks that he had in a big binder. You see, in the days before ATMs, he would often write himself a check so he could get cash out of the bank on the corner, and Mabel knew a walk to the bank meant a walk for her. My dad would joke that she loved money.

I, as a middle schooler, was not the first to discover how a dog's behavior could be manipulated by pairings with stimuli that had started out as meaningless to a dog. Anyone who has had a pet and a can opener knows the drill. Ivan Pavlov himself I'm sure was not the first to pick up on the funny associations dogs make. But he was the first to study them.

There is a direct link between the work he did and what we do at School For The Dogs in Puppy Kindergarten. Pavlov is also on my brain when someone tells me that their dog has seemingly started to hate men wearing hats.

Born in Russia in 1849, Pavlov was a physician who studied digestion by experiments he conducted on dogs. He spent years surgically removing dogs' esophagi and replacing them with tubes that he'd use to gather their gastric juices externally, to study the rate of production and chemical properties of the fluids he collected.

Pavlov's most famous contribution to science started with a practical problem. His laboratory was set up like a factory, and the dog-machines were turning on before they should—a man in a white coat entering the room was enough to get the dogs' gastric juices flowing. So Pavlov tested different ways to elicit these "psychic secretions," by pairing food with various stimuli, buzzing a buzzer, for example, and then giving the dogs food.

By repeatedly pairing a neutral stimulus, like the sound of a buzzer, with something that was innately meaningful to the dog, like food, he saw that he could turn almost any previously meaningless thing—buzzer, man in white coat, and so forth—into a "conditioned stimulus," or a stimulus to which a dog could be taught to respond in an automatic way.

This form of learning came to be known as "Pavlovian conditioning" or "classical conditioning."

FUN FACT

Pavlov's most famous studies are popularly thought to have used a bell for the conditioned stimulus, probably due to a mistranslation of the Russian word for buzzer. When creating pairings with an unconditioned stimulus, it's useful to employ something staccato and quickly perceived. A bell, which has a ring that may be heard by a dog longer than it can by a human as it trails off, would not have been a great choice for setting up learning situations in a lab.

Classical conditioning can be very broadly described in three words: *This equals that.* Or, if you prefer: learning by association. You see plastic golden arches on the side of the road and your stomach grumbles. You see a police car's lights behind you and your pulse speeds up. Thanks to repeated pairings, a stimulus that you were not born knowing about (golden arches, a car with flashing lights) has become a reliable predictor of something meaningful and carries information about what behavior your body should engage in.

The ability to learn this way is crucial to survival, whether because an animal learns that the rustling of leaves may be a reason to hide or that a painfully loud beeping noise means there is a fire. Harnessing some of the power of classical conditioning rather than letting our dogs and ourselves always be just at its accidental effect can streamline training. It can also give you a new view on how punishment is perceived by dogs, as we'll discuss in chapter 11.

Predicting the Future to Stay Happy and Safe

It can be tricky to try to predict the future, but that sure doesn't stop us from trying. As humans, we have complex ideas about time: past, present, and future. Language certainly helps us predict, with pretty good accuracy, many possibilities of the very near future, at least enough so that we can try to direct our paths accordingly. Without even being aware of it, our brains are constantly processing what's going on in the environment and trying to figure out what is going to happen next.

Just stop and follow your thoughts for a moment, and notice all the thinking that relates to something that will be happening in the near or far future. Now consider all the *things* that are helping to trigger those thoughts: the ring of my phone, for instance. It indicates the possibility of a conversation in the near future. My knowledge about ringtones was not included in the original package of me, but after having heard lots of rings in my life, followed by lots of phone conversations, the two are inextricably linked in my mind. Even the words on the screen are stand-ins for all the things I associate with them. But vagaries abound, since a single word can be associated with countless things, and associations may be different from person to person. Fortunately, with words, we agree on enough associations to make conversation possible.

Dogs are always trying to predict the future too. In a way, dog training is simply teaching dogs associations that will help them predict whether something will be good or bad, pleasant or unpleasant. Or, on an even more basic level, to learn shortcuts to help understand if something is safe or dangerous. If we assume we are generally pretty good at knowing what is going to be safe and good for them, this work can often be easy.

We can help dogs sort the good and safe from the bad and dangerous.
Without our help, they don't always know which label to put on things.

Understanding classical conditioning is crucial to good dog training. Specifically, it helps us improve our dogs' quality of life—and with that, their behavior. It can help us:

✦ Socialize puppies and introduce adult dogs to things we want them to like
✦ Change feelings about scary things
✦ Teach certain behaviors like come and drop it
✦ Practice being generous with rewards we dole out

Criterion Zero

Let's start with that last point. Remember, learning is happening whether or not you want it to be happening, planned or unplanned. Your dog is making associations all the time, and those associations are going to affect their behavior. So, we should try to keep this in mind all the time when we are training. If doing something all the time and forever sounds daunting, we can start small, with the simplest training exercise there is.

STEP 1: Go and reward your dog. With a treat, or a toy, or a head pat. Something they like. Right now. Go. Meet you back here.

Mission accomplished? Great. That's all this exercise asks of your dog. The next part is for you.

STEP 2: Now ask yourself what associations your dog could possibly have made with that desirable thing that just appeared: Lying splayed on the ground like a bearskin rug? Being around a human? Sniffing the couch cushion? You can't know the answer, since your dog can't talk to you. But you can make some guesses.

STEP 3: Then ask yourself what your criteria were for your dog. What did he need to do to get the good thing? Your answer should be: nothing. This is the starting place. I call it Criterion Zero. Often, we overlook Criterion Zero and try to start too far along, with too advanced criteria, especially when we are welcoming new dogs into our chaotic households.

To describe Criterion Zero, I sometimes reference a parable I made up about a country cousin visiting a city cousin.

Imagine you lived in New York and you had a cousin visiting. Cousin lives in a secluded log cabin somewhere and doesn't have much big-city experience. On day one, you bring cuz to Times Square, and you really want them to like it. It might be smart to work up to that level of craziness, but you can't: You live in Times Square! Lucky you! Unlucky cousin.

That's kind of what it is like when you're ushering a puppy onto the city streets for the first time. Consider that their previous idea of the world may have been that it could be contained within the living room. Their personal Times Square is the city street. And it just happens to be populated by a species that is more than triple their size and doesn't speak their language, and they are getting to experience all of this for the first time while being led around by the neck.

Now imagine that you're in Times Square with your cousin, and you ask them if they'd mind doing your taxes right there. Or play a hand of bridge. Or solve a Rubik's Cube. These requests probably won't be met with enthusiasm.

If you want them to feel good about Times Square, maybe you shouldn't ask them to do anything more than just *be*. Maybe throw in a massage or ice cream. Now we're cooking with gas.

I see people make the Rubik's-Cube-in-Times-Square mistake with dogs all the time. I live on a busy avenue in the middle of Manhattan with two little girls who love anything fluffy. For this reason, I try to leave my house with dog treats on me. Frequently, one of them will want to say "hi" to a dog on the street; they've learned to get a treat from me and to ask the owner if the dog can have it. More times than not, the person turns to the dog and insists that he or she "sit."

"Sit," they'll say, while tugging up on the leash. The dog, meanwhile, is trying to investigate my daughters and also not get stepped on by the steady stream of pedestrians, or people hailing cabs while drinking green juice or looking at their phones while walking. The dog owner might as well be asking the dog to do their taxes.

"Frank, sit! I said *sit*!"

This is where I jump in.

"Frank, be cute!" I'll say. Then, immediately: "He did it! Give him the treat!"

The stranger doesn't know that I'm a dog trainer. And he probably doesn't know I'm in the process of training their dog. But I am. I'm "training" the dog to do exactly what he is doing, which happens to be existing in a way that I think we can all agree is cute. With Criterion Zero, I am not concerned with getting the dog to do anything in particular. I just want him to feel good about the situation he's in, as that's setting the foundation for teaching good behaviors and avoiding bad ones.

Frank was learning long before he came upon a dog trainer. He was learning about being on the sidewalk, about walking with a strip of nylon tied to his neck, about buses rushing past and three-year-olds approaching. He was learning how to behave in this environment, with the environment itself being the teacher—*Ouch! Manhole covers are hot on paws! Avoid!*

More than anything else, he was learning how to feel about everything around him, and all those feelings were influencing his behavior, now and later.

We tend to think of dog training as being all about an animal *doing* something: sit, leave it, get off, stop jumping. But I suggest setting the bar a lot lower to start with. The process of learning involves honing and whittling and adjusting—a never-ending process of shaping behavior that has to start somewhere. To knit, you need to be able to hold a needle; to bake a croquembouche, you need to know what an oven is. And to do either of these things, you need to, first, well, *be*. And feel good about being.

At the root of all behaviors is a single common denominator: a living animal who exists. Before you move on to getting a dog to behave in the ways you want, it'll behoove you to focus on the absolute smallest ask you can possibly make: this is Criterion Zero.

Pavlov himself had no criteria for the dogs he trained to associate food with a buzzer. What were they *doing* when he came in with their food? Were they whining? Barking? Peeing? We don't know! That's because it was not relevant to the experiment. Murashka the little spitz wasn't getting rewarded for her really good "sit." Once she heard the ringing sound, Pavlov was going to give her food no matter what. Even if she hadn't been salivating, the food was still going to appear.

With young humans, we are usually good at approaching behavior in this way. We naturally help kids make good associations before we focus on honing their behaviors. We don't say, "Hey, crying baby, if you stop crying, I'll feed you." If a baby is crying, we're more likely to try to change how the baby is feeling—by giving her a bottle or a favorite toy or singing a song—than we are to make good things contingent on her refraining from crying. We don't stop to wonder if we're rewarding an undesired behavior. We change the emotion by giving the baby something desired without making that reward contingent on behavior. And what happens? We get a quiet baby.

Just like with kids, it's important to think about the way a dog *feels*, before—long before—we think about how we want a dog to behave. A dog that is feeling comfortable is more likely to do good learning in that place. If she is fearful, we are not setting the stage for good dog training. Rewarding for existing makes a comfy foundation for everything to come. Establish that foundation, and you can slowly start raising your criteria from zero to, for example, existing and not jumping, existing and sitting, and, eventually, existing and "sitting" when you ask her to.

This shaping of behavior, from simply existing to existing plus behaving in all kinds of desired ways, is a lifelong process. That process starts with creating a world of things the puppy feels good about and depends on us working off our proverbial tails to create good associations. If we don't create good associations, we may have to be extra clever later on as we try to use conditioning to change associations. This is sometimes called *counterconditioning*, and it is more work than creating good associations from the get-go, which is why puppyhood is a key time to be thinking about Criterion Zero. If you're just starting to understand training and your dog is out of the puppy stage, don't fret: this kind of conditioning is key to helping dogs of all ages exist more comfortably in our worlds.

File Under "Good"

In the second, third, and fourth months of a puppy's life, the filing cabinet of the canine mind is particularly wide open. This is also right around the time that we commonly bring puppies into our homes. From the moment you welcome a dog into your home, you can picture them trying to figure out how to categorize everything: good or bad, or safe and not safe. We can help a puppy do this using classical conditioning.

Thanks to language, we humans have incredibly advanced ways of understanding safety versus danger. While dogs can learn to make associations with specific words, there are faster ways to communicate with them when we're trying to teach them about the world using classical conditioning. The best way to "tell" a dog that something new is "safe" is by pairing the experience of that thing with something the dog likes. Very often, that's going to be food.

You're already training your dog with food, but you might not be training anything very useful. You could say that many dogs are inadvertently "trained" to love being in the kitchen, since that's where they're fed. And they're trained to love bowls on the ground if that's how their

51

food is usually delivered. By the same token, you can use food to create other associations that are more useful to your dog and you. Indeed, one easy way to work on "socializing" a dog is simply to consider where he is eating—even better, where, when, and with whom.

Creating Associations with the Three Ws of Food

You can use meals to create good associations by thinking about food in terms of when, where, and who:

+ **WHEN** are you feeding your dog? Present a meal when you're about to go out, or even if you're just going to hop in the shower, to help your dog create good associations with you not being present.

+ **WHERE** are you feeding your dog? Solidify your dog's interest in being in a crate by feeding meals there (with the door open); give a meal in the elevator or bathtub; or bring lunch to a bench in a busy park and feed your dog one piece at a time to forge good associations with all the novel stimuli.

+ **WHO** is feeding your dog? Teach your dog to be comfortable with all types of people by having a variety of people feed your dog. Ask a neighbor's toddler to put the meal bowl on the ground, or have an extra-tall friend come by, tossing shredded cheese as she arrives.

In its simplest form, socializing a puppy, or acclimating an older dog to a new situation, involves being thoughtful about the associations your dog may be making, and building resilience. A good way to do this can be to have treats on you and make sure to present them whenever anything, or anyone, comes into your dog's zone of perception. In our Puppy Kindergarten classes, we have a unit where we play a variety of sounds: A car siren! Give your dog a treat. A baby crying! Give your dog a treat.

We put out a variety of objects—windup toys, umbrellas, skateboards, handheld vacuum cleaners—and sprinkle treats on and around them. Sometimes we put treats on large crinkly aluminum baking sheets, and they gobble them up while they walk over them. We have a costume bin on hand too, and dogs take bits of hot dogs from dog owners who volunteer to wear hats or googly eyes or walk with crutches we keep on hand for this purpose.

Of course, for some pups, a bit of freeze-dried chicken is no match for a Manhattan financial advisor kneeling on the floor wearing a fez and Groucho Marx glasses. A dog who is scared might refuse to eat, which is a good indicator of stress, but he also could eat and be stressed. God knows I've eaten when stressed! Signs of stress may be subtle: A dog who suddenly freezes, yawns, scratches an ear, or licks her lips is likely feeling less than peachy about a situation. We will talk more in chapter 14 about specific signs of stress. My point is that there is more finesse to socialization than tossing treats. It's crucial to go at your dog's pace and to work at introducing your dog to new things when they are relaxed. Bombarding a dog with hot dog slices while they're terrified is not what good socialization looks like. No dog is ever going to feel good about every situation, but we can work at incrementally building comfort with new things by being smart about creating associations and letting our dogs set the pace.

Feeling Good about You

The other day at a Puppy Playtime I was running, a woman said to me, "Remember the first time Billie was here and she hid behind me the whole time? And now look at her! She's a total social butterfly!" I nodded along, but the truth was that I didn't remember. So many dogs begin like that in Puppy Playtime that I no longer have great recall for specific instances of this transformation.

My theory as to why so many dogs go from wallflowers to windup toys in playtime is that we let them spend as much time with their human as they want. It's not unlike attachment parenting. No puppy is pushed into the fray. If a young dog seems to want to sit in his person's lap, or under her chair, or just wants to sit in a corner alone, we let them do just that. What's more, we tell the dog's person to keep the other dogs away if puppers jumps in said lap, or under said chair. We want to create safe human bases. We want the dogs to feel protected. Incrementally, they will feel comfortable venturing a bit farther from the human. If those experiences go well—with people creating situations where they can go well—dogs gain confidence exponentially.

While this may be most observable within the defined time and space of Puppy Playtime, it's something that I believe is happening all the time in relationships between people and dogs. There is a common denominator in most of the associations your dog is making: YOU! So, the more good things that happen with you present, the more your dog is learning to feel good about you. And that is always a good thing.

A word of caution, however: Some dogs will get overly attached to one person. This can lead to the dog feeling anxious whenever that person cannot be around. In chapter 20, I'll address how to help a dog deal with difficult things, like tolerating being alone or having the self-control to not grab the Christmas ham even though it's right there and no one is looking. But for now, just remember that you can—and, really, should—create a kind of family of humans that your dog feels good about. Your dog can still be yours, but I suggest broadening your idea of "ownership" as you think about what really is best for your dog. There may be times you need to leave town. Or your life may take an unexpected turn that makes it impossible to have a dog at all. If you have people who are willing to be uncles and aunties to your dog—people with whom your dog has already had good experiences—it'll be less stressful to find extra care. And the more people your dog feels good about, the easier it will be for her to feel okay about new people, and to create good associations with all the things that their presence brings with them. Otherwise said: You can't introduce your dog to every person who smells like Drakkar Noir, but Pete smells like Drakkar Noir and he's an okay guy, so maybe this new neighbor who is going to watch your pup next weekend is an okay person too. We humans make assumptions about people based on ties that are weaker than that. It's why some people won't date Scorpios.

Generalize, Generalize, Generalize

In the past, dogs were often kept so that they could guard property. One good way to produce good guard dogs? Don't let them know there is anyone who doesn't look like you, until they're on the job.

If I'm correct in assuming that you didn't get a dog to scare off palace intruders, then it's probably a good idea to think about how you can help your dog feel okay around new and harmless stimuli, especially people. We can't introduce our dogs to every single variation of person out there, but every person introduced properly is money in the bank that other people will be received warmly. These introductions are largely about having other people give your dog good stuff—a stranger hands your dog a treat; a neighbor stops by to give him his dinner.

Some of our clients hold puppy parties, inviting a wide variety of friends with the goal of ending up with a selection of people who look different from each other. One client, who had just moved to a rural area, put up a note on the library bulletin board that asked, "Want to meet a puppy?" and included her phone number. She did the same thing on the town's Facebook group. Our trainer Erin Whelan tells clients in the city to practice "stooping" with their dogs—sitting on the stoop with your dog and giving them a treat whenever anyone passes by. If you don't have a stoop, it could be the couch in your building's lobby, a folding chair in a supermarket parking lot, or the outdoor seating area at Panera Bread. Let the puppy explore all these people on his own terms and let him get lots of goodies for bravery. After all, he isn't just learning that people have different skin colors. That's just *one* thing. He's also learning that some people have glasses and long hair, while others have shoes with pointy heels, or hats, or canes. Some are loud. Some are tall. Some smell like cigarettes. Some have beards. We take these things for granted, but your puppy probably had no idea there were so many people who could be so different from *you*.

It's important that your dog has these kinds of interactions as a puppy, if possible, because (news flash!) mental rigidity tends to increase with age. The earlier your dog establishes a wide definition of "people," the easier it will be to accept entrants into this category that may come at a later date. Puppies who are cloistered are much more likely to be nervous around anyone who doesn't look like *their* person, although that doesn't mean counterconditioning can't help change your dog's feeling about your new seven-foot-tall neighbor. Ideally, however, there will be enough other information in their mental filing cabinet of past good experiences to help deduce that, based on prior experiences with many kinds of people, the bearded fat man in boots and a red uniform is probably an okay dude.

Fear and Counterconditioning

"I think that if you whipped a dog five or six times to the sound of a violin, it would begin to howl and run away as soon as it heard that music again…"

—RENÉ DESCARTES

PUPPIES ARE PARTICULARLY sensitive to making erroneous associations that may lead to fear, and like associations with good things, their fear can become generalized to include all new things. Babies can experience the same thing.

This was demonstrated in the Little Albert study led by John B. Watson in 1919 at Johns Hopkins University. In an experiment that is cringingly unethical by modern standards, he trained a baby to fear a rat.

Nine-month-old "Little Albert" was first exposed to a variety of things with which he'd had no prior experience: a monkey, a rabbit, a rat, some yarn, and a burning newspaper, among other things. Archival footage of the experiment shows his initial reaction to these things as either happy or neutral.

After several presentations of new things, Watson then presented the rat for a second time, but this time, he did so while also clanking a large piece of metal near Little Albert's head. The kid freaked out, obviously. A fear response to a loud noise is an instinct.

The third time the rat was presented, this time with no clanking, Little Albert had a fit. With one loud noise, he had conditioned the baby to fear the rat. But that wasn't all: When the first set of objects was presented again, he was scared of them too! And he was scared of new things that were presented that related to a rat even abstractly, such as a dog and a fur coat. Fear of the fur coat then generalized further, with Little Albert becoming scared of a Santa Claus mask.

Again, from the perspective of evolution, these broad generalizations can make sense. One red berry made you sick? Let's just avoid all red berries to be safe. In humans, this sometimes results in stereotyping. I think it's safe to say that we have all been guilty of making some large blanket judgment about something or someone based on one experience that may have been an anomaly.

Watson's interest wasn't dog training. But he was well aware that these phenomena cross species lines. "The behavior of man, with all of its refinement and complexity, forms only a part of the behaviorist's total scheme of investigation," he said.

Remember the Nice Blue Monster

Imagine, for a moment, that you were sitting peacefully reading a book, when all of a sudden a blue monster bursts through the door. Terrifying!

You scream as loud as you can. But then, instead of attacking you, it gives you a hundred dollars.

That wasn't what you were expecting. It leaves. You go back to your book. But then, the same thing happens again! And then again!

After a few times, you're actually pretty excited to see that blue monster.

Note that if someone had been watching this whole thing unfold, it might have looked as if the monster had been paying you to scream. Indeed, sometimes, this is what good dog training is going to look like from the outside: like you're pushing treats into the face of a dog who isn't behaving. However, by focusing on the association and not on the current behavior, we can often change the root cause of the behavior.

If you're not scared of the blue monster, you won't scream at the blue monster. A lot of behaviors we don't like in dogs stem from fear. If we can take away the fear by creating a new association, the behavior will very likely change. It will very likely diminish.

This can, of course, be done without food or money. When my older daughter was two, she would cry when we drove through tunnels. So, we started throwing "tunnel parties" in tunnels, which involved me and my husband crazy dancing in our seats to "Hooked on a Feeling" until the car saw daylight. Now she gets upset when we visit my in-laws in Jersey and take the bridge. She is the Holland Tunnel's only fan.

Habituation and Sensitization

Sometimes, animals can learn that something they previously feared *isn't* scary. They can unlearn their fear. I have a dog mask that I use sometimes for making Instagram videos, and when I first got it, I walked into the living room wearing it. My younger daughter, Marigold, who had just turned one, started shrieking. An understandable reaction! I took it off quickly. The next day, even the sight of it tucked inside a drawer was enough to make her scream. But then my older girl put it on one day after school and refused to take it off for the better part of four *Peppa Pig* episodes. Marigold cried, but then somewhere halfway into the first episode, she made peace with the weirdness of life and curled up next to her dog-headed sister. This is called *habituation*.

Sometimes, however, you can be scared of something and more exposure to the stimulus just makes things worse. Many dogs, for instance, get scared when smoke detectors go off. The owner of a dog named Simon likes to guess at his interior monologue in these moments. "The bad beep-beeps make loud when you least expect it!" he says. "He especially hates when the battery in one of them starts to get low and the smoke detector uses its dying gasps to cry out desperately…*beep*. Then ten minutes later: *Beep*… The first beep, he's cautious. By the second beep, he is visibly startled. By the third beep, he is trembling in terror as he waits for the robot overlords to overtake and torture us only to be delivered by the sweet relief of death."

This is called *sensitization*.

My dog Amos was also wary of beeps. Once, when the neighbor's alarm went off when she wasn't home, I fed cheese to him whenever he looked toward where the noise was coming from, and then settled into doing relaxation exercises with him (more on this in chapter 21). Eventually, he habituated to the sound.

But then one night while I was eating Indian takeout and watching TV, the smoke alarm went off, and the apartment was soon filled with smoke and firemen. There was an electrical fire in the wall of my bedroom. I whisked him (and my cat) outside, where we found ourselves surrounded by loudly beeping fire trucks. After that, I don't think even a pot of cheese fondue would've changed his feeling about smoke alarms. Fair enough.

If your dog is in fight-or-flight mode, tossing treats—even really delicious ones—might not do much. If a dog is too scared to eat, that is information about their fear level—information you can use to lower the intensity of whatever the blue monster may be. That said, it's possible for a dog, or a human, to be wildly distraught and to still eat and not have the one thing and the other necessarily connect. When my dad died, I ordered a dozen Doughnut Plant doughnuts, my favorite, and I ate half of them. I don't think it changed my feelings about losing my dad. But it did take my mind off things for a moment. Sometimes, something along those lines may be the best we can do for a dog. We can't always control everything about a dog's environment, but we can at least help redirect the emotion, counteract a potential bad association, and water down the intensity of the event, even just a little bit. It's not the best we can do with food in training, but it's not the worst.

Ideally, we are able to acclimate a dog to potentially scary things at manageable levels, pairing them with something great. Then, little by little, we gradually—*gradually*—up the intensity of the potentially scary thing. Over many repetitions, the animal learns that whenever that thing appears, good things happen. Eventually, the process produces a neutral or positive emotional reaction to the sight of the previously feared or disliked person, animal, event, object, or place.

Then we can start teaching a reliable replacement behavior, but first we need to get the animal in a state of mind where they can learn around this particular stimulus.

Two desensitization tips:

1. **VALUE MATTERS**: The more memorable the food treats you use, the faster the emotional response will likely occur. Think ham, hot dogs, chicken, turkey, cheese, etc. Variety is important, and you can rotate to keep your dog interested. If a toy is more valuable, use that.
2. **HAVE PATIENCE**: Your dog's response is involuntary at this point. You are working to change it, but until your dog is feeling like they're not in danger, it's going to be hard to get them interested in sitting just because you happen to think sitting is important at that very moment. Keep at it and let your dog set the pace.

Desensitization Exercises

We bring dogs into our homes without their consent. Because they're not choosing their environs, I believe it's our job to try to help dogs feel good about things they are going to have to encounter in our human world. Think about anything in your dog's perception that could potentially be scary to them, then think about how you can preemptively help them learn not to fear the sounds, objects, and sensations they may not be able to avoid.

I suggest you make a list. You can start by listing potentially scary things in your home. Since I've probably known more dogs than you have, and have seen some common (and often unexpected) fears, I'll throw out some ideas:

✦ Microwave beeping
✦ Vacuums
✦ Guitars
✦ Tea kettles
✦ Hair dryers

Now think about how you can introduce your dog to these things at a level your dog can handle. Not all at once, obviously! It might mean simply starting out by giving your dog treats when they're in the same room as the guitar, if they show any trepidation around it. Notice your dog's reaction as you increase proximity to the thing. If you see signs of stress (see chapter 13), literally take a step backward with your dog, and try to get them comfortable at that distance. If a dog shows any signs of fear around a guitar, you probably don't want to play her your favorite coffeehouse set just yet. Some dogs might be fine with the sight of an object they haven't seen, but its sound might be another story.

Also notice your dog's reaction to the thing in different contexts. A switched-off Roomba minding its own business in the corner is very different from the autonomous dirt-sucking rover it becomes when it's "alive."

Next, take stock of potentially scary things outside. I'll start you off again, with some objects many dogs find frightening in an urban environment:

+ Skateboards
+ Scooters
+ Motorcycles
+ Bikes
+ Wheelchairs
+ Revolving doors

While you cannot control many things outside, you can be prepared to change associations and create new narratives, even just a little bit. For a dog who has not yet encountered much of the outside world, having lots of treats on you—and giving them when something potentially scary appears, like a skateboard—and keeping walks short (just long enough to eliminate) and rich in rewards is a good way to work at forging the kinds of happy feelings you want your dog to have in a world that sometimes cannot be predicted.

Handling

Lastly, consider the fact that dogs are often touched in ways that they may not be thrilled about. This is especially true when they're having to wear clothes or equipment, such as a harness or muzzle, or deal with grooming, or veterinary- or husbandry-related routines.

Classical conditioning helps you train in a way that lets dogs offer consent rather than having them feel like they're just victims of their circumstance. A great place to start is a simple collar touch.

1. Touch the dog's collar.
2. Give a treat.

Repeat. That's it. When I run Puppy Playtimes, I usually have puppy owners practice this four or five times in half an hour: go to your dog, grab its collar, and give a treat. I want those puppies to think having their collar grabbed at any point, by anybody, is no big thing. Even if it's during playtime! What's more, a collar grab doesn't mean the end of fun stuff! It means a treat and then more playing. So, come on over here human and grabby grab. This is the idea.

In fact, my playtime mantra is "Collar! Name! Treat." The truth is the collar and the treat are the important part. The name is there to make it a baby step toward shaping a name recall. The dog got rewarded after you said his name! The fact that you had him by the collar when you called him is okay. Every behavior is allowed to be that easy at first.

Come and Drop It

"Machines that love, machines that make a choice for someone, machines that are jealous, machines that are fearful… Never would Descartes have meant us to believe it!"

—MADAME DE SÉVIGNÉ

FOR MANY PEOPLE, dog training means teaching dogs to do what you tell them to do. Sure, it's great to have a dog who understands what you want, but that stuff is high school, and I think most people should be starting out at a much more basic level. Better to begin with a situation where the dog gets good stuff no matter what. At least most of the time.

Imagine two people, each standing in front of a different soda machine. Now imagine you're trying to teach the behavior of emptying out these people's pockets (a behavior humans are being trained to do constantly, in fact).

One soda machine is a regular soda machine: You put in money, and out comes your soda. Sometimes it jams, but almost all the time, *a dollar* equals *soda*.

The other soda machine is set up like a magic claw: one dollar gives you the opportunity to use the motorized crane to maneuver up, down, left, and right to pick up the soda and navigate it to the slot that will dispense it to you.

THIS OR THAT?

So, the first machine is a sure thing, where beyond putting enough money into it, the behavior is irrelevant. Did they put the money in with their left hand or right? Was it a bill or quarters? Who cares! Just like you don't care if your dog drops something from his mouth onto this part of the floor or that part of the floor, or if he does it by pushing it out with his tongue or opening his jaw. You just want the thing out of his mouth, like the soda company just wants the money. They get the money because the consumer knows that money equals soda, and quickly too. *Plink plunk.*

Now, there may be the occasional glitch. But if the system breaks on the ninety-ninth try, the person will probably shrug it off and will continue to put money in the machine—quite possibly for a while.

Dogs don't care about soft drinks, but I think about soda machines when I teach a dog a "drop" cue. I say "drop" and my dog get a treat. She conveniently empties her mouth in order to receive her ersatz soda.

The other machine requires both a degree of skill and luck. Even with excellent hand–eye coordination, you still might only get the soda to the slot every second or third time. And there is a time lag too. *Plink, ggrrrrr, rrrrrr, rrrrr,* and then, maybe, *plunk.* If I were interested in teaching someone the fine skill of maneuvering a claw crane, then this would be the machine to use. Ditto if I wanted to be a lot leaner in how many sodas I was giving out. Slot machines are a good example of the kinds of long-duration behaviors that can be maintained by an unpredictable delivery of rewards. But let's not turn into greedy casino owners yet. We can afford to be generous with our learners, at least to start out.

And, in some training instances, a simple *plink plunk* will get the job done.

The Special Come

"Come" (often referred to as a "recall" in dog-owner world) is one of the most important things a dog can learn, and it always, *always* should be followed by something good. It's a bad idea to call your dog to come if you're going to do something she is sure to dislike. Your "come" needs to net a party every time, even if you feel like you're rewarding a behavior that was kind of sucky, or if you feel silly doing a jig for your dog when all they did was take a few steps toward you in a small room. Sometimes, we talk about practicing a "special" come because it's wise to use a distinct cue that your dog will be unlikely to mistake for anything else. For many dogs, human words are spewed around them all the time to the point where they can turn into static (habituation!) rather than information. For that reason, I think it's a good idea to teach this special come with a nonverbal cue. If you can use a sound or other signal that will travel a great distance, all the better. Many trainers like to use a bell or a whistle, as these are distinct sounds that most dogs don't hear very often. If you're going to use a word, choose one your dog probably hasn't heard—one School For The Dogs' client says "Godzilla!" for come because, in her home, he is not a frequent topic of conversation.

Any kind of food reward will work for this exercise—even bits of ham or other slimy stuff I don't usually recommend—since you'll have both hands free to deliver the goods. While it's wise to sometimes practice this with high-value treats, keep in mind that you'll want to do this exercise frequently. So, if sometimes you're just using your dog's regular dry food, that's fine too.

STEP 1: Go to your dog, with treats hidden in your hand and your whistle in your mouth. (If you can whistle really loudly yourself, then you probably don't need a whistle. I hate you.) Your dog should be no more than two feet away. Blow the whistle (one blow, or two or three swift ones, as long as you're consistent each time). Then drop treats at your feet. You don't have to drop just one. This is an exercise where you are allowed to reward your dog in a stupidly generous way for doing next to nothing. "But she didn't even come," you say. "She was already at my feet!" I know! Doesn't matter! That's how easy this needs to be. Was she existing in close proximity to you? Yes? She deserves a treat Bat Mitzvah.

STEP 2: For one week, practice the above level, a minimum of fifteen times a day in at least three different but familiar places—different rooms or your yard or the hallway of your building, for instance. This should take no more than a few minutes a day, and it should be incredibly easy for your dog. Of course, you could do more. If you want to, you could feed an entire bowl of kibble in this way one piece at a time. Just make sure you never show a treat until after you whistle.

STEP 3: Toss a treat five feet away from you in a familiar place. This first treat is a freebie. When your dog gets the treat, blow the whistle, then drop a treat at your feet. Repeat for a week, a minimum of fifteen times a day in the same locations as before. If your dog is reliably running back and forth between you and the tossed treat whenever she hears the whistle, start tossing the first treat ten feet away, then whistling and delivering one at your feet. If your dog seems to not be getting the picture, go back to step 1.

STEP 4: Once you get to the ten-foot point, try tossing the treat five feet and then running five feet in the other direction while she goes for it. Whistle when you arrive at your destination, then deliver the treat five feet away in the other direction, again running the opposite way and whistling when you're ten feet apart. At this level, you're adding speed to the game, and you're building excitement. Now she is getting to run for the treat, *and* chase you, *and* get another treat. Best game ever!

STEP 5: Once you're working the fourth step, you can concurrently go back to step 1 in new locations.

STEP 6: In one of your original locations, furnish a friend with treats and a whistle, and stand ten feet away from each other. Take turns blowing the whistles then tossing treats at your feet. If this is confusing to your dog, have your friend move closer to you until your dog is eager to run back and forth between you.

STEP 7: Have your friend start running ten feet in the opposite direction right after your dog gets treats at your feet. Your friend should then blow the whistle and do the treats-at-feet thing.

STEP 8: Increase distance! You can also start grabbing your dog's collar while they are eating the treats you're giving. There may be times when you will need to do this, and this is a good time to help her create a good association with that sensation.

REMEMBER: You are never working your dog to a point of failure in this exercise. If, at any point, your dog seems uninterested in the exercise, either postpone the training session or go back to the prior level or try using better treats or both.

Parable of the Prodigal Dog

✧ **QUIZ:** Which matters more in the "special" come: The whistle or the reward?

✧ **ANSWER:** The reward.

I want my dog to come when called. I also want her to sometimes come on her own because she knows it's always going to net something good.

I think Jesus understood this dog training concept. In the Bible's Parable of the Prodigal Son, a boy asks his father for money, then quickly goes off and squanders it. Destitute, dirty, and downtrodden, he eventually returns home. Upon arrival, Dad doesn't chastise. He doesn't say, "Great that you're here, but I didn't actually say 'come.'" He doesn't ask why it took him so long to return. What does he do? He runs *to* his son, envelops him in his arms, and makes a meal of fatted calf in his honor.

Does Prodigal Son's "come" behavior need some work in the bigger picture? Sure. But if that first come was met with scolding instead of celebration, what reason would he ever have to come back again? You can't teach a better come if, after the first trial, your subject doesn't see the point of coming at all.

The Prodigal Dog's come should be such a surefire success that, if you need to, you'll be the father running to your dog. He should not be judged for a lackluster recall; he should not be given a bunch of other tasks to do upon arrival (unless it's doing the dishes with his tongue).

He shouldn't be ignored just because you didn't ask for him to come. Just be generous with that fatted calf, and you'll have a dog worthy of Jesus's training.

Drop It

A dog knowing how to drop something when asked can be useful when out on leash walks (if he picks up an unsavory item) as well as being a behavior all dogs who play tug or fetch should learn, since "fetch" quickly turns into "chase" if your dog won't drop the ball. A human equivalent of this exercise is the phrase, "Huge sale, drop everything!" The store is hoping that you'll stop everything else you're doing and run (or click) to the store. It's a more effective sales method than saying, "If you come to my store, maybe I'll give you a deal." The latter involves a contingency. The former doesn't, since the sale isn't happening because of you—but its existence impacts your behavior. When teaching drop it, you're aiming to be Target on Black Friday.

To start, you will be conditioning your dog to the words "drop it." For now, they need to learn it means *you* drop stuff. Have a treat pouch or bowl with a bunch of small treats ready, or have them hidden in your hand. If your dog is distracted, you can do this exercise using a pen or tether or crate. It's crucial that your treats remain out of sight until you say the words. Saying "drop it" and giving the treats at the same time will render the words much less meaningful. The thing you want to have imbued with mean- ing (the words "drop it," also known as the conditioned, or learned, stimulus) *precede* the stuff that has innate meaning (food, aka unconditioned stimulus). Pairing in the other direction or concurrently won't work as well.

TOOLS: High-value treats and an object your dog likes to have in his mouth, such as a bone or a rope toy.

STEP 1: Approach your dog and say "drop it" just once, in a clear voice and then immediately toss a small handful of treats on the ground in front of your dog. When he has finished eating, repeat again. Repeat this exercise thirty times over the course of one or two sessions. When your dog starts to look to the ground every time you say "drop it," it is time to move on to the next level. If not, keep going through this level until he is.

STEP 2: Once your dog is reliably looking at you or the ground when you say "drop it," you can bring out a toy or chewy or something else your puppy likes to have in his mouth. If your dog tends to run away when he gets his toy or chewy, then it's best to have him tethered or crated or penned for this, as you don't want to have to chase him to start the exercise. Once your dog is engaging with the toy, say "drop it" and toss the handful of treats on the ground, just as before. If your dog doesn't immediately drop whatever is in his mouth, use some better treats, give him a less exciting thing to chew on, or do both.

STEP 3: Begin inserting a slight delay between your "drop it" verbal cue and the presentation of the treats. You should still give the treat even if your dog doesn't drop the thing, but they usually catch on pretty fast. If you're waiting longer than five seconds between when you say "drop it" and when he drops the thing from his mouth, make the delay between your "drop it" and the treat shorter, or try upping the value of your treats.

> **STEP 4:** Repeat until your dog has a strong enough association with "drop it" that they release whatever they have. When practicing in a new location, or with a new toy, or with a new person, start the whole exercise from step 1 each time.

But Isn't It a Bribe?

We often expect dogs, and people, to do the right thing because they want to, or out of a desire to please, or an ability to understand that doing a hard thing today will pay dividends later. It is, in a way, expecting animals to perform on credit. Sometimes this works. In my experience, a lot of dog owners new to training will spend a lot of time waiting for a behavior to occur for the reasons they want it to happen, rather than using what they have on hand to get the desired behavior going in the first place. Truancy laws are an example of this: We expect people to send their kids to school for all the right reasons and fine them if they don't. Offering the reward before a behavior occurs *can* seem like a bribe, and it may be, in some cases. But a reward can get a behavior going, and then once it's happening, you can start rewarding the behavior after. All the while, you're creating the right associations.

A decade ago, I was taking the odd assignment to write wedding announcements for the *New York Times*. Thanks to this gig, I went to a wedding held in the actor Ethan Hawke's townhouse: The bride was his mother, Leslie Hawke. Leslie used a kind of Criterion Zero approach when working with poor families in Romania, where she moved in 2000 when she joined the Peace Corps. She saw that many Roma families with young children never sent them to school. The schools weren't nearby and, having had no education themselves in some cases for generations, many parents didn't see the point. How could she train the behavior? She offered the parents food vouchers just for showing up with preschool-aged kids. "Most illiterate parents don't read or talk much to their young children—and they haven't a clue that early formal education is important. That's why we give them an incentive. It gets their attention," she said. Most of the kids ended up attending daily; more than 70 percent of the preschoolers went on to primary school, where there were no vouchers.

Associations + Beyond

By now, you can see that Pavlov cannot be escaped! Even if we innately understand classical conditioning, we aren't usually tuned into how we can use it, or how it impacts us and our dogs. Associations are powerful motivators of behavior. Some associations cannot be avoided, but others can be developed by design, by you, and this makes them useful in training. However, learning by association is only part of the training picture. When you're the one wearing the treat pouch, sometimes you'll want to set certain behavioral criteria for doling out rewards. This will involve a kind of conditioning that was codified in America in the 1930s: operant conditioning. It's how someone gets really good at maneuvering the magic claw. And it's how we, and dogs, learn to get better at everything we do.

If This, Then That

LEARNING BY CONSEQUENCE

> "Learning is connecting. The mind is man's connection system."
>
> —**EDWARD THORNDIKE**

AT THE SAME time that Pavlov was in St. Petersburg theorizing about animal learning, a researcher in New York City was too. In the 1890s, Edward Thorndike, a psychology professor at Columbia University's Teachers College in Manhattan, put cats in boxes for the sake of science.

Thorndike installed various simple levers and switches inside slatted boxes about the size of your basic cat carrier. The levers could be manipulated, from the inside, to force the box open, and Thorndike tried showing the cats how to open the box himself, before he put them in it. They didn't get it. He tried guiding their furry little paws to the switches for them (cutest science experiment ever). He had them watch other more learned cats get it done. None of this proved effective. Basically, everything we learned from *Garfield* was wrong.

What he found was that, at some point, some kind of flailing or accidental movement of the cat would trigger the mechanism for the box to open. Following the first accidental successes, the cats' subsequent escape times got faster and faster—the more times the cats had success, the better they were at succeeding.

He referred to the behaviors that worked to get the box open as being "stamped in" and behaviors that didn't work, "stamped out." He was seeing that, at least in a slat-boarded box microcosm, behaviors were selected because of how they worked to improve the subject's chances of improving things for themselves in a specific environment. Thorndike called this the "Law of Effect":

> Of several responses made to the same situation, those which are accompanied or closely followed by satisfaction to the animal will, other things being equal, be more firmly connected with the situation, so that, when it recurs, they will be more likely to recur; those which are accompanied or closely followed by discomfort to the animal will, other things being equal, have their connections with that situation weakened, so that, when it recurs, they will be less likely to occur. The greater the satisfaction or discomfort, the greater the strengthening or weakening of the bond.

I'd like to pause for a moment to point out that, on the one hand, what Thorndike "discovered" must have been observed anecdotally, outside the cat lab, at some previous time. Half of all history tells the story of people doing something that works well for immediate personal gain. All animals—including ones that do not write papers and get tenure, whether fingered, finned, or feathered—spend much of their time trying to do what "works." In fact, one definition of "insanity" is doing something repeatedly without regard to whether what you're doing is working. But, at the time Thorndike did his research, no one had ever codified behavior in this way. The field of psychology itself was hardly old enough to rent a car, and the world's experts in the field were still in their corners arguing whether it was better to measure intelligence by testing someone's hand grip or studying the bumps on their scalp.

You probably don't need to put your own cat in a lockbox to understand that an animal's successful attempt at something, accidental though it may be, can lead to figuring out the problem faster in the future. However, at least in dog training, many still have the idea, by default, that behavior is solely caused by the thing that happens right before it. It's as if, when you utter the word "sit," the word jumps out of your mouth and pushes your dog's butt to the ground. If one "sit" doesn't work, you will often see someone repeating the word, sending out a verbal army of "sits" to get the job done.

When a command doesn't produce a behavior, people often take this as a dog's inability to understand the thing that was supposed to make the behavior happen—the "sits" jumped out of the mouth and did what they were meant to do, but the dog was too [stupid, stubborn, distracted—circle one] to comply. For me, dog training gained a lot of clarity when I started to consider the importance of both antecedents—the things that come before—and consequences—the things that come after—as they impact behavior. An approach to dog training that focuses on the antecedents and consequences that sandwich behavior is both elegant as well as effective.

Criterion Something

Science fiction writer H. G. Wells was a Russophile, and in 1927, he wrote about visiting Saint Petersburg and meeting Pavlov, whose work was not yet well known in the United States. The piece appeared in the *New York Times* magazine and was read by a longtime H. G. Wells fan, B. F. Skinner.

Skinner, originally of Susquehanna, PA, had just graduated from college where he'd studied English, but he was starting to realize he was more interested in understanding behavior in a way that went beyond what could be contained between the covers of a book. He read the work of Thorndike and Watson and soon found himself analyzing his own behavior in a new way. Packing, he realized, related to Thorndike's Law of Effect. In a note he wrote to himself at the time, he observed that, "At first one throws things into a suitcase in no order whatsoever and with the immediate consequence of not having enough room for everything and the deferred consequence of wrinkled clothing or a burst tube of toothpaste…" Deep thoughts.

Skinner arrived at Harvard's Department of Psychology for grad school the next fall, eager to see if he could build on Pavlov's work to try to understand universal principles of learning. Young Skinner found a mentor in the head of the physiology department who was interested in measurable characteristics, focusing on the observable behaviors of his experimental subjects rather than what he could not see—what the behaviorists referred to as the "black box" that is our internal "self" and "mind." This idea set Skinner on fire.

When it came to the study of instincts, Skinner's plan was similar to Pavlov's, essentially: He was going to watch his animal subjects eat. In the beginning, he was mostly using white rats, asking questions like How long did it take them to eat? How fast would they go to their food?

He set up a circular track that, on one side, was closed off by a door that opened onto a food hopper. When the rat was done eating at the hopper, it could go through the door to start the revolution again and get back to the food hopper. Each revolution was recorded by a seismometer-like device Skinner had hacked together. His dissertation was about how the speed of eating was subject to environmental and physiological influences. For instance, hungry rats ate faster at first and then slower as the meal progressed.

If this is not the research he is known for, it might be because it's something most of us discover whenever we visit a Cheesecake Factory.

It wasn't until after he had gotten his PhD that Skinner realized the major thing that separated his work from that of anyone before him: the door.

You see, Pavlov's dogs, as we discussed, were not required to do anything in particular. When they heard that buzzer, they got food. Eventually they salivated when they heard the buzzer. Nothing was contingent on anything they did or didn't do.

Skinner's rats didn't have it quite so easy. They were not required to do anything hard, but they had to do something: open the door. In all his experiments up until a spring day in 1931, every time a rat pushed the door, the rat got food. But then one day, while Skinner was out, a feeder jammed. When Skinner returned, he found that a rat had gone bananas trying to get the feeder to work again. Kind of like when you swipe or tap your credit card to pay for something and it doesn't work. You don't give up. This thing is just supposed to work regardless of what you do, and when it doesn't work, you start trying out all the different things you might be able to do to get it to work again.

Skinner's rat's failed attempt at getting the food hopper to work was, for Skinner, a eureka moment. "It was a Friday afternoon," he would later write in his memoirs, "and there was no one in the laboratory who I could tell. All that weekend I crossed streets with particular care and avoided all unnecessary risks to protect my discovery from loss through my death."

This was the beginning of a decade where Skinner started codifying what he came to call *operant conditioning*.

Skinner had discovered what happens when a reward or punishment becomes contingent on what the animal is doing, what I think of as Criterion Something. Over the next six decades, Skinner would go on to demonstrate how environmental control and different schedules of reinforcement could result in animals learning to do anything within their physical ability, and then some. He went so far as to train a fleet of kamikaze pigeons to guide U.S. missiles. But we're getting ahead of ourselves. For now, let's consider what this kind of learning has to do with getting your dog to sit or wait or stop begging at the table.

Choose Your Adventures

Your average day presents far more choices than all the *Choose Your Own Adventure* books put together. At any moment, you aren't just choosing to do one of two things, you are choosing to do one thing out of a nearly infinite list of doable things. If you're reading this, it means that out of all the possible choices that have presented themselves to you in your life, you've made enough good ones (and had enough luck) to at least keep yourself alive so far. For that you can thank something that you and your distant single-celled ancestors have in common: the ability to use past success and failure to guide future choices. Dogs have this ability too.

Animals use associations to figure out what things are good or safe, or bad or unsafe, often sorting things into these categories based on connections they suspect exist, not necessarily based on the animal's own actions. Pavlov's dogs learned to associate food with sound, independent of any behavior on their own, just like the refrigerator door opening equals my dog's dinner, in her mind.

Say, however, she whines at the fridge right before I go and get her some food.

Her own action (whining) had a consequence (my feeding her) that, in this case, because she very much likes being fed, makes it more likely that she will whine at the fridge again.

This is *operant conditioning*, because the subject (my dog) is *operating* on her environment (in this case me) to effect change (the appearance of food where there was none before). The word *operant* comes from the Latin word for "work," and for our good dog training purposes we can think of all *doing* as forms of work. Indeed, this is why anyone does any kind of work! If you do something that works—if it gets you something you want or makes something you don't want go away—you're more likely to do it again. If it doesn't do either of those things, you're less likely to do it again. That's operant conditioning in a nutshell.

Operant conditioning is the kind of learning that most people think about when they think about dog training: sit, stay, heel, etcetera.

From the dog's perspective, much of training breaks down into a tidy if/then statement:

"If I sit, then I get a treat."

"If I heel, then I get to keep walking."

"If I leave that thing, then I get this thing instead."

If this/then that is a form of learning by consequence. The overarching goal of this book is to show you how to use your dog's fine-tuned ability to learn from consequences to get the behaviors you want. When the consequence of *that* turns out to be a happy and well-trained dog, you've built a Möbius strip of enjoyable coexistence that can last your entire lifetime together.

In the world of dog training, there is a division, and sometimes derision, between those who take a top-down approach to changing behaviors and those who want to use methods that are as gentle as possible, usually making use of teaching technologies rooted in the science of behavior. I've heard members of the former group refer to the latter as people who are "pushing" operant conditioning on dogs, as if it were a tool we could choose to take out of our toolbox or not. I've also heard trainers talk about going "beyond" operant conditioning, as if the codi-fication of a natural science were limiting them.

In fact, operant conditioning, like classical conditioning, cannot be avoided and is always in play. Whether or not we do it on purpose, we provide consequences for our dogs that they probably think are based on their behavior all the time. These laws of learning work on us whether we believe in them or not, however aware we are of them. The choice isn't between operant conditioning and something else, it's between inten-tionally and skillfully using operant conditioning to the benefit of our dogs and us, or letting it happen willy-nilly, shaping our dogs' (and our) behavior in ways we didn't plan and may not like.

In the next chapters, we'll break down operant conditioning into its components to better understand how to make it work for us as we train our dogs.

Negative Reinforcement

NOT AN OXYMORON

"Admitting the need for self-defense is not shameful, nor is the acknowledgment of vengeance as a reaction to coercion. Natural law governs our reactions when others shock us."

—MURRAY SIDMAN, *COERCION AND ITS FALLOUT*

BY DEFINITION, REINFORCEMENT is anything that encourages a behavior and punishment is anything that discourages a behavior. Every behavior that is reinforced is more likely to happen again. Every behavior that is punished is less likely to happen again.

How do you tell if something is being reinforced or punished? This may sound like a question for the ages, but it isn't a philosophical conundrum.

If it's happening more than it did before, a behavior is being reinforced.

If it's happening less, it is being punished. At the same time, consequences are either *positive* or *negative*, depending on whether they involve something being added to the situation or taken away. Remember, in math and science and good dog training "positive" and "negative" aren't emotionally or morally loaded terms. "Positive" simply means addition and "negative" means subtraction.

As a good dog trainer, positive reinforcement is my home base. But it has not, traditionally, been the go-to training method for many trainers. I think that is because it is widely misunderstood. But to be fair, punishment can be misunderstood too. Let's take a closer look at how reinforcement and punishment work, starting in the lower-right quadrant of the operant conditioning grid with *negative reinforcement*.

Negative reinforcement is a major reason dogs show aggression: growling, barking, and snapping are all behaviors that can make something undesirable—whatever that is—go away. On the one hand, at least in a limited sense, it works. Negative reinforcement is also the quadrant that most popular dog training has lived in over the last few centuries, which is why I'm starting with it. Let's get this over with.

In 2017, when School For The Dogs started a program to teach aspiring professional dog trainers, I liked the idea of having our students work with a noncanine species of animal, something that had been required by the Karen Pryor Academy program I attended. I had worked with my cat. But I didn't want to make our students go out and get another pet if they didn't already have one. I daydreamed about alternative subjects who could maybe be trained in their own environments: pigeons in the park? Rats on the subway tracks? Ants in a farm? Then one day a friend who is a middle-school science teacher mentioned buying snails online. You could buy snails online?! Of course you can! This led me to peruse the odd world of mail-order invertebrates. It didn't take me too much scrolling to find the perfect animal for our students: planaria.

Planaria are simple flatworms made up of ten thousand cells or so, roughly the size and shape of a grain of wild rice. Darwin studied them. Tiny though they may be, they have a nervous system and a kind of primitive brain. They can be found all over the world under rocks in rivers and ponds. But if you don't have one of those in your backyard, you can get planaria on Amazon.

I ordered a few dozen, and they came in a little cup with a twist cap and some petri dishes. Using some air-drying putty, I made a wall between the two sides of the dish with a small door in it allowing them to go from one side to the other—a two-room suite, if you will. Could I teach them to go from one side to the other? I tipped the dish to get them all on one side, tapped the dish, then put down treats on the dish's far side. The Google told me planaria like to eat water fleas. Sadly, I had none. So, I tried bread crumbs, and bits of banana, but they didn't seem enthusiastic. They also eat such tiny amounts of things that a bread crumb was like food for a month. Not great when you're trying to get in your training reps. Before I went too far down the rabbit hole of trying to find the perfect training treat for my pet worms, it dawned on me that there was one thing they really seemed to *not* like: bright light. This realization led me to become a kind of flatworm sadist, experimenting with them using something I don't usually suggest be included in the go-to toolbox for new dog owners: negative reinforcement.

When behavior is affected by negative reinforcement, something undesirable was either avoided or escaped by engaging in a behavior. Skilled trainers can use very mild negative reinforcement, often in the form of a retreat: the scary person backs away when the dog (or horse— this is a common horse-training technique) is not going ape. It can work. But it's usually not where we start out with our clients. Planaria, on the other hand…

So, I covered one side of the petri dish rooms with black construction paper, tapped the dish, then hit them with the light on my phone on the other side. Tap tap, light! Tap tap, light! Over the course of a week, I trained them that a tap meant it was time to skedaddle to the east wing.

Once, on a flight to a dog training conference in Illinois, I sat next to a couple who were thrilled to learn that I was a dog trainer and wanted to tell me about a neat trick their poodle could do: they had taught her to go sit on the lap of their daughter's giant Elmo doll.

I was all: Tell me *everything*.

Turns out that they'd bought a collar that made a high-pitched noise they couldn't hear, and it could be operated by remote control. They turned it up as high as they could whenever the dog sat anywhere in the room *other* than on the Elmo doll. Sitting on the Elmo doll made the sound stop.

"That's a good example of training using negative reinforcement," I said. They looked at me quizzically.

"How could it be negative?" the wife said. "She loves that doll!"

Does she love the doll, or does she love not having to hear that noise? If sitting on the Elmo doll itself was positively reinforcing, they wouldn't need the collar. Negative, I explained, in this instance means that something is removed from the scenario—in this case the high-pitched noise. While reinforcement refers to the fact that the desired behavior, sitting on the doll, is being improved upon every time the dog realizes that the doll is the place that frees her from aural pain. The dog loved Elmo like I love taking Aleve when I have a headache or putting on gloves when my hands are cold. If taking the pill makes the pain subside, the behavior of taking the pill is reinforced. The difference is nobody gave me the headache to teach me the cute trick of taking a pill. Nobody made the cold get me to put on my gloves. If they did, we might call it torture.

There is a type of training called "Force Fetch," popular in some gundog circles, that involves ear pinching but with the purpose of getting a dog to hold onto a bumper so that he can learn to hold prey in his mouth. The ear is pinched while the bumper is put into the dog's mouth, and the pinch is released when the dog clamps down on it.

A dog could be taught to drop something with an ear pinch, too. If he discovers that dropping the thing results in you leaving his ear alone, the dropping behavior is encouraged.

But as we saw in chapter 7, we can teach a dog a "drop it" without pinching his ear. So why would we use negative reinforcement, knowing we have a painless alternative?

Downside: The Bare Minimum

Behaviors trained with negative reinforcement tend to be lackluster. It's one reason people pay bills late. It's why we usually don't send the government any more taxes than required. Animals trained with negative reinforcement generally put in *only* as much effort as they need to avoid, or escape, something undesirable. I saw this phenomenon in action with my friend's kids. The older one was a great student, always trying to achieve the best possible grade to better his chances of getting into his top-choice college.

He didn't get into his top-choice college.

When his younger brother started high school a year later, it seemed like he had learned that there was little point in trying to reach for whatever brass rings were presented to him: the feeling of achievement when you see an A or the line that trying hard at school will make you successful for the rest of your life. Instead, he was motivated to just not fail. To this end, he downloaded an app in which he logged the grade he got on every paper he wrote and every exam, and it would calculate the minimum grade he needed to get on the next ones in order to pass the class. This approach was reinforced. He got accepted everywhere he wanted to go.

Downside: Negative Reinforcement Will Be Associated with You

One major bummer about using negative reinforcement is that it does not endear your learner to you. I experienced this firsthand the last time I ever had dinner with my dad. It was September, and I was just back from Italy, where I'd gotten engaged. My fiancé and my dad and I were all at my dad's favorite restaurant in SoHo. He was asking about our wedding. We explained we were keeping things small. A brunch reception at the restaurant across from the temple. Did I invite Uncle Jim, he asked. Yes. And Cousin Paula? Yes.

Then he paused.

"And your siblings?"

My father had three children before me with his first wife. They were a lot older and grew up in another state. I wasn't on great terms with them. Anyway, didn't I mention it was a small wedding?

Never before had I heard him raise his voice during a meal.

"Why are you punishing me? You're an animal trainer! You're not supposed to use punishment!" he bellowed.

I excused myself to go to the bathroom and breathe. And cry.

There, I thought: *I'm not trying to train my dad! I'm just a woman with a guest list!*

I was also frustrated that he seemed to think "punishment" was just the opposite of being nice. As I saw it, I wasn't trying to punish him at all. Rather, he was trying to use negative reinforcement to control my behavior.

When I went back to the table, he told me if I wanted him at the wedding, I had to invite my half-siblings. Invite them, and I could make the dad-not-coming-to-my-wedding thing stop.

It really hit me, in that moment, how attempts at coercive control can get compliance, but rarely do they make the dog want to take his trainer out for a drink. Or invite someone to your wedding.

No matter how well negative reinforcement works to get a certain behavior, if you're the one pinching the ear, or putting on the collar that shocks, or causing the scary sound, by the laws of learning, your dog will likely associate you with that experience. So we have to ask ourselves, is that the relationship we want?

Confusing Terms

While the word "negative" is busy being misunderstood in the corner, "reinforcement" is on the other side of the room getting confused with niceness. In the section called "Affection" in *Cesar's Way*, Millan explains how Americans use kisses and belly rubs to "reinforce" bad behaviors. "Share your affection only with a mind that is calm and submissive," he writes. As someone who didn't get her teeth cleaned for two years after her dentist kissed her on the lips, I can tell you that affection isn't always reinforcing.

Creative uses of the word abound in this field. In their 2020 book, *The Art of Training Your Dog: How to Gently Teach Good Behavior Using an E-Collar*, for example, the authors refer to three shock levels delivered by the collar. At the least extreme is the "education level," which a dog can "just barely feel at any given moment but gets his attention" (they don't explain how we know what the dog feels). At the most extreme is the "interrupter level," for "when the dog fully understands what we're asking but decides not to comply" (they don't explain how we know what the dog understands or how we know that the lack of desired response comes from their will to disobey). In between these two settings is the supposed "reinforcement" level, a kind of Goldilocks "just right" sweet spot that is "harder to ignore than the educational level" but not "painful" or "disturbing," according to them. They do not say how a shock has any effect at all if it is not disturbing. And the word "punishment" appears not a single time in the book.

Punishment

"From the time of Plutarch and Pliny and probably long before, it was believed that young bears were brought forth as shapeless lumps and that the mother licked them into shape. From this came the idea of licking some young cub into shape, and since the chief shaping object, formerly, was the rod, the word 'licking' came to mean a beating."

—BERGEN EVANS, *THE NATURAL HISTORY OF NONSENSE*

THERE ARE THREE types of consequences that will make your dog less likely to do something:

1. Doing it results in something undesirable happening.
2. Doing it results in something desirable being taken away.
3. Nothing happens.

Straightforward enough. However, the technical term describing the first two of these consequences is *punishment*—a word no one seems to want to have associated with them. Trainers who use punishment may refer to themselves as "correction based" or "balanced," the latter being a popular term among dog trainers who incorporate both reinforcement and punishment in a training plan. They tend to give "corrections" or "reminders."

I think the word itself is part of where things get tricky and where we need to rethink our snap judgments when it comes to dog training. Just like people wrongly associate the word "positive" with smiles and sunny attitudes, "punishment" is misunderstood and swept under the rug because we have been conditioned to associate it with pain, misfortune, and discomfort. Further confusing the matter is the counterintuitive behavioral subcategory *positive punishment* (the upper left quadrant of our operant conditioning grid), which marries the two most misunderstood terms. If "positive punishment" gives you the contradictory mental image of a mean school principal wearing a tie-dye shirt and singing "Don't Worry, Be Happy," me too.

Positive Punishment

Recall the first of the three types of consequences in the list in the previous section: doing it results in something undesirable happening. This is positive punishment. If a behavior results in something undesirable and the dog stops engaging in that behavior, that behavior has been positively punished. *Positive* means something was added, not that punishment is swell. *Punished* because the effect is, by definition, to decrease the likelihood of the behavior happening again.

Except sometimes, punishment *is* swell—this may surprise you coming from a "positive reinforcement" trainer like myself, but thank goodness for punishment! You and I are alive today to talk about this because we, and our ancestors before us, have evolved in such a way that we can get information from our environment that tells us not to do something, sometimes. Punishment can be a real lifesaver. My dad used to tell the story about how his Doberman got a face full of porcupine quills. You know how many times she did that? Once. Any animal who doesn't find certain things punishing may not thrive long enough to pass down those tendencies to the next generation: people born unable to feel pain, for instance, live in constant danger.

There's a difference between punishment that comes from interactions with the environment and those that are intentionally arranged by someone. In most of the history of modern dog training, humans have been the someone. This is most likely because doling out punishment can be extremely reinforcing for, well, anyone who is doing the punishing. Even if the punishment wasn't effective in the long run for changing a behavior, that leash jerk made the dog stop pulling right now, and that makes me feel like I'm in control, like I did something that stopped a behavior I didn't like. I *feel* like the punishment worked, and that's a reinforcing feeling. My leash-jerking behavior was therefore reinforced and will happen again if a similar situation arises, which it probably will. If it doesn't work all the time, that doesn't even matter much: I hardly ever win scratch-card lottery tickets, but I still buy them.

Punishment can also stop working, usually because the object of the punishment becomes used to the punishment. So the punisher needs to regularly amp up the intensity of the punishment. Fun times.

Likewise, if you're punished by having something taken away, it can become ineffective if you eventually find there's nothing left to be taken. This always makes me think of the mournful lyric famously sung by Janis Joplin in "Me and Bobby McGee" about how freedom is what you have when there's nothing left to be taken.

When a behavior is encouraged or discouraged because of consequences that involve something being taken away, it's actually, technically, not *bad*. It's *negative*.

Negative Punishment

In everyday language, "negative punishment" sounds like the worst! So, it may surprise you again to learn that negative punishment, in behavior science and in dog training, can sometimes actually be a gentle way to change behavior. Negative punishment is never my first choice as a trainer—that's positive reinforcement, which we'll get to next—but, very occasionally, it may be my second.

Anna Ostroff, a one-time School For The Dogs client who has been working with us as a trainer for over six years, recently worked with a dog who couldn't tolerate anyone being near his human. He was fine at daycare but became aggressive to everyone around as soon as his owner came to pick him up. Same thing at the vet. He could only tolerate Anna at a distance of ten or so feet when his human was present, and he wasn't happy about it. After working together four times, Anna had an idea: She told his human to leave the room. Alone with just Anna, over ten minutes or so, he relaxed. He took treats tossed at him. He was able to do some training exercises with her. It was impressive progress! When his person came back, he seemed elated, but then he turned and barked and growled at Anna. She told the owner to go away again. After a few repetitions, he was able to be in the same room with both of them together. He had learned that barking at Anna made the good thing, his favorite person, go away. That's the negative. It ended up being a way to discourage barking, which is why it was technically punishment.

Is It Really Punishment?

Your dog jumps on you, and you yell "no" and push him down. Your dog jumps again. Did he want your attention, regardless of your tone and word choice? It's one possibility. We can ascertain whether the behavior has been effectively punished by looking at whether it keeps happening. Sometimes you can stop a behavior in the moment, which may be positively reinforcing for you. But the behavior doesn't decrease over time. So then you are having to continually raise the oomph of your punishment. Exhausting. And, taken to the extreme, terrifying.

Likewise, we can inadvertently punish a dog when we mean to reinforce a behavior. To a dog who is fearful, for example, a new person approaching with a treat to reward the dog's sitting may actually be punishing the sit.

Then there are the times when an attempt at punishment turns into a cue. Turning your back to a dog who is jumping on you may discourage your dog from jumping. However, too often, it becomes a little dance rehearsed over and over, as the dog learns that your turning your back in moments of excitement is a cue for her to sit, and to get all the good stuff—attention, treats, praise, etcetera—that happen when she sits. And how does she get you to turn your back? By jumping on you.

It's interesting to me that in my personal library of many popular books about dog training published over the last century or so, almost none of them use the word "punishment." It's there. It's just called something else. I don't think this is because people are ashamed they're using punishment and excuse it by calling it something else. I think it's because they truly don't understand it as being a part of a science of behavior.

For example, in his 2021 book *Training Your Dog the Weatherwax Way*, R. Ruddell Weatherwax, grandson of Lassie's trainer, never recommends "punishment" per se, but he does recommend training protocols that rely on punishment as defined by operant conditioning. In a chapter called "Bad-Behavior Training," he suggests throwing an object onto a hard floor behind a dog who is barking. "It could be something they love, like a toy, or something they acknowledge or respect, like car keys or a chain collar... The very moment the correction tool lands, you say 'No!'

in a strong voice." He says the dog should then be praised and fed. "In essence," he explains. "you're marking the good behavior in the mind of your dog. If they begin barking again, then the reward is withheld. There is no punishment for bad behavior; just reward for good behavior." It's as if refraining from using the "p" word makes it invisible.

A few years ago, I interviewed the original Timmy, who played opposite Lassie's titular heroine on TV in the 1950s and 1960s. His name is Jon Provost. I asked him about Lassie's trainer. "I never saw anybody that trained and used the methods that Rudd did. Rudd was always praise and reward," he told me. "His dogs were treated better than his wife."

Curious to learn about what seemed to me an early uncredited hero of reward-based training, I tracked down Weatherwax *grand-père*'s book *The Lassie Method*, published in 1971. Indeed, he never advises using "punishment." But he does suggest developing the ability to "mean talk." To teach a dog to be alone, for instance, he suggests leaving your home and then lurking outside the door to see what happens. If the dog starts to bark, "bang open the door and roar at him: 'No! No! What do you think you're doing! No! Quiet! Quiet!' Browbeat him for a good two minutes no matter how repentant he looks," he writes. "The next time you have to rush in, slam a book or a newspaper to the floor, grab his neck and give him a shaking and the most scorching Mean Talk you can. Each and every time he brings you back hereafter, make him think you're a hair's breadth from dismembering."

The Problem with Not Teaching What to Do

We all like to have some idea of what we can do to make the world around us safe and comfortable for ourselves. When we use punishment as a teaching tool, we are telling the learner what not to do, but we aren't telling them what *to* do.

I've seen dogs appear paralyzed in this way in many a dog training reality TV show, with the dogs finally appearing to be reformed simply because they are literally hardly moving. Punishment has provided those dogs with a lot of information about what not to do but no insight on what they should do, so the dog does as little as possible, the only thing that feels safe. A dog in this state, to many eyes, can appear to be quite well behaved.

What's more, punishment-focused training may end up punishing behaviors that we don't realize are actually helpful. A dog who is punished for growling, for instance, may learn to not give that useful indication of discomfort and to instead go straight for the bite.

With humans, we have language to explain to someone what we're punishing them for (a helpful notice on my windshield explains I've been fined for parking in front of my work after 8:00 a.m. on any weekday). And, if we are feeling nice, we can explain to someone what they can do in the future to avoid punishment (the meter cop explains I can park around the block where they only clean the streets on Tuesdays). Of course, we all know what it is to be punished for no rhyme or reason. It's even less fun when you get fined and you don't even know why.

With dogs, that's what most punishment probably is like. We can only hope that they're making the right association: that they understand they're being punished for the thing we think we're punishing them for. If we're lucky, they do, which we can deduce if the behavior stops happening. However, we may never know all the other things that were inadvertently being punished at the same time. For instance, you yell at your dog for peeing on the carpet (for the sake of this thought experiment, we are pretty sure your dog doesn't construe your vocalization as a reward; he doesn't like being yelled at). If any time has elapsed since the urine and the carpet encountered one another, you very likely will be punishing your dog for approaching you as you walk into the room. If your punishment is meted out with *perfect* timing, there is still no guarantee that he will understand your wrath has to do with his pee. And all the other behaviors that are happening in that moment are being punished too: being near you, looking at your boots, existing in the living room, and who knows what else.

For this reason, I've often counseled puppy owners that it's better to just ignore a puppy who eliminates in the wrong place rather than yelling or trying to stop him mid-business (which probably is scary to him, given that peeing or pooping puts anyone in a rather vulnerable position!). Otherwise, a puppy may learn to associate *fear* with *peeing or pooping in front of you.*

When we punish dogs, we can inadvertently cause associations that lead them to have fears that we didn't intend to create.

Beth Berkobien, a colleague of mine in Texas, told me about her late Rottweiler who soiled himself in fear whenever his feet touched rubber. It started when they were training for an Obedience title, and a trainer at the facility where she was bringing him suggested that a remote-controlled "electronic" collar would help "clean up his heel." She used the shock collar twice.

The place had rubber floors.

He never got over the fear. Seeing her dog so scared effectively punished the behavior of training that way. It's why she became a positive reinforcement trainer.

We're wired to hang on tightly to associations with anything that may be dangerous—it helps keep all animals alive. But causation doesn't always equal correlation. That's complicated enough for humans to understand. Dogs have superstitions too, but they usually don't involve lucky underwear. They almost always involve a misunderstood association that leads them to think that something is bad or dangerous when it isn't. A dog who has been hit may, for example, take any kind of hand-raising as a foreboding sign, even if it's just a kid raising his hand to answer a question. A dog who runs to say "hi" to the UPS man and hits the invisible fence may now associate the driver with the shock.

Sometimes these connections will never be known; other times we may discover them by accident. School For The Dogs' cofounder, Kate Senisi, once did a virtual session with a French bulldog puppy who bit anyone who tried to put on his collar and leash at walk time. This can happen when dogs have a fear of going for walks, but his humans reported that he ran from the collar even before they had ever attempted to bring him outside. After some observation and further questioning, Kate learned that the collar itself was the thing he seemed most afraid of. She asked if he was okay wearing any other collars and was told the only other collar he'd ever worn was an electric collar, which they were using to keep him off the couch. This puppy had learned a fear of collars in addition to or instead of an aversion to the furniture.

I recently asked Kate how she explains to clients that their attempts at punishments are ineffective. "I tell them if they're trying to punish their dog and it's not working, then they're just being annoying." I had never thought about it in this way, but I realized she was right. At least, when I think of people in my life who I label as "annoying," it's the telemarketers of the world and nagging relatives who are always trying to get me to do something I don't want to do, or to stop doing something, usually without success. But I comply just enough of the time to reinforce their behavior.

At School For The Dogs we avoid using "aversives" with dogs because, I'll say it again, when we choose punishment or coercion, even mild, we risk creating a bad association that may end up looming much larger than the good and right associations we work to forge. What makes this especially heartbreaking is that too often, these wrong associations may have to do with the person in charge of the whole game: *you.*

Thank goodness dogs are as forgiving as they are. Here are some things I have imagined I'd say to dogs I've met, if they spoke English:

"Oh, that umbrella? It's just a little weird when it opens, but it's not going to hurt you."

or

"Yes, I was yelling, but not at you."

or

"I didn't like the way that walker jerked you around, but not *all* people who wear Doc Martens are scary."

The Punishment–Reinforcement Seesaw

If you're engaging in a behavior that gets punished, you're likely experiencing several aversive events. There's the punishment itself, but there's also the removal of what was reinforcing the behavior in the first place.

You will start to notice this hopscotching between the quadrants of operant conditioning when you consider behavior in terms of reinforcement and punishment. Remember the dog with the Elmo doll and the high-pitch sound-making collar? The stopping of the sound (that we can surmise was unpleasant) reinforced the behavior of sitting on the doll; the presence of the sound punished, or discouraged, all behavior that was not sitting on the Elmo doll, in a positive punishment–negative reinforcement seesaw encouraging the behavior the dog's people wanted from both ends (and resulting in their behavior being positively reinforced, because their scheme worked).

Likewise, negative punishment and positive reinforcement correspond. One game I play with dogs is called the "elevator game," which you can do whenever you're giving a dog a meal (or a toy or anything they desire that you don't mind them having), assuming your knees are up to it, since you are the elevator in this game. I ask a dog for a sit. Once they're sitting, I start bending down toward them with the food. I'm positively reinforcing the behavior of sitting by approaching with something delish. But, if the dog tush pops up, the "elevator" reverses—I straighten, the food recedes from the dog's perspective, and I wait for the dog to sit again. When the elevator goes up, the behavior of doing something other than sitting is being punished, by literally removing the good thing, in this case being close enough to eat (negative punishment). When the elevator goes down, it positively reinforces the sitting by delivering, or beginning the process of delivering, the food.

Last summer I went to a conference run by Vermont-based trainers Sara Matters and Debbie Jacobs. During a lunchtime conversation about how positive reinforcement trainers sometimes use punishment, I mentioned the elevator game. Debbie hadn't heard of it, so I explained, and she looked at me with a furrowed brow.

"Why do that?" she said. "Why not just set the dog up to get it right and only work at levels he can handle?"

It dawned on me that she was right: it is possible to avoid using negative punishment, to teach such a thing, so why was I going there? Was I compromising my values as a good dog trainer? Taking the easy way out rather than setting up my learner for success? I had to ask myself some serious questions.

In the next chapter, we'll talk about just that: setting dogs up to succeed and showering them with delights when they do. And I'm hoping that if there is some cosmic scoreboard keeping track of such things, my efforts at explaining this to you will temper the fact that I have sometimes punished my dog by raising her food bowl when she stopped sitting as the dish came toward her.

Punishment of any kind is not in my or any of my positive reinforcement training colleagues' go-to toolboxes, and I hope it won't be in yours. However, punishment is part of life, and you cannot control everything in the environment that may end up punishing your dog. You also will very likely punish your dog, sometimes, if not as part of a training plan then simply by ending a game before your dog is ready to retire or leaving the house when your dog really wants to come with you. When I told my husband about feeling ashamed for sharing my elevator game strategy, he said, "So basically she never uses punishment and you do?"

No, it's not that simple. Both of us are committed to finding ways to avoid overusing negative reinforcement and punishment in training. Both of us believe in something like the Hippocratic oath as it pertains to working with dogs: first, do no harm. However, there can be gray areas.

The fact that dogs are so willing to do our bidding, even when we are sort of jerks about it, means that it can be very easy to pick whatever training method seems effective without taking into account how humane it is.

Good dog trainers tend to assert that in order to be maximally humane, training interventions should be as unobtrusive as possible. In the coming chapters on positive reinforcement and managing your dog's environment to get the behaviors you want and not get behaviors you don't want, you'll see what this looks like and what a joyful approach to training it is. Punishment can be so mild it's hard to argue it's doing harm—like turning your back on a jumping dog or returning to a stand during the elevator game. My conversation with Debbie reminded me, however, that even a mild punishment still creates an association between me and something the dog doesn't like. And why would I want that?

Every dog owner will sometimes punish or negatively reinforce their dog, intentionally in the context of a training session or just accidentally in life. I think the best we can do is to commit ourselves as much as possible to using positive reinforcement. It's like putting so much money into a joint bank account of love and trust that the occasional withdrawal won't be a big deal.

With positive reinforcement, we assume our dogs already want to please us, and it's our job to show them how.

Positive Reinforcement

FEEL THE LOVE

> "To people schooled in the humanistic tradition, the manipulation of human behavior by some sort of conscious technique seems incorrigibly wicked, in spite of the obvious fact that we all go around trying to manipulate one another's behavior all the time, by whatever means come to hand."
>
> **—KAREN PRYOR, *DON'T SHOOT THE DOG!***

A COUPLE BLOCKS from where I grew up in Manhattan's Chinatown, there is an arcade called Chinatown Fair. My parents were divorced, but in the 1980s and '90s, on special occasions, we would take a trip *à trois* to the rather dingy (and super ding-y) Mott Street arcade. We weren't there to play pinball or *Ms. Pac-Man*, however. We went to see a chicken play tic-tac-toe.

It cost fifty cents to challenge the chicken, who stood in a clear box that had backlit red Xs and Os on a hashtag board, maybe a foot high. Once your coins plunked in, the chicken would go to a control board behind an opaque panel to peck her first move. Then you'd put in yours, pressing a button to indicate your choice. The chicken always won. If you were lucky, you might get a draw. (If you were *really* lucky, she would lay an egg.)

I'd ask my dad how it was done. "She's a smart chicken," he'd say.

Later, over a plate of General Tso's, he'd look down and say, "This chicken was less smart."

A few pinball machines over, a different chicken would step up on a platform in her clear box and do a little dance when you paid. The world's purest peep show!

My dad was able to explain this one with more clarity. The plate she danced on, he said, was giving her electric shocks which made the chicken look like she was dancing.

That seemed reasonable. Inhumane, but reasonable. But the one who played tic-tac-toe was a mystery. The people who ran the arcade weren't going to tell. Google didn't exist yet. Even my dad didn't know.

Fast forward thirty years, in a converted warehouse in a suburb of Boston, I'm filming myself in slow motion delivering a cup of bird feed to the beak of my very own trained chicken.

Maybe you're wondering why I, or anyone, would train a chicken. The number one question I got when I told anyone I was heading to Massachusetts for a week to train chickens was: "What on Earth are you training them to *do*?" This speaks to the way we think about training, as being something with a subject and an object, often a problem to be solved, possibly with some kind of salvation granted. "Do they need your help?" asked one friend. "Or are they being bad?"

Neither. They were being trained because I wanted to learn how to train them. Any benefit to them was not the point. I was there to hone my own skills. In some ways, training a chicken is like swinging with a weighted bat. If you can train this flighty animal that has no interest in your affection or attention and would like to just not be killed, you'll look with fresh eyes upon the Cavapoo who thinks your toes taste great.

In other ways, chicken training is much simpler than dog training, clearing away a lot of the emotional and cultural static that surrounds everything about dogs. Few people worry about the power struggle in the chicken–human relationship. I wasn't there to make friends. Either we're hanging out because we're training, or we aren't hanging out and we aren't training. There's no cuddling on the couch afterward. I also had total control over pretty much the only thing the chickens cared about: food. We have less control over all the things our dogs want.

Bob Bailey, who started the program, has trained over ten thousand individual animals and over a hundred species, almost entirely using positive reinforcement. But it was Parvene Farhoody who was running the clinic I attended. Farhoody was working toward a doctorate in behavior analysis and learning processes. She had studied the art and science of chicken training with Bob Bailey himself and developed the latest version of this workshop with him, but Bailey had had some health issues so Farhoody was leading it solo. I told her about the Mott Street birds and she nodded. "Those were Bob's."

I was, for a moment, speechless. The last thing I expected when I arrived in Taunton, Massachusetts was to solve the mystery of the tic-tac-toe chicken.

When I flashed back to the present—where I was surrounded by people teaching color differentiation to hens—I told Farhoody about my dad's explanation of how the chickens were made to dance using electric shocks.

"You can't force a chicken to do that," she said. "You have to use positive reinforcement."

A Virtuous Cycle

Positive reinforcement is something I knew a lot about before I truly understood what it was. It was why I did things I liked to do. It's so simple really. I went to restaurants I liked. I hung out with friends I liked. I tried to find work I liked. Life was basically an effort to do things I liked and figure out how to do more of those things. My behavior was being molded by positive reinforcement all the time, though I didn't call it that or give it much thought.

Sometimes life was also about avoiding annoying stuff or figuring out how to do something in the easiest, least painful or difficult way. But if I had to choose between motivating factors, I would choose doing things I like.

And I know my dog is like this too.

Whenever you do anything because there is some kind of potential gain, you can thank your ability to learn from positive reinforcement.

If a behavior is positively reinforced, it means that something desirable was added to your situation making it land on the positive side of our imaginary X/Y axis, were we plotting this—and the likelihood that behavior will reoccur has been encouraged—the reinforcement part. Welcome to the upper right quadrant. It's a nice place to be.

Behaviors are positively reinforced when engaging
in them results in something desirable.

Behaviors may be reinforced with attention or food or access to a desired spot, or with any number of signs or sounds that have taken on meaning thanks to repeated meaningful pairings via *classical conditioning*. (Recall Pavlov's dogs and their buzzer.)

Once you train your eyes on how it's possible to reinforce behaviors you want without having to even think about getting rid of behaviors you don't want, once you see the enthusiasm with which a dog in training will participate in the process, it can alter your point of view of everything and make you ask questions that leave you shaking your fist at a society where we are so controlled by mandates and fines, coercion and force. Because positive reinforcement works so well and feels so much better!

We tend to think of freedom as binary. You have it or you don't. I live in a "free" country, but is it total freedom? I guess it depends where you draw the line about what you can tolerate. I'm free to not pay taxes if I'm okay with going to jail. When I'm doing something I don't want to do because I fear the consequences of not doing it, or when I stop doing something I want to do for the same reason, it doesn't feel like freedom. It feels like I'm stuck between the proverbial rock and hard place, picking the least painful option.

My dog has had little agency in her life. She didn't choose where she'd live or with whom. I control what she eats and when. She can't even pee on her own schedule. And yet, I want her to do things I want AND I want her to want to do them. In a world of positive reinforcement, this is possible.

Total freedom might sound like it'd produce anarchy, but good dog trainers know that shaping behavior using a reward-based system can create reliable, predictable habits and interactions that the learner is excited to have in their repertoire. Once we understand the science, the only limitations trainers will have with a dog are their own skill set and willingness to practice. Plus, of course, the dog's physical abilities.

Reward the behaviors you like, and you'll get more of those behaviors. Can it all really be so simple? Roughly speaking, yes.

Can you create good associations by giving your dog food or other things they desire that you can control? Yes.

Can you change behaviors that way for the better? Yes.

What happens if you accidentally reinforce the wrong thing? Not much more than a piece of jerky. Dogs are a lot more forgiving than, say, a chicken, and unlike with punishment, the worst that can happen when positive reinforcement goes wrong is an extra treat. It might mean no immediate visible improvement with the behavior you're focusing on, but nonetheless a good association has been made with you, the bearer of good things. That piece of lamb lung or kibble is a coin in the bank account that is good things associated with you, which can improve your dog's interest in letting you be their guide through this crazy human world.

It's simple. But it's not easy.

The Amazing Brelands and Baileys

Bob Bailey is fond of pointing out: "Training is simple but not easy." It isn't easy, since it can take time, patience, and ingenuity to train an animal. But much of it comes down to creating opportunities for behaviors you like to happen, then rewarding those behaviors. Over and over. It makes me think of knitting. You're never really doing more than making loops. Simple. But, until you do it a lot of times, it's not easy.

"Training must be worthwhile for all—for the animal and for the trainer. The animal must get something it wants or needs. The trainer must get behavior or some other satisfaction out of training," writes Dr. Bailey on his website, in black text on a yellow background, looking very year-2000 html-y. It is so full of wisdom that I have it bookmarked and visit it once a month or so. "Reinforce often, especially early in training."

Bailey's page reads, to me, like a guide to navigating many relationships in life where we are trying to encourage certain behaviors, whether we are working with dogs, chickens, parents, children, employers, employees, and even partners or spouses. Choose your own animal. I mean, is there any relationship that we care about at all in which we *wouldn't* like to have some influence?

Bailey is in his late eighties and lives in Hot Springs, Arkansas. He's on my screen, wearing a blue Hawaiian shirt with dolphins on it. When I ask him what he is proudest of, he tells me his marriage—he's been a widower since 2001—and his three sets of twins. This is sincere and sweet, but it takes me by surprise, because, being familiar with his career, I thought he was going to say something like "training a dolphin to rescue military gear."

When his wife, a groundbreaking and influential trainer—both a mentor and a partner to him—was asked a similar question in a filmed interview in 1992, I figured she'd talk about her considerable contributions to developing and refining the ways in which a great variety of species of animals could be trained—over the course of more than five decades, she trained everything from killer whales to cockroaches. But she too gave an answer that surprised me: "Our biggest contribution," she said, "was training people."

Her name was Marian Breland Bailey, and when she says "our" in that clip, she isn't referring to her and her husband; she's referring to her and her husbands. She was widowed in 1965, the same year Bailey began working for her. They married in 1976.

Bob Bailey grew up in Van Nuys, California, and studied biochemistry at UCLA. "My idea of a trainer was a guy with a whip, a chair, and a gun in a lion cage," he tells me. But that had changed by the time he met Marian Breland, who had been an undergraduate student in a University of Minnesota class taught by a thirty-five-year-old B. F. Skinner. What she learned about operant conditioning in that class would change the path of her life. She married a fellow grad student—Keller Breland—who had a similar passion for what Skinner was teaching.

The Brelands left academics in the 1940s to use what they'd learned in Skinner's lab to train animals for commercial purposes. They called their business Animal Behavior Enterprises, and they soon had remote-operated feeders and a staff of trainers conditioning animals by the dozen. "The Brelands had the idea that they could mass produce behavior," Bailey explains to me. "If they control the contingencies, if they controlled the environmental conditions, if they prepared the animal, if they adapted the animal to what they were going to experience out there, they could produce hundreds of animals." This sounds nefarious, until you realize that much of what they ended up doing involved dressing up chickens and ducks who would perform amusing—or astounding—tasks in enclosed displays at roadside attractions and amusement parks.

The Brelands didn't use positive reinforcement to create behaviors out of nowhere. They simply encouraged existing behaviors and brought them under stimulus control—a fancy way of saying that they created situations where the animals would engage in the behaviors at the right moment, in the right place. The chicken dancing was only doing the kind of scratching that chickens do innately, probably to crush seeds and grain. What made it magical was the chicken doing it on the stage, just after the music started playing.

The Brelands' coin-operated machines were shipped around the world, with ducks from Tokyo to South Dakota in identical little pale-yellow rooms, turning on identical pink lamps and then banging out tunes on identical tiny Schoenhut pianos. They would be rewarded only after plunking the piano keys a certain number of times.

Think back to our discussion of the magic claw soda machine, which requires a specific behavior (operating the claw) to convert your money into a refreshing beverage for you. In the Brelands' world, the ducks learned that they could convert coins into duck food, if they behaved a certain way. And the ducks did so with enough reliability to build a business that, by the early 1960s, was already well into its second decade.

In 1954, *The National Humane Review* wrote, "We think the animal training methods being used by the Brelands are a gratifying development. Wide applications of the Breland theories and techniques could eliminate many vicious training methods. What Mr. and Mrs. Breland preach and practice is this: to train an animal, make the animal enjoy what you want it to do. In a single word: kindness."

Despite ringing endorsements of this kind, dog people weren't interested in buying what the Brelands were selling. The young couple approached dog food companies about bringing their techniques to pet owners, but they were sent home. These companies already had trainers on their staff, and they were getting just fine results. Look at Lassie! "The Brelands were threatening essentially the working lives of people who were out there using coercion as their primary means of training dogs. They were trying to introduce the idea of using reinforcement," Bailey explains. "Which is totally contrary to the idea at the time, which was that the animal was supposed to do what you wanted. And if not, you provided a punishment to this animal. That was accepted."

They also continued their research, in situ, writing about the ways in which operant conditioning could be used to train such a wide variety of animals. Their 1961 paper titled "The Misbehavior of Organisms" married the field of ethology to behavior in a way that hadn't been considered by the behavior scientists who hadn't left the laboratory. Ethology is the study of what animals do to survive and thrive and reproduce to survive and thrive some more—to earn a living, if you will.

It was in this groundbreaking paper that the Brelands coined the term "instinctive drift," describing how, in some cases, learned behaviors would be disrupted by an animal's instinctive desire to do something else, usually relating to food. After many repeated pairings of an object and reward in the form of food, the association with food would be so intense as to trigger instinctive food-related behaviors. For instance, some raccoons, when they tried to train them to put coins into a small wood bank, would begin to treat the coins as if they were lunch, washing them with their hands. What the Brelands were suggesting was that no animal was tabula rasa. Instincts—those preinstalled life-sustaining behaviors—are always part of the picture and cannot always be fully overridden.

Principles of learning that may be easily applicable from one species to the next cannot account for the particular behaviors that have evolved to create that particular species' instinctual behavior patterns, especially behaviors relating to food and sex. To teach effectively, we need to understand how the animal has evolved to earn a living. (Whenever I see people conspicuously fondling money, I think about those raccoons).

After a career of training chickens for tic-tac-toe (a retired unit is currently preserved at the Smithsonian), dolphins for the Navy, cats for the CIA, and seagulls to retrieve objects from miles away, Bailey tells me what he found motivated the animals he worked with: food and security, he says, were the most potent things.

"People keep trying to make it more complicated," he says again. "Training is simple, but not easy. Those of you out there who are teaching it, teach it simply. Teach it as simple steps, not complicated steps. That's my word to the world."

In 2010, the same year that I first used a clicker, Cesar Millan released his book *Cesar's Rules*, which, contrary to its title, contains wisdom and, well, rules, from other famous animal trainers. One of his interviewees is Bob Bailey

"I think trainers philosophically oriented toward 'correction' or other punishment euphemisms, can default under stress to coercive procedures which, in my view, often create more problems than they solve," Bailey says, in a chapter of Millan's book called "Rewards, Punishment, and Everything in Between."

I asked Bailey about Millan. "Millan is just a phenomenon, like so many others in the past," he said. I got the sense he thought his discussion with Millan had transformed his training style. "If you look at his first season and look at his last season, you will see a dramatic difference in Cesar Millan's behavior. You will see that he has changed *his* behavior," Bailey said.

I'd like to believe this, but I have a feeling Bailey hasn't actually watched the show in the last decade. I have. If you watched the latest season of his latest show and took a drink every time Millan says anything even remotely related to behavioral science, you'd wind up stone-cold sober, which is my least favorite way to watch Millan. But I didn't want to get into it. I try to not argue with old men in dolphin shirts.

Instead, I mentioned to him that I had done an iteration of his "Chicken Camp" and had spent a week training a chicken to peck at a yellow dot.

"But, afterward, what did you do?" he said. "After you taught the discrimination? What did you do?"

I thought about it and remembered the final exercise of the week: We had to teach the chicken to *stop* pecking the yellow dot. To anyone who might have been watching through the window, it wouldn't have looked like much had changed. But we went from using clickers and bird feed to train one behavior to training another behavior: The second behavior was just the behavior of not doing what the chicken was doing before. The difference was subtle but important—and a reminder that you can elegantly get one behavior to stop by teaching another. An absence of one behavior is never simply an absence; it is always going to be another behavior.

"All that stuff that you did before was in preparation for that," he said. Then he said something that sounded a little Cesar Millan-y: "You learned about yourself."

Indeed, I had.

I learned I love training chickens.

Getting Rid of Behaviors without Using Punishment

"Nothing happens, nobody comes, nobody goes, it's awful."

—SAMUEL BECKETT, *WAITING FOR GODOT*

MY MOM'S DOG used to pee on the rug, and it would drive her crazy.

"He just went out!" she'd say. "There's no reason!"

Sorry, Mom. There was a reason. It just may be hard to tell what the reason was.

To understand this concept in terms of my own animalness, I consider the fact that there is some kind of reason why I'm doing everything I'm doing right this moment. Things I did previously in my life that I regret? Current me might no longer remember my reasons, but past me had them. Many of the reasons behind many of the things I do are not going to be obvious to anyone but current me.

Now, do I get asked "what are you doing?" and then "why?" all the time? Yes. Especially by my toddler. And School For The Dogs' cofounder, Kate. In our relationship, I'm the risk-taker and she sometimes finds herself trying to put up speed bumps.

Have I sometimes done things she hasn't liked? Yes. But she always asks me an important question before she tries to get me to change course: "Why did you do that?"

Too often with dogs, we forget to ask that question: Why are you doing that annoying thing? Instead, we jump straight to needlessly labeling the issue, or we combat the problem before considering its origin.

If your dog is doing something you don't like, first try to figure out what the reason is. Is it being reinforced by something in the environment? That might mean that the barking makes the bad guy in the hallway go away, or that you give the dog attention in the form of saying "No barking." Is it self-stimulating? Is it a behavior that stems from fear? In the discipline of applied behavior analysis, these kinds of questions are involved in doing a "functional assessment" of the issue. Good professional dog trainers are skilled at doing this, but you can do it too. What are the observable events that precede the behavior? What are the consequences? What is the reason?

Even if you can't figure it out without some professional help, you've at least found questions to ask. Whatever the answers, there is one thing I'm sure it will not be: no reason.

If you can determine that the behavior is a response to a specific cue in the environment—an antecedent, like, say, the doorbell or a dog that looks a certain way—you can start to figure out how to restrict exposure to that cue. And/or to create good associations with that cue. If you can figure out what is reinforcing the behavior, you can think about how to remove the reinforcer. There's a technical term for that: extinction.

Extinction

Growing up in New York City in the 1980s, subway cars were like folk art museums on rails. Each car was covered in brightly colored graffiti, no two alike. But where some New Yorkers saw charm, others saw vandalism. And some saw it as a problem that, visually, triggered feelings of fear. Classical conditioning on rails.

It wasn't hard to figure out who committed these crimes. Most of the people were literally writing their names on the cars. They'd get caught, and there was a punishment that fit the crime: they had to clean the cars in police detention. But it was sometimes more of a reinforcer than a punishment, as it gave the graffiti artists the technical behind-the-scenes of the paint-removal process, which helped them figure out how to make more durable graffiti. Mistakes are learning opportunities, indeed.

When he took the position of president of the New York City Transit Authority in April 1984, David Gunn announced the Clean Car Program.

The program started by creating "clean cars." Cars that received this designation would never leave the terminal with graffiti on them. Within two hours of entering the terminal, a clean car got cleaned. In this simple way, Gunn trained the graffiti artists. He took away any chance that their art would be sliding through the boroughs on display to millions of subway riders each day. Why put in all the effort—jumping fences, risking arrest—to make art that won't be seen by anyone, that will not have an effect? The Clean Car Program was an exercise in extinction. It worked.

Ignoring Stuff

It's a common misconception that positive reinforcement training entails just ignoring stuff you don't like, in the hopes it will go away, and rewarding everything else. The reality is that it's not so simple, as ignoring behavior you don't like isn't always practical or possible. Maybe you can ignore the whining at the dinner table, but is everyone else willing to ignore it too? Nobody can ignore your dog lunging at the neighbor's dog in the elevator. Ignoring a dog who barks the whole time you're at work may not be effective, neighborly, or humane. As a trainer, I rarely suggest making use of extinction, even if it seems benign because it is in some sense the path of least intervention. However, dragons that way lie and it's more complicated than it first seems.

Every behavior has some function. The function may be to get attention or access to something we want or need or to escape something we don't want. We avoid things that feel bad, and sometimes we do things that just feel good.

But what happens when the reward goes away? You probably will stop doing the thing. Possibly forever. Possibly for just…a long time. (There can be spontaneous reoccurrences of behaviors that have undergone extinction. Like when you ghost someone and then suddenly they call you after years.)

It's happened to all of us, which is why you probably know that when you're the one engaging in a behavior that is undergoing extinction, it can be kind of sucky. It's not a lot of fun to suddenly find the faucet that was reliably giving you good stuff has been shut off.

If you're the one making use of extinction, it's facing the uncomfortable fact that you may be getting rid of the behavior without getting rid of whatever was causing it. I think of this when my friends explain to me how well the "cry it out" method works with kids. It may get the crying to stop, but maybe only because the kid has learned crying doesn't work anymore. Crying is a behavior babies (and dogs!) engage in to try to get their needs met. It's their "flight attendant call" button. Ideally, I think we want the animals in our care to feel like they can let us know how we can meet their needs. Let them learn the button doesn't work and you may end up with a passenger who finds a less polite way to get your attention.

In this way, trying to use extinction to get rid of a behavior without addressing the cause of the behavior can lead to Whac-A-Mole–type situations. Before he met me, my husband and his ex had a papillon, and their neighbors complained about his barking. So they put a training collar on him—sold to them by a pet-store clerk who assured them it only used "static electricity." The collar got rid of the barking, but they then came home to find thousands of tiny paw prints near the door. They set up a video camera to figure out why and found that "he would jump over and over again in front of the front door. For hours. Like hundreds and hundreds of times." But at least the neighbors weren't bothered!

If extinction isn't always the quickest way to get rid of behavior, it may be because most individuals, given the right circumstances, may go on doing x behavior for a very long time without reinforcement. An animal like me, for example. Last summer, I spent about a week playing a game called *Road to Paradise*. I'm ashamed to tell you it was located inside of the Starbucks app. The game involved lining up certain shapes and colors to gain "stars." I am perfectly able to make coffee, but I really like it when other people make it for me. So, I wanted the stars that playing the game would earn me to use toward free drinks.

I got five bonus stars at first ("Whoa! You just won five bonus stars!") and calculated that this would translate into about an eighth of a cup of coffee. I was going to need the whole cup. So I kept playing. And playing. Not to brag, but I had the feeling I was actually pretty good at this game. ("Forecast: sunshine and bonus stars all summer long.") But I kept not getting any more stars. Instead, I was winning opportunities to play special types of moves in the game. Then, like Skinner's rat denied access to the food hopper, I started to play with great intensity and ingenuity. Maybe you only win stars if you play when you're inside a Starbucks? No. What if you log into your account on a different device? No. This is a kind of "extinction burst," and it is sometimes a way trainers can get their learners to try new things. But, when you're the learner, it can feel sort of sucky. Eventually, I looked up the rules online and when rewards are intermittent, animals can keep behaving for long periods of time without reinforcement. You can train behaviors with scant rewards over long durations of time this way. But if that kind of stinginess is your preferred training method, you have to be very clever about not letting too long of a period pass without a Starbucks star. After a while, the behavior can undergo extinction, and you'll find your animal's tendency to click on your app has completely stopped. And she is forced to make her own French press.

If you are even going to think about trying to use extinction properly in training, you must keep in mind that consistency is key. Whatever reinforcer has been maintaining the behavior needs to be taken away forever, truly. Reinstating the reinforcer, even just once, can cause the behavior to return, possibly worse than before. You can choose to simply ignore a dog for jumping on you. This might not be a bad idea, but another person giving the dog attention for jumping even just once may be enough to maintain the behavior. And there are rewards for jumping that have nothing to do with anything you have control over. Jumping may put a dog at prime crotch- or mouth-sniffing heights, for instance.

You can ignore a dog for barking, but if the barking has nothing to do with your attention, your taking that away will not have an effect as punishment or extinction, especially when the other side of the seesaw is weighted with reinforcers, like making the person in the hallway go away (happens EVERY time!) and engaging in an instinctive behavior selectively bred for countless generations—barking must feel good. Again, to shape your dog's behavior, it's important to understand your dog's reason. Or to try.

Extinction can be part of the process of training, especially in the beginning, to help your dog figure out what works when and where. But, the more proficient you become with positive reinforcement, the less failure your dog will experience, and the less need for extinction. In his 1989 book *Coercion and Its Fallout*, behavioral scientist Murray Sidman describes how to approach a way of teaching that could avoid it.

> The only way to eliminate extinction from the teaching process would be to eliminate failure. We will, of course, never completely do away with failures but technical developments have made the goal worth pursuing. One of the most exciting accomplishments of behavior analysis has been the discovery of ways to teach without producing failures... New applications of errorless teaching techniques are continually being discovered and refined. What makes errorless learning possible is effective programming. This is something the teacher has to do, not the pupil. 'Trial and error' still exists but the feasibility of errorless learning has shifted both the trials and the errors from the learner to the teacher.

Once you recognize extinction, you may recognize behaviors undergoing extinction in your own life all the time. And you may sometimes find yourself trying to use it to change your dog's behavior (convenient in that, like the plot of many episodes of *Seinfeld*, it is often about doing nothing).

But there are also other options, ones that might make you think about stopping behavior while also still being a good friend. Like many a plot of *Friends*. That's where we are going next. *I'll be there for you!*

Negative Reinforcement Revisited

Let's revisit our hypothetical barking dog. Imagine you approach this dog, and the dog starts barking at you. If you wanted to try to let the behavior undergo extinction, you could just keep standing there. Maybe covering your ears. While you're getting barked at, you also should be praying that something in the environment other than you is not reinforcing the barking behavior.

Eventually, the dog may realize barking isn't going to get you to budge. But it's not going to be a lot of fun for anyone involved. And it won't endear you to the neighbors.

The kinder and more efficacious move might be to negatively reinforce the behavior. Rather than waiting for the dog to try everything else and then give up, try leaving when the barking *begins*.

But isn't that rewarding the behavior I don't want? Yes! For this reason, if you're putting together a carefully constructed training plan in a well-managed environment, this probably isn't going to be your initial move. Better to try to set things up so as to avoid the behavior to begin with. But in the real world, negative reinforcement may be a starting point. The "reinforcer" is going to be the removal of whatever is upsetting the dog: it's "negative" because something is being subtracted from the situation, but it's "reinforcement" because it's encouraging a behavior. So what is the behavior you're encouraging? The behavior your dog was engaging in to try to make the scary thing go away! Ideally, the very *start* of the behavior. You're teaching the dog that giving you just a bit of information about not liking something is enough. The dog doesn't have to go all cuckoo bananas about it. It's a surprising way to have both the trainer and the trainee working toward communicating in a way that is polite and respectful.

Incompatible Behaviors (and Beyond)

In 1984, a 52-year-old marine biologist named Karen Pryor wrote a book called *Don't Shoot the Dog!* The book isn't about shooting or about dogs. The title comes from a section of the book where considers how to deal with hypothetical problems involving something happening that you don't like, such as a neighbor's dog barking. There are lots of ways you could get the dog to stop barking. One of them is shooting the dog. Pryor suggests, of course, not shooting the dog.

In a section called "Untraining: Using Reinforcement to Get Rid of Behavior You Don't Want", Pryor recommends a litany of other ways to go about curbing barking, without resorting to punishment, negative reinforcement, or extinction. Among her suggestions are:

SHAPE THE ABSENCE OF THE BEHAVIOR

The process of doing this will be clearer when we go into more depth about what shaping really is. But, for now, think of it as possibly starting with our negative reinforcement example—backing off early on if that seems to be why the dog is barking, then either positively reinforcing anything other than the unwanted behavior or, sometimes, positively reinforcing a weak version of the behavior—an initial quiet bark, for instance. I once had such success with this method with a client, Wiggles, that she started to do a "silent" bark, just opening and closing her mouth in moments she used to bark, then looking at me for approval. I eventually cued her to do this when I pointed the remote at her and said, "Mute."

CHANGE THE MOTIVATION

This usually involves helping a dog not be fearful. "Barking dogs are lonely, frightened, and bored. Give exercise and attention by day so that the dog is tired and sleepy at night, or provide another dog to sleep with at night for company," writes Pryor. "Or bring the dog inside."

PUT THE BEHAVIOR ON CUE AND THEN DON'T GIVE THE CUE

Pryor herself calls this one a "dilly" and, when working with dogs and owners, I agree. I certainly have had dog trainer friends who have worked with their dogs to create splendid "bark" and "no bark" cues, for instance. But I really can't think of a time where walking through how to do this with a newbie client hasn't seemed like the long way to take up a mountain. Early in my career I tried to teach a neighbor to do this in a half-hour session and then had to spend a decade listening to her out my window yelling "Quiet!" to the dog while the dog barked. It punished the behavior of me trying to teach all but the most advanced students to do this.

As you learn, in the next part of this book, how to teach specific behaviors with positive reinforcement, you will at the same time be able to train behaviors incompatible with behavior you don't want on the fly. The dog who is trained to go to his crate way over there to enjoy a peanut butter–filled toy when the doorbell rings is a dog who is not also going to be barking at the door. Being in a crate in another room is incompatible with being at the door; licking peanut butter is incompatible with barking. You will also find yourself rewarding so many desired behaviors, with teaspoon- or pea-sized reinforcers (depending on the size of your dog), that there will simply be fewer hours in the day that your dog will have to spend doing annoying stuff. Instead, she'll be trying to figure out how to do more of the things that have been positively reinforced.

We humans are architects of our dogs' space and of their days. We dictate what their schedule will be, whom they will socialize with, and when they will be allowed to urinate. We decide what they eat, where they sleep, and what kind of medical attention they are going to get. We shape their environment—or rather, our environment, the one we share with them—and environment shapes behavior. In the next chapters, we'll go full positive reinforcement, and I'll show you how you can reward the hell out of behaviors you want, and simply not have a lot of undesired behaviors in the first place. My point here is there are many ways to stop behaviors you don't want from happening, no firepower required. Most powerfully:

✦ You can reward alternate behaviors.
✦ You can construct environments where the behavior is unlikely to occur.

Positive Interrupters

There are inevitably times when dogs do things we don't want them to do, and we don't have the luxury to sit around and think about how to rearrange the environment or reward an alternate behavior, because we need them to stop doing the thing they're doing right this second. This was me when I noticed Amos pancaking himself to get under the kitchen cabinets at my neighbors' place a beat after they told me they'd just put out rat poison.

In that moment, I wasn't concerned with teaching him to never approach rat poison again. I didn't care about punishing the behavior, and I certainly wasn't thinking creatively about safer and more appropriate activities that he could do the next time we visited my neighbors. I just wanted the behavior to stop. I wanted to get him away from the rat poison. First, I screamed—instinct at work!—which at least got his attention. Then I threw a steak on the floor.

This was before I knew anything about dog training—before I understood what a positive interrupter is. A positive interrupter is, essentially, a version of the come and drop it that I outlined in chapter 8—remember the "drop-everything sale"? Instinctively, I made a drop-everything sale that Amos couldn't resist, with steak at the low, low price of 100 percent off.

At School For The Dogs, for a more planned example, we have a "break" cue we use during play. We say "break," but it could just as well be "party time" or "baba ghanoush" or "get over here you little monster"—doesn't really matter as long as it's consistent (and succinct is probably better). "Break," take hold of your dog's collar, and give him a treat. We practice this over and over when the dogs aren't doing anything wrong or dangerous, so that we can use it if we need to sometime when they are.

Before we start chasing dogs and trying to get them to come to us in vain while they're occupied and don't want to be bothered, we condition a word that means, essentially, I have good stuff, come get it. We do this in low-intensity moments, from close distances—at first the owners go to their dogs—and work up to being able to call a dog out of play.

This rat poison incident occurred a few years before I started the dog training part of my life. I hadn't developed any kind of cue like "break" with Amos. But I did know that whether I was encouraging or discouraging a future behavior didn't matter. I just needed him to stop what he was doing, immediately. I'd do the work in the future to arrange things so

that it wouldn't happen again, rather than rely on teaching him to avoid
ιαl poison ohould he ever come across it.

Since an important part of our job, when we have a dog, is to keep
them safe, it's invaluable to have a kind of emergency switch you can flip
in those rat poison moments. If you haven't taken the time to condition
something like "break," it's a good idea to start with a highly noticeable
stimulus that is likely to get your dog's attention, just like I did.

PART THREE

Do Try This at Home

Dog Language, Part One

GIVE ME SPACE

"The dog has seldom been successful in pulling man up to its level of sagacity, but man has frequently dragged the dog down to his."

—JAMES THURBER

IF I'VE TALKED more about chickens, flatworms, canine TV stars, and subway cars than you expected from a dog book, it's because I am currently pitching Netflix a show about flatworm TV stars and chicken trainspotters. But also because I wanted to beat you over the head a little bit about something I certainly did not understand until well into my adulthood: the science of behavior is species agnostic. Behavior is lawful. We can apply the overarching principles of behavior science to help us improve our lives with other species, and this kind of interspecies ease of translation makes me feel the way I do when I lose hours watching other examples of ease between species. Sloths playing with puppies, or whatever. It feels good.

As a dog trainer, understanding this has given me great relief. There is no reason to take any of it personally. Your dog is simply doing what works. You are too. If you've so far used methods that you can now

define as involving punishment, it's because those behaviors were reinforced. Don't punish yourself for it! It's why I wrote this book, so that you
would know there's an alternative.

Using positive reinforcement, we can do a lot to help dogs want to
do what works for them *and* us. We can train without pain, using our
brain! Being part of that dyad, in the role of trainer, can be profoundly
rewarding to us humans too. My behaviors have been positively reinforced in ways that have brought me here, writing this for you. Positive
reinforcement is why we have been able to build School For The Dogs
into the business it is. We are positively reinforcing both the dogs and
the people. We're certainly not forcing them to spend their money, and
the behavior of spending money on good dog training (and associated
treats and tools) is certainly not something we try to punish. They come
back for more and recommend us to friends because they want to.

Whether you're here to improve your relationship with your dog
or you're starting from the ground floor, you can look to the science of
behavior for guideposts—ones that aren't covered with cobwebs of myth
and misinformation. We can take our understanding of the work that
Skinner did in the lab (though he too used it in his life) and use technology developed by his students to apply the science in specific ways, with
a specific species, with maximum interspecies ease. We can train dogs
to live comfortably and happily in a human world.

However, before we discuss how to use classical and operant conditioning in training, I want to make sure to address another part of the
story. While we're interested in how behaviors are selected for in the
moment we're living in, it's also important to consider what behaviors
have been selected for over generations to make the particular species
that you're working with.

In most schools, someone studying animals takes classes in two departments: behavior science, often found in psychology departments, and ethology, usually under biology. Ethologists ask, "What behaviors have been learned, and what behaviors have been baked in to help the species thrive in that particular environment? What behaviors have been selected to make it possible for members of this species to get along and feed themselves? How have they been able to expend fewer calories than they consume, keeping it going long enough to pass along their genetic material to another generation?"

This is where things become not so species-non-specific, or even individual-non-specific, and where we need to think carefully about the tendencies of the animal in front of us. The more you know about dogs in general, and your dog in particular, the better your training will be.

I tend to think of dogs as animals first, individuals second, and breed as a distant third. Too many people are quick to jump to the differences between a border terrier and a Borzoi and lose sight of what they have in common as animals and as dogs, not to mention how two Borzois might differ from each other in extreme ways. You also can't separate the behavior from the environment. A member of a certain breed who has certain tendencies in one environment may have very different ones in a different environment. I roll my eyes a bit when someone calls and asks if we have experience training pugs, because they really want to work with someone who understands pugs, or when people tell me they're getting training advice from one of the breed-specific books that they keep near the register at big pet stores. Breed-specific information can be a starting place for understanding your dog's particular tendencies in the broadest way, but I wouldn't put too much weight in it. Your dog may not have the same exact set of tendencies, or tolerances, or interests as a dog of the same breed who lives next door, any more than you can expect me to be like my genetically similar family members.

What defines me as a human is more salient to getting to know me, I think, than assuming I am like my Uncle David. That said, many breeds of dogs do engage in certain behaviors that have been bred or developed over generations, and knowing what those behaviors are likely to be is helpful if you're getting to know a new dog or seeking out a purebred. Sight hounds, for example, usually like to run: they were bred to outrun prey over long distances. Dachshunds often want to dig: they were bred to burrow for badgers.

No species has been bred to be as diverse, and to live in as many varied environments, as dogs have. A Mexican hairless will not have the same exact behavioral repertoire or needs as a Great Pyrenees. Fortunately, I don't think having a bibliography of all possible preinstalled behaviors is strictly necessary. Spend some time with a dog, and you can see their tendencies for yourself. Also, fortunately, breed to breed and dog to dog, they all have more in common than they don't. Dogs of any mix of breed communicate with each other, and as our goal is to get our dogs to feel good while they do what we want them to do, it's helpful if they can communicate with us too. Good dog training partly depends on us being able to read signals of stress or contentment, and for this we need to learn to, well, speak dog.

Dog Body Language

When I was about six, in the mid-1980s, a toy hit the market that seemed to me like a high-tech miracle: a stuffed animal that talked. The commercials made Wrinkles the dog seem capable of carrying on a two-way conversation. I was an only child with few friends and two cats who were lousy conversationalists and a dog that mostly wanted to hang out with my dad. I made it clear to my mother: I *needed* a talking dog or a little sister. We kept getting mail about how we could help an orphan in a far-off country for only one dollar a month, so maybe we could just bring one home? She got me the stuffed toy.

I was thrilled, but Wrinkles did not prove to be the buddy I hoped he'd be. He said, "I like you" with a weird electronic lilt. He laughed when tickled, and when I pushed a little plush femur into his mouth, he made a slurping sound. He didn't ask me about myself or talk about

Dogs may shake when they're wet, but a shake-off can also be a displacement behavior.

the world as he saw it or discuss his feelings with me. Overall, Wrinkles proved to be less interesting than our actual dog, Mabel, whose internal thoughts I would guess at, and narrate, in the Miss Piggy–pitched baby talk I'd decided was her voice. Little did I know, Mabel was talking to me all the time. Just not with words.

For their part, your dog probably already is doing graduate-level work in the field of interpreting how *you're* feeling based on *your* body language.

The best way to get good at reading theirs is to use something most of us were born with, with an heir to spare: an eyeball. Of course, it's also very helpful to have ears, a mouth, fingers for scritching, and some liverwurst. But often, eyeballs are enough.

Use your eyes to get to know how your dog behaves when he is happy, when he likes something. You'll also get good at spotting signs of fear, so that you can help get your dog out of fear-inducing situations and reintroduce the blue monsters incrementally and appropriately. You can give your eyeballs a head start by knowing what to look for. Being even mildly conversant in dog body language will help prevent unwanted behaviors from happening, especially ones that can stem from fear and lead to danger

I don't claim to be fluent in dog language—as a nonnative speaker, I will always have more to learn. But I've spent enough time watching dogs over the years to appreciate the ways in which they express themselves and clue us into their internal world without any words. Dogs are talking to us, and to each other, all the time.

Learning about dog body language can literally save lives. More than four million Americans are victims of dog bites every year, with at least half of those being children. Some of those bites are fatal. A handful of people die from dog attacks each year, and many bites result in dogs being euthanized when, in many cases, some basic knowledge of dog body language could have prevented these incidents from occurring.

Fear and Discomfort

There's a Roald Dahl short story that ran in the *New Yorker* in 1949 called "The Sound Machine." It's about a man who invents a special box that allows him to hear sounds at pitches that would never reach the human ear. The first time he tries it, he is in his yard. As soon as he turns it on, he hears a "throatless, inhuman shriek, sharp and short, very clear and cold." In the garden next door, Mrs. Saunders is pruning her rose bush. The sound was the death cry of a rose.

My friend Kiki Yablon turned me on to this story. She's a dog trainer too. "I think about that story all the time," she told me. "You start to see all these little moments of misery." I knew what she meant. Working with dogs and people, there can be so much suffering and misunderstanding. I have a black rectangle on my wall and another in my pocket that I could use to dial up any number of lauded dog experts working with the canine equivalent of screaming roses every minute of the day.

Context is key to reading any particular body part or move. The good news is that dogs don't have a whole lot of moves—they're not, like, doing TikTok dances. They wag their tails and lick; show their teeth and growl. However, there are a lot of contexts. And, just like even identical twins may have different mannerisms from one another, every dog has their own special repertoire of physical "language". So, instead of talking about lots of dogs, or lots of contexts, I'd like to focus on just one dog. An N-of-1 study. Her name was Holly.

A Case Study in Body Language

We're in a Los Angeles backyard, bordered by white vinyl fencing, and there, standing in a patch of half-dead lawn, is our young heroine. She is beautiful, blond, and about to lose her shit.

This is Holly, a two-year-old yellow Labrador retriever who guards her food. Six inches away from her food bowl is Cesar Millan. He's crouched in a position that can only be described as Neo from *The Matrix*, ready to dodge bullets in a Warrior One yoga pose. He is frozen, staring down at a dog who is saying with every silent body part, "Leave me the fuck alone!"

To be sure, Holly has good reason. Prior to his crouching-tiger move, the Dog Whisperer had encouraged her owner to poke her with a broomstick, then he literally squatted over her food bowl and used his pursed fingers to jab her in the neck. He followed this up by approaching her, low and menacing, with his hands out in what I would call the universal sign for "I am going to throttle you."

I never met Holly, but at a glance she seems like a peach. Resource guarding is common in dogs. And in humans! No one likes it when someone takes their stuff. Holly's behaviors are most likely meant to keep people away from a highly valued resource. My approach in this situation would be to work to show her that she doesn't need to worry about anyone touching her food. Millan has a more top-down approach, focused on the aggression rather than looking at its cause.

We can train to stave off guarding by creating lots of good associations early on when anyone approaches a puppy's food bowl. But some dogs are going to resource guard more than others. My guess is that Holly just came into the world running an extra-large "this is mine" program, because that behavior probably had some benefit to her forebears, born into situations of scarcity rather than surplus. But, bless her: she does a lot to try to defuse the situation long before anyone has puncture wounds.

For instance, over and over in this episode, we see her licking her lips. Mouths are communication devices, don't cha know. We humans also do a lot with our mouths when we are stressed. We bite our lips and purse them. We cover our mouths. Dogs don't have much in the way of lips, or hands, but they have luscious tongues, and they use them sometimes like big pink flags of surrender. If your dog hasn't just been drinking, and hasn't just been given some peanut butter, and suddenly has a tongue that is trying to windshield wipe her own face, it might be her way of using a very good inside voice to ask you, or another dog, to give her some space. True dog whispering, if you will. The polite response? Give the dog space! But that is not the Millan "way." He has a different read on the situation.

"It's relaxation," he says, kneeling in front of her.

Shortly after coming at Holly with his my-hand-is-a-dog-mouth hand (again), she is showing some *piloerection*. Don't get too excited by that term. It's the fancy way of referring to the puffed-up hair you sometimes see on a dog's back when they're aroused—a mammal's way of trying to appear bigger than they are. Humans have a vestigial variety of this in the form of goose bumps. Porcupines, which raise their quills, have the extreme version. It's more apparent on some dogs than others. Earlier in the episode, when her owner comes at her with a broom handle, it's particularly noticeable on Holly. She also displays a textbook paw lift. Dogs lift a front paw in moments when they seem like they are feeling unsure. It's as though one paw is ready to find the nearest exit, but the other three are still assessing the situation.

About halfway into a three-minute clip of this 2012 episode of *The Dog Whisperer* on YouTube, "Showdown with Holly," on the Nat Geo Wild channel, she looks over her right shoulder. Makes sense, there's probably a camera there. But you can see the whites of her eyes here. This kind of canine side-eye is something you see when a dog may be feeling unsure, usually accompanied by stiff posture. It's as if they're trying to be invisible, and they think no one will see them if the only thing moving is their eyes. Trainers often call this either "half-moon eye," because the white on the side of the eye is the shape of a crescent moon, or "whale eye," I do not know why. I have never been eye-to-eye with a whale. But I've seen dogs do this, and I roughly translate it as: *Give me some space, dammit. I'm not whispering!*

Millan, who has just gotten through explaining that he did his weird pose and hand jab because "her brain got stuck," is now attempting to further explain this dog's pathology. He goes to put his palm on Holly's nose. "It's relaxation," he says. "It's an understand—"

Boom!

Holly clamps down on his hand like she means it. They're momentarily a flailing unit. You can see her teeth. You can see his teeth. She's growling. He's kicking her. The kicking doesn't look particularly effective, but she decides to spare him. Really, her restraint is impressive.

Millan looks down at the camera and says:

"I didn't see that coming. I didn't see that coming."

Maybe because he was busy "whispering" rather than reading what Holly was saying. Just before the bite, Holly's owner Hyrum Lai had said, "I can see her ears dropping, that's usually what she does before she does something."

※

Before exhibiting behaviors that could be dangerous to others and themselves, the vast majority of dogs do us (and each other) the favor of exhibiting postures, expressions, and behaviors that are attempts to alleviate stress, defuse situations, and warn off unwanted advances. It's safe to assume that most dogs understand that aggression is a calorically expensive activity that usually isn't worth the cost. When wolves and other canids are observed in their natural habitats, high-ranking members of the pack can be seen defusing situations, not stoking them. They cool themselves down and communicate "I mean no harm!" in ways that, once understood, are hard to miss. Unfortunately, as we chaperone our dogs through our worlds, we too often ignore their pacifying efforts, or, worse, we completely misinterpret them.

Aggression in dogs is no small topic, and this book is not big enough to address some of the really difficult work that skilled trainers I hire do to help dogs and their owners every day at School For The Dogs. But I hope to help the dog behavior novice start to develop an eye for signs of discomfort and work to give dogs some space when they need it. Counterconditioning and managing the situation are the next steps. The first step is often simply to give the dog some space.

Give the dog some space.

And don't, like, poke a broomstick into a stressed-out dog's face. Okay? Just don't do that.

Behavior issues are the number one reason that adult dogs are surrendered to shelters. In too many cases, "behavior issue" is a nice way of saying what a dog has done to people with their teeth.

A distressed dog doesn't need a teacher. They need a savior. I want my learner trying to understand what I want, not deciding whether to fight or flee. Often, fleeing is impossible, especially for dogs who are carried or leashed. Or cornered in a yard. And what do they do if they can't get away? Teeth! Do some dogs end up like this because of how they're born? Probably—or at least with a propensity to either have a showdown or try to disappear. In any case, these are self-protecting behaviors, and any number of circumstances might put a dog in the state of just being an animal trying to survive in a world they didn't choose. In my experience, exceedingly rare is the born-sociopath dog who goes with no notice from happy-go-lucky to taking a chunk out of a stranger's hand.

Let me just go on my soapbox for a moment and say it as I see it: We do dogs a massive disservice when we train them in ways that could even possibly cause distress, and we—all of us, not just dog owners—further screw things up by not learning the very basics of seeing when a dog needs some space. We do ourselves a disservice too. Because, sometimes, our stupidity about this stuff means that humans get hurt. And families have to give up dogs they loved. Healthy, once-happy animals get euthanized or sent somewhere they didn't want to go. Everyone loses. If we could all become minorly conversant in some basic signs of dog stress, we'd all win.

SCHOOL FOR THE DOGS STRESS GUIDE

LOW LEVEL	MEDIUM LEVEL	HIGH LEVEL
Averted eyes	Staring	Drooling
Turning away	Hyper-vigilance	Escape attempts
Blinking	Scanning	Freezing

LOW LEVEL	MEDIUM LEVEL	HIGH LEVEL
Ears back	Leaning away	Pacing
Repeated stretching	Low tail	Panting
Tongue flicks (lip licks)	Mild facial tension	"Pancaking" or flattening
Scratching	Moving away	Yelping
Self-sniffing or licking	Repeated tongue flicks	Sweaty paws
Shake-off	Slow approach	Facial tension
Sneezing	Stiff muscles/body	Trembling
Yawning	Whining	Tucked tail
Weight centered backward	Whites in the eye	

A Flick of the Tongue Is Not What You Think

If you're looking to kill time, search any stock photo site for the words "dog" and "tongue," and you will find yourself with lots of scrolling to do. If dogs were this interested in our tongues, it'd be weird.

A tongue flick may be adorable, but it is also something else: a good indication that a dog is uncomfortable and perceives a situation as possibly threatening. A camera thrust in a puppy's face—coupled with a toddler's arm thrown around the dog or a pair of pajamas forced upon him—may result in some cute tongue for a photo. But, when you start to see it as a mild sign of distress, it can feel really creepy to see it pop up all over ads and social media, the accidental fetishization of a gesture that is meant to convey important information about discomfort.

Displacement and Self-Soothing Behaviors

Have you ever gotten mad and banged the table? It doesn't make a lot of sense. It wasn't the table's fault. This is an example of a displacement behavior. It's something animals do when they don't know what else to do.

Shaking off. Sneezing. Suddenly scratching an ear. These are all things I've seen many dogs do when they seem a little unsure or uncomfortable. A dog will suddenly stop and scratch his ear after a training session has gone on a while. Given the context, I interpret these as signs they need a break—signs of fatigue or frustration. Some dogs seem to get a very itchy ear when a greeting doesn't go the way they maybe wanted it to, or a social advance has been rebuffed. I've often seen this in Puppy Playtime when one dog has not accepted another's attempt to play, and the one who tried to initiate suddenly has this ear thing to attend to. It's the dog equivalent of being at a party where you don't know anyone, so you pretend to check your phone even though it's dead.

If the "Showdown with Holly" YouTube clip is all you see from episode 12 of season 9 of *The Dog Whisperer*, you haven't gotten a full portrait of the kind of bad day Holly is having. Earlier in the episode, Millan learns that she has been biting people who come near her food since she was five months old. Her humans explain that at first, she did so with her tail down, but now her tail is up and stiff. They seem sure this is significant. Millan interprets. He says she is saying, "I am unsure about how to be, right? How to go from primal behavior to domestic behavior. I really don't know how to do it." Got that? I'm not sure I do. But Holly's owners, Lai and his wife, nod along.

A lot happens to Holly in the episode before where the YouTube clip picks up. There's the whole thing where Lai chases her around the yard with the broom, sticking it in her face like he's jousting. Then Millan brings over two dogs she's never met before and lets them run off-leash into her yard. He approaches all three dogs with a food bowl of kibble, shaking it around like he's popping corn. No one is allowed access to it. Only his dog, Junior, Millan says, is looking at him in the right way. He calls this moment "the ritual of claiming." The shot ends with Millan doing his little air-punch to Holly, in front of the two other dogs, who look like they'd like to peace out. All three are taking turns stooping their heads low and lifting a front paw.

Eye Contact

With the other dogs still roaming Holly's yard, Millan stands between her and the food. She has her tail between her legs, and he stares her down. She is darting her eyes, but then she backs away from him. He is triumphant. "I got the imprint that I want to achieve. It was really fast."

Millan puts away the other dogs and returns with yet another bowl of dry food, which he places between him and Holly, and they lock eyes. He gives her his best blue steel. She is wagging her tail! But she looks maybe … confused? "See that eye contact?" he tells the camera. "That's bad."

Is it? Knowing what happens a moment later, I'm going to agree with Millan on that one. Everything that is happening right now is bad. But eye contact certainly isn't *always* bad. I've spent some of the best moments of my life making eye contact with dogs! Might it sometimes be "bad"? Yes, I suppose. Remember, context matters, and when you've had the afternoon Holly has had, everything is going to suck. The part that happens next makes me want to cry: Holly kisses Millan. Sometimes dogs will lick as an attempt to push something away when they're uncomfortable. Other times, I think it can be a last resort—a kind of grand appeasement gesture. *I am but only a weak puppy beneath you, strong one!* Of course, it can also be a sign of affection, but I don't think that's what's going on here. I think Holly is just throwing out whatever she's got. Millan reads it differently. "That's submission," he says. "I'm going to let her lick me because he [sic] is showing submission." Don't get me started again on dominance and submission. (Do reread that section in chapter 3 if you've forgotten.)

Then Millan brings Lai into the yard, the two of them hovering over the dog's food bowl on the ground. Millan, kneeling at Holly's eye level, beckons her to the bowl but then says "shht!" when she approaches. She looks up to her owner.

"He's addressing it to you," Millan says, "because he knows I'm claiming right here." Millan can feel Holly's energy, but he can't remember her gender pronouns.

"Right," says Lai.

I hope Hyrum Lai reads this, so that he will know I crown him the unsung hero of this episode. At every step of the way, he shows he's picking up on what Holly is dropping—or at least trying to.

Millan doesn't reply to this statement. Instead, he declares, "He knows that the only energy that is not assertive is yours. Because he sees my energy, even though it's closer to the food, which makes me a better target for him…"

And then suddenly Millan pops up and stares the dog down like he's murdering her with his eyes.

Cut to commercial.

Poor Holly. She had issues to begin with and is now getting all kinds of mixed signals from new people—Millan, but you also have to account for the presence of the off-camera crew that came with him. Plus two random dogs. And then the more quotidian stressors: the Lais' toddler running around waving a Chuckit!, and Lai with the broomstick. Trainers call this "trigger stacking," a pretty self-explanatory term. Dogs who experience one stressor after another can end up snapping from the compounding stress. I'm sure you don't know what this is like.

Is the Lais' son in danger? I think so. As a parent, this would make me scared. According to Millan, the problem isn't an inability to understand Holly. It's their inability to take charge and to let go of their fear. "What I did here right now is to claim the food and claim you... If you touch your son with the energy that he's seeing right now, your son becomes a target."

After the bite, a bloody-handed Millan takes Holly to a corner of the yard and stares her down for more than five minutes (a chyron tells us how long it's been).

Eventually, a détente is called for. Millan goes back to his trailer. But, before he departs the Lais' home, he says, looking at his bloodied hand outside his trailer, "You know, the worst part about being bitten is the energy the dog gives you when he bites." He stumbles backward—a visual representation of how the dog's bad qi was the really painful thing, not the punctures the canines made in his wrist. "When they're biting, they're also giving you their negative energy. That's what really threw me off."

What throws *me* off is that this dog was doing everything she could to try to get out of what must have felt like a threatening situation. She showed a textbook's appendix worth of behaviors meant to do everything from appease to defuse and even seek help—there's a pre-bite moment when she gazes up at Lai for help, and it sears my soul.

Dog Language, Part Two

HAPPY BODIES

"A dog teaches a boy fidelity, perseverance, and to turn around three times before lying down."

—ROBERT BENCHLEY

WHILE IT'S CRITICAL to be able to read body language that says a dog is not comfortable, you'll also want to get to know what your dog looks like when things are going well. Play, in particular, often gets mistaken for aggression, and I've seen many dog owners get stressed out at dog parks and chastise their dogs when what's really happening is healthy, beautiful, and actually very necessary.

Play, your inner Puritan might ask, is necessary? Yes! Especially for young dogs. Physical play helps juveniles from many species get stronger and hone their motor skills, and it serves as a form of social training, teaching animals codes of social behavior and helping them understand where they fit into their community. Research by University of Colorado ethologist Marc Bekoff indicates that play teaches animals a sense of morality. By roughhousing, animals create social bonds and learn what behaviors are acceptable: how hard they can bite, how roughly they can interact, and how to resolve conflicts—all lessons they can generalize to other situations.

This is yet another big thing that humans and dogs have in common. University of Tennessee Professor Gordon Burghardt's Surplus Resource Theory attempts to explain, among other things, why mammals, like humans and dogs, are more playful than, say, reptiles. The theory posits that humans and other creatures who enjoy tennis balls have better energy stores and a greater capacity for sustained vigorous activity; longer periods of freedom from threats and food shortages due to parental care; a susceptibility to boredom; and an environment full of novelty. As humans, we have the perfect conditions for playtime. In fact, our acquisition of pet dogs who arguably serve no useful purpose when it comes to our survival could be considered an extension of our desire to play. In turn, we've provided dogs with food, shelter, and safety, and these conditions, together with dogs' own natural energy resources (and, as we will see, susceptibility to boredom), make their environments super conducive to playing. But they're not playing Marco Polo or chess or Minecraft. Their games help to hone the skills they'd need should they ever have to fight for survival, Katniss Everdeen style. This might be why a lot of dog play looks like fighting.

In an adult dog's life, they may need to bark really loud to scare off an enemy. They may need to dig to hide something. Or search for food. Or tug an animal apart. And it'll certainly be helpful if they can hump. Dogs keep doing these things into adulthood even when their survival doesn't depend on it, probably because they've evolved to be perma-puppies. On the road trip to the kind of maturity we see in wolves, today's dogs pulled over at the rest stop and got lost in the ball pit. And that's okay. Just like it's now (debatably) okay for grownups to join kickball teams and play smartphone games on the subway.

But dog play can easily be misinterpreted as fighting and aggression. It also sometimes crosses a line and drifts into dangerous territory where dogs harm each other or people. Familiarizing yourself with normal dog play and getting a sense of where that line is helps to keep everybody happy and safe.

A good way to learn about dog play is to visit a dog park. Without your dog. Here is some of the body language you might see.

BUTTS UP IN THE AIR

There are few things I love more than to see dogs sending each other whole-body invitations for play. We call this position a play bow, and it is a happy sight! When Kate created the School For The Dogs logo, she used a silhouette of her late, great pit bull, Disco, play bowing: butt up in the air, front legs flat on the ground, tail up, ready. I saw Disco in this position many times, and it was like he was smiling with his whole body.

Other dogs may bow in a way that puts them totally flat on the ground, head down, with tail wagging either high up or low to the ground. Besides the tail, which may or may not be in motion, dogs are usually quite still before and during a play bow, a physical posture observed in other canids and some other mammals as well. It's a stable position from which the animal can quickly move into other positions, but it is also a nonthreatening position, as it puts the inviting animal's head lower to the ground than the invitee, hence *bow*.

Dogs bow to each other, but they also bow to humans. Either way, we can read it as a sign that they come in peace. Why is this important?

Perhaps because, with dogs, playing can so often resemble fighting. Initiating play with a bow, a dog is saying, "Hey, whatever happens from here I mean no harm, okay?" Research suggests that "rapid mimicry," which may be what is happening when another dog responds to a play bow with a play bow, is a way for playmates to get on the same emotional and behavioral page, a shortcut for creating empathy, which can lead to safer, more successful play.

A play bow is also a kind of a stretch. Stretching can feel so good—I can tell you this from experience! Happy is the dog doing a bow stretch, or the other kind of stretch in the other direction, back legs all long. A subcategory of the latter is the stretch that happens with eyes looking at you, or with paws on you. I love this kind of dog hug.

TAIL WAGGING

In 2015, a company called TailTalk hired School For The Dogs to provide dog actors for a promotional shoot for their product, which they were billing as the "World's First Dog Emotion Sensor." It was basically a bracelet that attached to the base of a dog's tail and reported, via Bluetooth, the speed and angle as it wagged, with the goal of helping a dog's humans understand how a dog was feeling. The product—which ended up never being commercially produced—had a conceptual flaw that was understandable, in that it reflected the way in which people too often think about dogs: one isolated body part at a time. Can you learn something from the speed and directionality of a tail wag? Quite possibly. But it's like interpreting a person's feelings based on their thumbs. They may occasionally put a thumb up or down to signal approval or disapproval, but more often thumb movements have to do with movements in other parts of the body (what are the other fingers doing?) and context (is the thumb being raised by the side of the road?). A tail wag happening in conjunction with ears down may mean something different from one with ears up. It can mean something different at the dog park than it does at the vet.

There are studies you can read about what different types of wags might mean, and different speeds. However, broadly speaking, let's just say that there are lots of different types of wags, lots of types of tails, and many environments where wags happen. For that reason, in my book, a wag should neither be dismissed as unimportant nor glorified as a sole signifier of anything sinister or happy. It's literally the tail end of a body that is telling us a lot from head to toe. Right, Holly?

OTHER PLAY BEHAVIORS

Chasing is a common dog behavior, although it can be concerning if it becomes too intense. It is important to watch out for any signs that the play has become too rough, such as yelping, whining, or mouthing. Is one dog being chased to a hiding place and then doesn't want to come out? That's a sign that the chase is probably not consensual.

If you have any doubt about whether both dogs are cool with the game, break it up. What you'll have at that point is information: If the dogs rush back to play with each other, that's information that they're both feeling good about things. If either one retreats and tries to crawl up your pant leg, that's information that the play isn't consensual. If you're not sure if your dog is enjoying being chased, better be safe than sorry and give your dog a break from the aggressor. Remember how learned behaviors can drift into innate food-seeking behaviors? A similar drift can happen with behaviors that start out as play: animals or kids who move quickly and make high-pitched noises can suddenly seem like they'd be good to have for dinner. It's why I think it's a special thing for our clients to be able to have playdates in the presence of a dog trainer. People learn what to look for to keep everyone safe and happy.

My favorite thing to see during play is lots of taking turns. Some dogs may always like being "it" or have a tendency to want to play on the bottom. That's fine. But usually, a good play pairing has lots of shifts in who is chasing whom, reversals of who is on top, and lots of little breaks, with each dog giving the other dog the time to take a second now and then.

HUMPING

People sure do think humping dogs are funny. Someone gave me a thumb drive that makes it look like a dog is humping my laptop's USB port. "Wally, you need to buy dinner for her first," says the woman with a Portuguese water dog that is trying to mount a Shiba Inu at Tompkins Square Park. Nearby, a tiny poodle is doing it just in the air. "Look, he's twerking," someone says.

Here is how I see it: Trace the path of why anyone does anything and you'll usually find that it relates to an inborn desire to figure out how to live long enough to procreate, and then to procreate. Our baked-in instincts help us do things relating to these goals, and sometimes those instincts get triggered a little liberally. Sometimes on the other side of that equation is going to be a receptive female. But more often than not, it's probably going to be a laundry bag or some dog in the dog park who would rather be chasing the ball.

Some dogs go through a humping phase and then grow out of it. If they're playing with polite dogs, they'll probably learn from others that it's kind of an annoying behavior in the context of play. But it is possible other dogs may not be polite. For that reason, it's a good idea to just get your dog off the other dog. No need to make a big deal of it.

Others may default to that behavior as a kind of displacement of emotion. Amos would sometimes hump when there were two dogs playing and it seemed like he wanted to get involved but couldn't figure out how. He also would sometimes hump my leg when he seemed like he wanted to leave the dog park. It wasn't the most endearing thing about him, but hats off to him for figuring out how to train me to jump up and take him home.

SNIFFING

You probably are already aware that dogs like to sniff things. Sniffing must be incredibly rewarding to dogs. The part of their brains devoted to sniffing is more than forty times greater than ours, as is the number of neural olfactory receptors. If a dog is sniffing, he is taking in information about the world. Checking his pee-mail, if you will. Can stress sniffing happen? Sure. But usually, a dog who is gathering information with the nose is happy doing just that.

LOOSENESS

When Amos was happy, his tongue hung out of his mouth and he'd hop about; when my current dog, Poppy, is pleased, her body wiggles and she rolls over in case you might be interested in patting her belly. Our trainer Anna Ostroff's dog, Ginger, smiles with the corners of her mouth up. Every dog displays their happiness in their own way. As a rule of thumb, what you're looking for is the opposite of stiffness. You're looking for looseness. Boppiness. Chillness. It isn't one thing to look for. It's myriad little physical signals that they're in the place they want to be, with the dogs or people (or both) they want to be with.

Be a Safe Base

After you've visited the dog park a few times alone and perhaps reread the previous chapter, you can go there with your dog. If you see signs that your dog needs space, from other dogs or other people or you or the tree, you should figure out how to help your dog get it.

If your dog is loose and happy running around like a goof with the other dogs, taking turns like a champ, bouncing around and play bowing, by all means stay.

Here's something else that might happen: Your dog may just want to sit with you. And that's totally okay. You don't need to push them into the fray. Dogs are allowed to be reticent to engage or to not want to "play" at all. The "run" in dog run shouldn't be an imperative.

During our playtimes for puppies, we designate all the people as safe "bases." If your puppy retreats into someone's lap or is seeking refuge under a chair, we'll let you know it's your job to help keep the other puppies away.

You have become a conditioned reinforcer. You are the provider of safety and sustenance and all the good things in life. You are Hyrum Lai! Minus the broomstick! Let your dog get confidence by the mere fact of being in your presence. Let her feel like she can approach the world with that basis of security.

DOG PARK TIPS

Dog parks aren't appropriate for every dog, and urban dog parks have their own unique challenges: they can be small and dense with a revolving population. If a park has dogs in it who don't want to be there, accompanied by humans who aren't particularly good at reading dog body language (and are lost in their phones to boot), things can go south quickly. So how do you

---

make sure your dog stays safe and happy at the dog run? Here are some tips to help you plan ahead.

- **ENSURE YOUR DOG CAN SIT AND WAIT BEFORE ENTERING THE PARK.** Allowing your dog to rush into the park leads to increased excitement, which can lead to inappropriate "over the top" greeting and play behaviors. Teaching your dog to sit and wait before entering the park allows some of that excitement to dissipate so they can enter more calmly. This will also give you the opportunity to observe how the other dogs in the run react to your dog before they even enter.

- **WALK BRISKLY INTO THE RUN.** Don't linger at the gate. Walk right in, using your body to split and walk between dogs to prevent them from all crowding your dog at once as you enter. Multiple dogs crowding all at once can be overwhelming for some dogs and can easily lead to conflict.

- **CALL YOUR DOG FREQUENTLY FOR BREAKS.** Practice calling your dog to come to you often throughout the visit and then immediately release them to go back into play. This will ensure your recall cue will work when you really need it. If you're using treats to reinforce, keep them hidden and make sure you practice with a trainer to learn how to deliver them stealthily; otherwise, you could cause a dog fight.

- **KEEP VISITS SHORT.** Dogs (especially adolescents) can become overstimulated or overtired when you stay too long. Being overstimulated or overtired can lead to less control over their bodies and thus the ability to communicate may deteriorate, which can lead to more conflict. Limit visits to fifteen to twenty minutes to be on the safe side.

- **KNOW HOW TO INTERVENE.** If you see something concerning, intervene by first physically walking in between the dogs' space, then call your dog to the gate and leave. Avoid grabbing a dog you don't know by the collar; you could be bitten. If there's already a fight ongoing involving your dog, start with loud noises for intervention, then try water (hose or bottle) or grabbing the hind legs, unless the dog is latched on. If you grab and pull a dog that is latched on, you could intensify the injuries.

- **MAKE LEAVING FUN.** Off-leash time may be the best part of your dog's day, which can make it hard for some dogs to leave. You can "train" a conditioned emotional response to leaving by making sure that your dog gets treats, play, and praise from you as soon as you leave.

The Training Triad

GOOD MANAGEMENT

"No punishment has ever possessed enough power of deterrence to prevent the commission of crimes. On the contrary, whatever the punishment, once a specific crime has appeared for the first time, its reappearance is more likely than its initial emergence could have been."

—HANNAH ARENDT

ONCE YOU UNDERSTAND how animals learn, the principles of good dog training, and how to read your dog's behavior, you are ready to set the stage for you and your dog and start working in the real world. Good dog training in action depends on three things:

1. Managing your dog's environment to set him up for success
2. Figuring out what is really reinforcing to your dog
3. Delivering those things with good timing

Management, rewards, and timing: I call this the Training Triad.

Build Your Own Cult

Early in the *Dog Whisperer* episode about Holly, Hyrum Lai says something very true, for her and for many other pet dogs: "Holly didn't have

a say about coming to our house. So we have to do everything we can."
As the ones with the thumbs and the bigger prefrontal cortex—and the
keys, money, and treat pouches—we are managing doggie environments
all the time, wittingly or unwittingly.

Unless things have worked out badly for you in life, your box isn't
as clearly defined as the tic-tac-toe-playing chicken's. Ditto your dog.
Nonetheless, we can do a lot to influence the opportunities a dog has by
controlling their environments.

This is what I mean by management. We are largely the designers
of our dogs' worlds. We manipulate inputs and encourage behaviors by
figuring out what motivates them and setting them up for success. In
this sense, humans truly are dominant. In our homes with our dogs, we
are almost like cult leaders. Power-wise, it's not an even relationship.
(Unless your dog can drive and open doors and fridges, I don't want to
hear about her being the "alpha.") But when a cult is really working, the
cult members *want* to be there. So, too, with your dog: ideally, we want
them to want to be part of good dog training.

Once we start paying attention to the ways in which we already control many aspects of our dogs' lives that affect their behavior, we will start
to see how small tweaks can make a big difference.

Setting the Stage: Managing Space

Type the name "Skinner" into a Google search bar, and the algorithm
is very likely to guess the word you need to complete your search is
"box." This is because Skinner put rats in boxes. He put pigeons in boxes.
To some, however, he is most remembered for someone else he put in a
box: his daughter.

"I have come across people who thought I was either dead or
crazy," Deborah Buzan told me. She is a painter who lives in London.

"Colleagues of my parents would come back from lecture trips abroad and would say that they met people who would say 'It's a pity about Skinner's daughter, isn't it?'"

When Eve Skinner was pregnant with Deborah in 1944, her husband wanted to figure out how to make motherhood easier for her. Here is how he put it, in *Ladies' Home Journal* the following year:

When we decided to have another child, my wife and I felt that it was time to apply a little labor-saving invention and design to the problems of the nursery. We began by going over the disheartening schedule of the young mother, step by step. We asked only one question: Is this practice important for the physical and psychological health of the baby? When it was not, we marked it for elimination. Then the "gadgeteering" began. The result was an inexpensive apparatus in which our baby daughter has now been living for eleven months. Her remarkable good health and happiness and my wife's welcome leisure have exceeded our most optimistic predictions, and we are convinced that a new deal for both mother and baby is at hand.

Bringing home a child, or a new dog, can feel like living with an adorable creature on a suicide mission, can't it? We baby-proof and puppy-proof our homes, sure, in all the obvious ways to keep really bad things from happening. By the same token, consider how we control parameters of their worlds—or could—that would encourage good choices, while also creating general feelings of safety and comfort. It doesn't require a physical box, but Skinner took good management to the next level and made a special box. For his daughter. It was basically a kind of climate-controlled raised playpen, enclosed but with windows.

Don't take "living in" the box the wrong way—Baby Debby Skinner was taken in and out of it throughout the day until she was close to three. He said she always showed an interest in going in, and never was forced to remain in it for long periods alone.

Buzan insists that people needed to understand that he wasn't experimenting on her. He wasn't training new behaviors. But he was preventing her from discovering other pastimes, like sticking her fingers in sockets, tumbling downstairs, or breaking the gramophone. I can tell you from experience that once your toddler discovers it's fun to spin all the toilet paper off the roll, or fish your birth control out of your purse and pop out all the pills, you dream about ways in which you can keep them from developing similar hobbies in the future.

We can set up our dogs for success by managing their environments and at the same time keep unwanted things from happening. Historically, in dog training, more emphasis has been placed on the latter. Most dog crates look more like prisons than Montessori classrooms.

Skinner's baby box, which he called the Air Crib, was filled with toys, and his daughter seemed happy to be in the thing. Skinner saw the whole

Skinner's youngest daughter, Deborah, in her Air Crib.

thing as a big win for environmental arrangement—one that could reap benefits for everyone.

"Many babies seem to cry from sheer boredom—their behavior is restrained and they have nothing else to do. In our compartment, the waking hours are invariably active and happy ones," he wrote. "The fact is that a baby will probably get more love and affection when it is easily cared for, because the mother is less likely to feel overworked and resentful of the demands made upon her."

You can think of the home you're in with your dog as a kind of box, with physical boundaries you have more control over than your dog does. Within that box, you can set the stage for safety, comfort, and the behavior you want.

To grasp the idea of this kind of environmental control, it may help to think of *The Wizard of Oz*. Did you ever notice in the movie that there's actually a red brick road right next to the more famous yellow one that Dorothy and her friends are on? Yet, they never leave the yellow brick road. We never worry about them wandering off. We never ask, "What about the *red* brick road?" We never even wonder where it goes. Our heroes stay on that yellow brick road because why wouldn't they? There's the promise of something compelling enticing each of them with every step (a heart, a home, a brain, courage), and so many interesting things happen along the way! This is how I think about management. Given a specific training end goal, be it sitting quietly, coming when we call, or peeing outside, we build a veritable yellow brick road for our dog to get there, a path of learning so obvious and appealing that the alternatives barely register. We create the conditions in which the behavior we want is the easiest thing for our dog to do, and the behaviors we don't want don't have much room to occur—a path, sometimes quite literally, as you will see, to training that is the path of least resistance. Follow the yellow brick road, Toto!

Good management is a matter of setting clear boundaries, but there's going to be such great stuff happening within those boundaries that ideally, your dog won't even realize the boundaries are there. It takes a little forethought, but the fact that we control so much about our dogs' lives means it's not hard to set things up this way.

On the flip side of the management coin, we manage the environment because we want to prevent a dog from doing things we don't want, recognizing that if given a chance to do these things, they can be reinforced by the doing. Peeing on the rug feels good. If the behavior of getting food off the counter is reinforced even just once, and it may become a behavior your dog will want to try out forevermore. By keeping a dog out of the room with the rugs and making sure there is never any unattended food on the counter, we ideally keep our dogs from discovering those hobbies in the first place, or else we can hope that the behavior will undergo extinction due to lack of reinforcement.

A CASE FOR DOG CRATES

A crate can be ground zero for managing space. You know exactly where your dog is when she's in a crate; and, equally important, you know where she isn't. You know she's not in another room chewing on the furniture, learning how much fun that is, leaving you to figure out how to get her to unlearn it later. And, critical to house-training, since dogs tend not to pee or poop where they sit or sleep, when your dog is in the right-sized crate you can be pretty sure she's not doing those things either. From a dog's perspective, a crate should ideally be a cozy, safe place to be alone, sometimes, but also sometimes a base from where they can feel safe about engaging in the larger world—your world. When it comes to traveling, a crate is a mobile home, so your dog has a home wherever you go.

Training a dog to go into a crate, we want to make sure that we are thinking about dog body language and smart conditioning. In this-equals-that terms of classical conditioning, we're aiming for crate = good and safe. Make the crate a place your dog wants to be. Put treats in the crate, and feed meals in it. Don't even start closing the door to the crate until your dog is happy to be in it on her own. Sometimes I'll play "crate FOMO," putting something great inside and shutting the door, to build interest in the crate. When excitement starts to peak, I'll open the door of the crate and let the dog burst in. I'm building the behavior of getting in there with excitement. Then I'll leave it open and let her hang out in there, or not.

Before you start leaving your dog alone in the crate, keep the crate with you and take it from room to room. If you have a small dog and a small crate, you can even have it on the couch with you, or put it on your desk. You can also build your dog's interest in the crate by feeding him his meals in it. When your dog is content being in a crate while you're around, you can start leaving him alone in it.

I never used a crate with Amos—it's not like they're compulsory. When I got Poppy, she was a puppy and I had a toddler, so it was a no-brainer. I fed her meals in the crate from the start, sometimes in training games, and she still often eats (and trains) in the crate. Sometimes with the door closed, other times not. She goes in on her own all the time. I move it around the apartment so that she can be part of what's going on but still have her safe spot.

Other Space Management Tools

White noise machines, door sweeps, and crate covers can help keep your dog from getting into the habit of barking inside, if they block out the stimuli that are your dog's reason for barking.

Outside of the boxes we live in, we cannot always control the environment with great precision. But if you have a dog who is stressed out by other dogs or skateboards, for example, you can make choices to, say, walk down quiet streets and walk at off-peak times of day. You can also make the choice to physically get in between your dog and something that might be scary—make your body a visual blocker.

Muzzles are another example of a management tool that can do a world of good. Some reasons we help people acclimate their dog to wearing a muzzle include:

✧ **IT CAN KEEP A DOG FROM BITING.** Even a dog with no bite history may benefit from wearing a muzzle, as there may be a time when they need to be restrained for medical treatment in an emergency. In those situations, a muzzle is sometimes required to keep everyone safe. If your dog is already accustomed to wearing a muzzle, it can be a less frightening experience.

✧ **IT CAN KEEP A DOG FROM EATING STUFF OFF THE STREET.** Do you want to know the cost of dislodging a chicken wing bone from your dog's trachea? I certainly don't. But I do know this: it's more than the cost of a muzzle.

✧ **IT MAY MAKE OTHER PEOPLE FEEL SAFE.** You might not think your dog is vicious, but I've never met a dog who isn't capable of biting. That possibility is really scary to some people.

✧ **IT IS ONE WAY TO MAKE OTHER PEOPLE GO AWAY.** Some people don't know that the best way to approach a dog is to let them come to you. On the street, they insist on coming to say "hi" to your dog, and may end up crowding him or scaring him. Or other dog owners let their dog approach in a way that isn't polite. A muzzled dog is a lot more likely to get a wide berth on the sidewalk.

TRAINING A DOG TO WEAR A MUZZLE: SCHOOL FOR THE DOGS' WEEK-BY-WEEK PLAN

- **WEEK 1:** Use food to create a good association with the muzzle by feeding your dog through it. An easy way to do this is to put peanut butter in it, then hold it and let your dog lick it out.

- **WEEK 2:** Add in the straps by having your dog eat treats or kibble through the muzzle with the straps loosely buckled.
- **WEEK 3:** Eliminate food as a lure and wait for your dog to put his nose in the muzzle before giving treats.
- **WEEK 4:** Increase the duration your dog wears the muzzle by treating him intermittently for up to five minutes while engaging him in other activities.
- **WEEK 5:** Generalize the training by taking your dog to new environments where he can wear the muzzle comfortably and confidently.

It's up to you to find a balance that works between management and training. Sometimes it will be obvious—decent parents don't try to train babies not to fall into the pool. They put up a fence. When the kids get a little older, the teaching can begin.

Could you teach your dog to avoid all power cords? Yes, but time and energy are finite, and I would rather put mine toward other things and just not let an interest in cord chewing ever develop in the first place. This is not unlike plugging up sockets rather than trying to teach a curious baby's roaming fingers that outlets are dangerous. There are no consequences, good or bad, to chewing power cords if they are made inaccessible to begin with.

Managing Time

Dogs spend roughly 50 percent of their time sleeping, which leaves only about twelve hours a day in which we really need to think about what the dog is doing. A puppy sleeps even more than that. When the dog is awake, we want to give her every opportunity to do the right thing.

Planning feeding times and walking times and making those parts of the day meaningful and enriching can go a long way toward having a happy, healthy dog. We can shape their behaviors by devoting more or less time to certain activities, especially for puppies. And by dosing exposures to new things just right.

Paying attention to your dog's schedule is pretty key when you're working on house-training. Dogs new to going outside should get many frequent opportunities to relieve themselves in the right spot but, new as they may be to everything this involves—being on a leash, being on pavement, a dog across the street, a garbage truck lumbering by—those outings should be pleasant and short. Even if bathrooming hasn't occurred. I'm usually a fan of frequent, short walks for puppies. Another benefit is that when walks are short, your dog will most likely learn to go right away. When you have an 8:00 a.m. meeting and it's raining, you will be very glad you taught her this behavior! If walks are long, your dog may learn to go after twenty minutes of strolling. Of course, food rewards can be part of this picture too, but even without edible reinforcement, we can go a long way toward getting behaviors we want by simply providing lots of opportunities for those behaviors to occur, and by being mindful about not letting new experiences go on so long that they become stressful or overwhelming.

It's also important that the opportunities you give your dog to go correlate as much as possible with the times that your dog needs to go. Puppies, especially, should get an opportunity to go in the right spot—whether that's outside on a leash, or in a yard, or inside on a pee pad or a grass patch—immediately after they eat and at regular intervals after that. If you can get your dog to the right place as soon as she wakes up from a nap, this will also encourage elimination to happen when and where you want it to. But you can also look for cues—body language!—that your dog is thinking about going. Watch closely when she does, so you'll know what to look for. Spinning a couple of times, or concerted sniffing—some dogs' signs are more obvious than others'.

Here are some ways you can manage how your dog is spending time:

TETHERING

If your dog is tethered to you, they won't have a chance to wander off to pee on the bath mat when you're not looking, and they will also be close enough for you to start reading the signs that they may have to go.

CRATING

Most dogs don't like to bathroom in the same place where they're hanging out, making a crate an invaluable management tool for house-training. This is one reason why a crate shouldn't be much larger than your dog. If you suspect your dog has to pee, you shouldn't have them in the crate. Start with short stints in the crate, and make sure you give the chance to potty in the right spot as soon as they come out.

CARRYING

If you have a dog that is small enough to carry, you can make sure he isn't going in the wrong spots by simply keeping him under your arm, or on your lap, or in a comfortable bag.

PENNING

Keeping your dog in a fixed space helps you manage where he goes, literally. The key is to pen off an area that is small and that, whenever possible, includes you, so you're there to spot the signs that it's time for an outing. The moment you allow your dog more spatial freedom, outside of the crate, carrier, or pen, bring him to the appropriate "go" spot right away. You might want to try different substrates to see what your dog likes to go on. Some like grass. Some like the feel of a metal manhole cover underfoot. Some like to go between two parked cars, like a little bathroom stall *en plein air*. Tip: If hallways, stairs, an elevator, and/or lobby lie between your home and your puppy's go spot, carry him outside so he doesn't have a mistake on the way out.

Managing Energy

Kay Rhee is an artist in New Jersey who sews sculptures out of felt: burritos with hand-stitched lettuce and limes inside; soft sushi rolls; fortune cookies; succulent gardens; and an entire dim sum spread, including a teapot, dumplings, and shrimp shumai. The detail of her craftsmanship, however, is entirely for the purchaser of these items—not for the end user. Each item contains little openings and folds that are meant to be stuffed with dry dog food. Dogs use their noses and paws in a game of treat-hide-and-seek that burns time, and energy that could hardly be put to better (or cuter) use.

At School For The Dogs, I have traced a lot of people's dog problems to what is likely a common denominator: boredom. Dogs evolved to kill things, chase things, help us, and guard us—to have jobs. If your dog's life involves little more than walking around the block a couple times a day and trekking from the sofa to the kitchen for breakfast and dinner, you have an unemployed dog who will naturally start making up her own jobs, jobs you probably don't want your dog to have—say, letting you know about every person that is in the hallway, or redesigning your coffee table with her teeth. Such creative behavior is part of what has helped dogs—and people—evolve to be such engaged, successful species. Part of the fun of being alive, for us and for our dogs, is problem-solving. Even when we're solving a problem that is not desperate for a solution. It's why we play *Wordle* or *Minecraft* or read two pages of strangers' opinions about whether the Dyson Supersonic hair dryer is really better than the InfinitiPRO by Conair.

Boredom isn't just bad for an animal's brain, it can be bad for health too. Economists have found a negative correlation between how early someone retires and how long they live. People who stay engaged in some kind of work, like volunteering, fare better. Money isn't the only reward we get out of work. So, since you're going to give the dog the food anyway, why not add in a work component, to make eating last longer and give it even more purpose?

When I was a kid, I used to regularly visit New York's biggest neurotic. Big as in 700 pounds. His name was Gus and he lived in Central Park. Gus was a polar bear.

He lived in a highly managed environment: a small icy enclave maintained year-round in a small corner of the Central Park Zoo, smack-dab in the middle of Manhattan. In the 1990s, when he was in his late single digits, he developed the habit of swimming in figure eights around his containment, over and over. He would do this in hours-long stretches for most of the day, and sometimes I would watch. I remember snapping photos of the bottom of Gus's foot pushing against the glass. I didn't know I was watching a display of animal suffering.

Gus's behavior was a sign of stress. He wasn't in anything resembling his natural environment. His life presented no challenges and little agency. There had been one thing he liked to do: hunting. However, because seals weren't accessible, he instead stalked children. He'd wait for one to smush a face up to the glass of his enclosure, and then he'd rush at them, claws out and mouth open. The zoo figured out how to manage his environment to keep him from engaging in that pastime. They put up some visual barriers, which is when Gus began swimming laps.

In 1994, the zoo called in a trainer who, according to *New York* magazine, was into "cutting-edge behavioral therapy." He clued them into the fact that "Gus is just bored and mildly crazy in the way that a lot of people are in New York." The solution? Changing up his environment, including food toys to keep him occupied.

Some twenty-five years later, I was sitting across the table from a fellow dog trainer, Ferdie Yau, and I asked him about his first job working with animals. It turns out he started his career by making work-to-eat toys for Gus. "We gave him puzzles, so for example we started giving him what looked like a big plastic ice float basically, and we cut holes in it and we hid toys inside of it. Inside those toys we'd hide food. We would put a puzzle inside a puzzle inside a puzzle, kind of like those little Russian dolls that you open up," remembered, adding, "It's just like working with dogs."

WORK-TO-EAT TOYS

In the 1970s, a Colorado mechanic named Joe Markham had a dog who was bored, and it was causing dental issues. The dog kept chewing rocks. So, Markham tried to get him interested in chewing, well, anything else. He gave him a rubber part from the suspension of a Volkswagen, and the dog loved it. He named it for the gorilla king who he imagined might use such a thing as an earplug: KONG.

Nearly fifty years later, the KONG company has sold fifty million of these chew toys in a range of sizes. My dogs had them growing up—they're fun for games of fetch because their shape makes them bounce unpredictably, like a football. It was only when I went to dog trainer school that I realized the real value of this toy is the hole that runs through its core.

You can smear peanut butter, cream cheese, liverwurst, or soft dog food inside a KONG. To extend the enjoyment time, put the food in and freeze it before you give it to your dog. There are people on Etsy who 3D-print little plugs that also act like stands so you can fill them with liquid (like bone broth, with or without kibble or some other treat mixed in) and put them in the freezer without the liquid spilling out. Run a large zip tie through the hole and you can affix it to the side of a crate or to the leg of a table.

The KONG is the proto work-to-eat toy. It established the category and has largely cornered it, even today. The company now makes many other toys that can be used with or without food, including work-to-eat toys for zoo animals.

Here is a rough categorization of the kinds of "work-to-eat" toys that many pet stores now purvey.

- ✧ **KONG-STYLE** toys are meant to be stuffed with wet food or peanut butter or the like.
- ✧ **PUZZLE TOYS** have doors and drawers and flaps behind which you can hide treats or food.
- ✧ **KIBBLE BALLS** are round or partly round toys that dispense treats or food as they move. Best for use with things that are dry.
- ✧ **SLOW FOOD BOWLS** are bowls with varied, interesting textures and paths designed with a dog's oral pleasure and interest in mind— landscapes for the tongue, if you will. Good for use with most types of treats and food.
- ✧ **SNUFFLE MATS** are like little washable toys, sometimes not unlike pretty rugs or even soft sculpture into which goes food. Your dog's nose goes into the shag or nooks to find the stuff. My dog Poppy loves snuffle mats! The deeper you embed the food or treats (or

even treat dust), the more snuffling is required. Best for use with dry food or dry treats.

✧ **LICK MATS** are similarly easy to use. These are, as their name suggests, mats designed to be well tongued. Usually, they're made of silicone rubber molded with different grooves of different depths. Sometimes they have suction cups on the back. You can smear them with wet food or anything lickable and wash them in the dishwasher.

DIY TOYS

When it comes to work-to-eat toys, personally I am a functionalist. I don't think our dogs care how they look, or what we spent on them. I have, many a time, asked a dog owner to get me an empty ice cube tray or a muffin tin from their kitchen during a session, so that I could sprinkle it with something to keep their dog occupied while I spoke to them.

CHEWING

Since our goal is to manage their environment to provide appropriate enrichment opportunities, we need to think about what our dog is going to chew. What, not whether. Chewing is a normal behavior—let it not be on the moldings of your home or your mom's hearing aids.

Here are some things dogs can and should be encouraged to chew:

✧ **BONES.** You can get chopped bones at pet stores or make friends with the butcher at the supermarket. Beef shank bones, large lamb or pork bones, knuckles. You want something that is larger than your dog's mouth. You can parboil a bone to soften and clean it, but avoid giving a dog cooked bones, as the heat will dry the bones making them more likely to splinter in your dog's throat.

✧ **YAK CHEWS.** These are very hard orange sticks that come in various sizes. They're made of yak's milk and lime. They were originally made in the Himalayas and sometimes are called "Himalayan chews."

✦ **ICE.** Just ice. Some dogs love it. You can also make ice from bone broth.

BULLY STICKS AND BULLY STICK SAFETY

Never did I think I would own a shop that does a brisk business in dried bovine penis. And yet here I am.

Bully sticks come in many sizes, and sometimes they're curled or braided together. Sometimes they smell really bad, as soon as they're moistened with dog saliva. Some are marketed as "odor free," which means they were drained and dried an extra-long time. Pro tip (or commonsense tip, when you know what a bully stick is): the more yellowy a bully stick looks, the more likely that it will smell bad.

Possibly stranger than my bull phallus mercantile is the fact that we also do big business in products that are meant to hold the bully stick so that it won't be swallowed by a dog when it gets chewed down to a little nub. For my podcast, I have interviewed three different entrepreneurs who are sure they've figured out the best way to house these chews with safety in mind. Our best seller at School For The Dogs, the Bully Grip, is like a rubber puck with a little asterisk cutout that grabs onto the end of a stick when you stick it through. Its creator was inspired to create it when her dog swallowed a bully stick and it had to be pulled out the other end. She showed me a picture. It was bad. Don't let that happen. Use protection.

AVOID: RAWHIDE

Avoid giving your dog rawhide. At least I do. Rawhide is usually hard and white in color. It is made from cow, horse, or deer hides, although other types of rawhide may be available. Sometimes, a dog chews off a piece that is too big and it can get stuck in the esophagus or in the intestines. I know people who've given their dogs rawhide every day of the week for years without issue, but I also know others who haven't been so lucky. Also, rawhide can contain chemicals like bleaches, formaldehydes, and arsenic-based preservatives. Yuck.

If you *are* going to give your dog rawhide, Nancy Kearns, editor of the *Whole Dog Journal*, gives the following good advice:

✧ Look for chews that are made in the United States. Check! A picture of an American flag on the package is not proof enough.

✧ Go for types that are made from just one solid piece of hide rather than a sewn-together Frankenstein medley, even if it is in the shape of an adorable booty.

✧ Avoid products that are super white or tinted with colored-barbecue flavoring.

Managing Energy with Play

"The child's parents take care of its survival problems and it is left with a great deal of surplus energy. Its playful activities help to burn up this energy," wrote Desmond Morris in his 1969 book called *The Human Zoo*. "Each bout of playing is a voyage of discovery: discovery of itself, its abilities and capacities, and of the world about it."

Ditto dogs.

Physical play seems to help juveniles from many species get stronger and hone their motor skills, while also acting as a form of social training, teaching young animals codes of social behavior and helping them understand where they fit into the social hierarchy of their community. By roughhousing, animals create social bonds and learn what behaviors are acceptable: how hard they can bite, how roughly they can interact, and how to resolve conflicts—all lessons they can generalize to other situations.

But play isn't just about the physical stuff. It's also about what goes on in our minds: the games we make up, the imaginary lands we create, and so forth. Human evolution seems to favor innovation and creativity. A child who creates imaginary worlds is a child who, on some level, is practicing for the unknown, but *possible*. He might become an intergalactic space traveler or a lion hunter. Or a teacher or a dad. Video games help with our hand–eye coordination, but they also can train us to think analytically, to be more aware of our surroundings, and to work better together. Right now, in schoolyards and rec rooms and on Facebook pages, kids are preparing for the future. But they're also preparing the future. Did NASA give kids something to dream about, or was it the consequence of childhood fantasies? I'd say, both.

As a perma-puppy, it's normal that an adult dog should still want to dig and chase and do all the things that might help him out should he ever find himself in some sort of proto-dog situation—a canine version of *Deliverance*. That's why, as a dog trainer, I love figuring out ways to make my dog's life as enriching as possible. Dogs want to play: to interact and engage, if not with us then with things we can put in the environment for them.

It's especially important for puppies to get playtime with toys, humans, and other puppies. Puppy play is all about practicing life skills, and learning social cues and boundaries in the process. Indeed, a danger of taking a puppy away from his siblings too soon is that he may not have learned the kind of bite control and inhibition that he would've given more time playing with his sisters and brothers.

CURATED PLAYDATES

Dog parks can be overwhelming to some dogs. Dogs tend to play best one-on-one. If you don't have a well-matched playmate for your dog, consider contacting a trainer and asking if they can help set you up with someone and their dog in your neighborhood. We do this kind of dog-friend matchmaking all the time for School For The Dogs clients. If they can't arrange to play at School For The Dogs or in one of their homes, they can check out SniffSpot.com, a site where people list their dog-friendly fenced-in yards that you can rent by the hour. These yards can also be useful if you don't have your own yard but want to throw a ball or a Frisbee for your dog in a private, safe spot.

Rewarding Environments

Once we set the stage for the behavior we want from our dogs, it's important to reward behaviors we like when they occur. Rewards, of course, aren't separate from the environment. They're part of it. And we humans have a lot of control over them.

Rewarding behaviors that you like starts with knowing what is rewarding to your learner. Otherwise said, you need to figure out what your dog is into.

The Training Triad

GOOD REWARDS

"Does the employee prefer recognition in private, public, or either? Will a thank you do? Does he enjoy the times when his peers are aware of good performance? How about occasional on-the-spot candy, free lunch, certificate for ice cream, small gift, etc.? Find out what works for individual employees. Establish an action plan that fits the needs of individual employees rather than trying to fit all employees into one big category."

—BOB NELSON, *1501 WAYS TO REWARD EMPLOYEES*

IN THE BEGINNING of the 1964 film *Mary Poppins*, the Banks children write their own advertisement for a new nanny. They're quite explicit; they want someone who has "a cheery disposition," "rosy cheeks," is "very sweet and fairly pretty" and will sing songs, bring sweets, play games, love them like a daughter and son, and ideally not smell like barley water.

In their robes and stocking feet, they sing their help wanted ad to their father. Sadly, George Banks isn't a very good animal trainer. He doesn't even look at what they've written. He hasn't considered why they are behaving badly. Perhaps their needs aren't being met? Perhaps he should be hiring women who lay off the barley water? Moments later, in swoops a young Julie Andrews, as Mary Poppins. *She* has read their list of desires. This has given her a clear understanding of what they want.

Mary Poppins describes herself as "kind but extremely firm," "practically perfect in every way." I don't know if she's perfect in *every* way, but I think she'd make a damn good dog trainer.

Not a year later Julie Andrews would be on screen again, playing another A-plus nanny, this time to the seven von Trapp children. As she traverses Salzburg, she belts, "I shall be firm but kind!"

When she arrives, the children's father informs her that she is the twelfth governess they've had.

"What's wrong with the children?" asks Andrews as Fräulein Maria.

"There's nothing wrong with the children," he says.

He's right. The issue isn't the children. Just like in good dog training, the issue is not the dog.

The moment they meet her, the children attempt to get the attention of their father by doing things they expect will displease her. If he is scolding them, he is paying attention to them—something he otherwise doesn't do. So, they put a frog in her pocket and a pinecone on her chair. Sometimes puppies really are annoying! But, she seems to understand that any reaction will reward these kids. So, she does all she can to stifle herself. She even goes so far as to thank them, in front of their father, for the "gift" they put in her pocket.

In this story too she soon figures out exactly what it is that her charges find rewarding: Pussy willows. Christmas. Bunny rabbits. Chocolate icing. No school. Pillow fights. Telegrams. Birthday presents. Any presents! These are a few of their favorite things.

Your job as a good dog trainer is to figure out a few of your dog's favorite things.

Once you have a well-set-up environment where your dog is likely to partake in lots of behaviors you want (and is unlikely to have a chance to do things you don't want), you need to be equipped with rewards to make it clear to your dog what it is that you want her to keep doing.

Dog trainer Kathy Sdao, who started out as a marine mammal trainer, wrote a book called *Plenty in Life Is Free*, the title a response to a no-free-lunch approach to animal training that strives to control every input, making everything a dog wants or needs be contingent on good behavior.. We don't have to go to that extent—and, if we're building a foundation for love and trust, we shouldn't. If I'm the god of my dog's life, I want to be like Kathy Sdao's God. She writes, "I've come to believe that [the nothing-in-life-is-free approach] contradicts the central miracle that I embrace: that I'm surrounded by countless unearned gifts from an extravagantly loving God. So, for me, one of these opposing ideas—'nothing in life is free for dogs' or 'grace is abundant for all creatures'—had to go."

Rewards versus Reinforcers

In the *Mary Poppins* books(on which the movie was based), there's a dog named Andrew, whose "ordinary days were filled with the kind of things most people have only on birthdays." He dined on oysters, wore fine overcoats, and "had two candles on his cake for every year instead of one." Thing is, Andrew didn't like candles. Or oysters or overcoats.

You get a "most valuable employee" award. You receive a passionate kiss from your boyfriend. Your soccer team wins and everyone gets taken out for ice cream. But if you hate your job and are planning to leave your company, or if that kiss is delivered in front of all your work colleagues, or if you're allergic to dairy, none of these things is likely to be reinforcing. A well-chosen reward is something that your training subject likes, but technically it is only a reinforcer if it increases the likelihood that whatever behavior preceded the reward's delivery will reoccur.

When is a reinforcer *not* a reward? When it's a negative reinforcer. Remember, from chapter 9, sometimes what increases the likelihood that a behavior will reoccur is when behaving in a certain way makes something "bad" go away, as when you buckle your seatbelt to make the annoying beeping sound stop.

Picking Rewards

One of the most important things you'll ever learn about your dog is what they like! In fact, you can expect to spend the rest of your life with your dog cataloging what they enjoy. No two individuals enjoy the exact same cornucopia of things—that is as true of people as it is of dogs. Some people like to sleep late and watch NASCAR. Some people like to wake up early and meditate. Bert likes paper clips; Ernie likes rubber ducks.

What pleases one person might seem perfectly punishing to someone else! I would not be caught dead running a marathon, or eating shark fin soup, or getting tied down with leather straps and whipped. But other people pay good money for the privilege of doing these things. Fortunately, your dog probably isn't into that kind of leather. But when you start paying attention to what your dog likes, you may be surprised. Some dogs prefer to walk away from the dog park than toward it. Some dogs really like having their bellies rubbed and others would *never*.

As you begin to take an inventory of what your dog is into, you can think of it as their currency system. What is your dog's hundred-dollar bill? What is his fiver? You'll need to figure that out. Because animals tend to do the things for which they regularly get paid and feel like they're getting paid enough.

Food Rewards

The main type of reward we use at School For The Dogs is food. Of course, you do not have to use food to train, but most dogs want to eat several times a day—and, if a dog enjoys her food, that means her food is

CHOPPED UP HOT DOG

AFFECTION

PRAISE

GOING OUT

BLUEBERRIES

NICE JOB

GOOD DOG!

BALL

BABY CARROTS

PEANUT BUTTER

CHEESE CUBES

BACON

OPPORTUNITY TO SNIFF ANOTHER DOG'S TUSH

DRY FOOD

acting as a reinforcer, even if you're not tuned into what behavior it is reinforcing. Much of the time, the reinforced behavior might just be bending over their food bowl. Why not use the food they're eating anyway to reward other behaviors?

When choosing food rewards, here is an important criterion: pick food treats that can be broken up into very small bits and delivered to your dog quickly. For most dogs, something the size of a pinky nail will do the job, or even smaller for small dogs. There's a practical reason for this: we want to try for many repetitions in every training session, and we are more likely to get them if we can deliver the food quickly and the dog can swallow it quickly.

If every time your dog did something right you gave him a whole pork chop, a single training session wouldn't accomplish a whole lot. For this reason, avoid food that crumbles when it's broken into bits, and anything sticky or slimy, as it will be harder to get from your hand to your dog's mouth.

Part of what we want is a dog who doesn't just get something right occasionally; we want them getting the desired behavior right a lot...and quickly. This is called *fluency*, and before we work on teaching anything too fancy, we want dogs who are fluent at a handful of important behaviors. You know how you can probably add two single-digit numbers in your head without much effort? That is a skill you learned and have done so often that it's second nature, and that's the kind of automaticity we want to build in training. The way to get there is to get a lot of successful repetitions in any given training session.

Our go-to treat at School For The Dogs is dehydrated lung of lamb. It is widely available in pet stores and online, thinly sliced, and breaks up easily into small pieces. It doesn't get your hands greasy, and it's relatively low in calories. It's also what they call "single ingredient"—an ingredient that happens to be loaded with iron and vitamins. It tastes like cardboard to me, but the dogs seem to like it.

Often, however, I've picked up treats at the corner deli on the way to a client's house. Hot dogs and string cheese are big money for many dogs. A single hot dog or Polly-O can yield at least fifty small treats, and if you freeze them, they don't turn gross in your hand. I've also gotten yellow American cheese, which I can ball up in the palm of my hand and pinch bits from.

Can you just use kibble? Yes. A reward does not necessarily have to be an extra-special treat. Many dogs will happily work for regular dry food. Some kinds of kibble can even be broken up into extra small pieces, making them easy to deliver and swallow. You can also stretch the value of kibble in training by mixing it with a few higher value treats; the occasional extra-yummy piece will help your dog stay motivated. However, some situations might require more valuable treats than others. For example, learning something in a new place or with distractions around may call for the thing your dog *really* loves, the fifty-dollar bill, if not the hundred.

Years ago, at the home goods store that used to be on the ground floor of my building, I picked up a little tube that was being sold as a portable salad dressing dispenser. I was fascinated: I never realized there was a market for such an item! Silicone and palm-shaped, to this dog trainer it was screaming to be filled with peanut butter (or cream cheese or liverwurst or baby food) and licked. You can deliver wet food in one of these tubes too, although it's small so better used for smaller quantities of richer stuff, in my experience. A larger tube, like a camping squeeze tube, would similarly work for something like canned wet food, or whatever you make if you have a blender and are creative in the kitchen.

TREAT BUFFET + TREAT LADDER

To figure out what treats your dog likes, you can try two methods:

- **TREAT BUFFET:** Put out six different types of treats around your dog and note the order in which he eats them to determine his preferences. Do three trials. What did he eat first? Second? Those are going to be your big bills.
- **TREAT LADDER:** Offer your dog two different treats and note which one he chooses first. Then pair the winner against a new treat to determine his preference order.

In my experience, meat, cheese, and peanut butter are the highest value treats for most dogs. But every dog is different. I've worked with dogs who've gone bonkers for peas, carrots, cucumbers, blueberries, and celery.

Where to Put the Treats

At School For The Dogs, we sell treat pouches that we have custom made, with hinges that stay open but also snap shut. They fit around the waist, like a fanny pack (or crossbody, the way the kids do these days). I also like a silicone pouch that clips to my belt. Use whatever works for you for easy carrying and quick delivery.

If you don't have treats physically on your person, you'll still want them out of your dog's sight. That might just mean having them in a bowl on the table higher than your dog can see. I often just keep them hidden in one fist. What you don't want to be is a Ziploc-bag-hand trainer—if your dog can see the on-deck treats throughout his training session, it will be harder later on to teach him to do things without waving around treats. You'll be conditioning the behavior to happen in the context that the reward is present, and you can see how this would be a problem for, say, a long-distance recall.

One of the simplest, most useful tips I can offer about using rewards with animals: set up direct deposit. This is how I pay my employees. I am not just concerned that they get paid; I want it to be a seamless process for them so as not to waste their time and energy on visits or calls to the bank.

With dogs, "direct deposit" is as simple as making sure your dog knows where to get the treat. Before you start training anything, consider where the reward is going to be available. Practice the treat delivery. Where are the treats going to be? In a pouch or in your hand or in your pocket? Can you comfortably deliver one at a time, or are they too slimy to handle?

Sometimes, you'll put food directly into your dog's mouth. Other times, you may want to put a treat on a plate or in a bowl to help your dog know exactly where to find it, no searching required, like drawing a target around it. If you're trying to get many repetitions quickly, you might want to put the treat in the same exact place each time. Other times, it may not matter that your dog is sniffing around looking for the treat you tossed.

If you're walking and rewarding your dog as you walk, you should also consider the precise spot where the treat will be delivered. I find it's useful to reward just by my leg, and sometimes I will even put a bit of tape at the spot as a reminder to myself where I want to deliver the treat. We call the place where the dog will receive the treat the "magic zone."

For certain behaviors, you can use the treat delivery to "reset" your dog. If you're practicing a sit, for example, tossing the treat a little in front of your dog can get her to stand up, making her ready to sit again. When practicing come, you can toss a treat some distance away, so your dog will again be in position to come back to you. Sometimes, I do "laps" with my dog, putting a treat on her bed when she's in her open crate. When she gets to the bed, she's rewarded with a treat in her crate, and back and forth. You can do laps between any two places.

One of my favorite training tools is the Treat & Train, a remote-controlled treat dispenser that sits on the floor and spits out any kind of uniform-sized hard kibble or treats. In a pinch, I've used peanuts and Cheerios in it. I can trigger it at a distance, which can be useful when training certain behaviors, such as recall, but also if I feel like training without getting up off my couch, or without getting my hands all meaty or cheesy. And like a bowl or plate, it also functions as a treat target since the treats always come out of the same place. My dog knows just where to go to find her yummies.

Don't forget, you can use regular meals in training if your dog eats regular meals. As we discussed, turning feeding time into training time just means being mindful of the who, when, and where of presenting the meal.

Nonfood Reinforcers

The reason that we mostly use food rewards is simply efficiency. In most cases, edible reinforcers will get you more successful reps with your dog in a short time than, say, throwing a ball for him. It's important to note, however, that you can use almost anything your dog enjoys to reinforce behaviors that you like. Part of the fun of getting to know your dog is figuring out what they're into! One dog might do anything for a ball. Another might love nothing more than getting to say "hello" to another dog or sitting in your lap. Games like tug can be a great reinforcer to teach an excited dog how to both listen to you and play with you at the same time.

Never underestimate that your attention is very likely reinforcing behaviors, be they wanted or unwanted ones. We can't always control signs of pique, but it's a good idea to try. Remember Fräulein Maria, stifling her displeasure at being made to sit on a pinecone. I call this going into "screensaver" mode. The late great dog trainer Dr. Sophia Yin called it "being a three-hundred-thousand-year-old stump." When a dog is not doing what I want and I'm frustrated, I find there's more power in being boring than in being reactive. I can't control everything about the situation, perhaps, but I can control my own reactions, and that can count for a lot. A puppy nips and you squeal, trying to imitate another puppy; a dog jumps on your aunt, who never pays attention to the dog, and suddenly she is yelling at her. We assume that our displeasure is understood as punishment by the dog. But we shouldn't. We should just note whether the behavior happens more or less in the future. If a behavior keeps happening, consider what reinforced it. Your excited reaction may have put fuel on the fire even if that wasn't your intention.

Does your dog respond to praise alone? Test it out. If the behaviors you're praising happen more and more, either it's working or there is some other reinforcer in play that you aren't taking into consideration. When using words as rewards in training, consider that higher pitches tend to be more attractive to dogs than lower ones, in the same way that a dog inviting play will usually whine or bark in a higher pitch, whereas a dog telling other dogs to go away will use a lower and louder bark.

"BUT MY DOG ISN'T FOOD MOTIVATED."

Every dog trainer has heard this, yet I have never met a healthy dog who isn't interested in eating at least some of the time, without the need to cook their interest by depriving them of food. A dog who will not eat is most likely a dog who is scared or unwell, which means you need professional help. Anorexia is a condition that can impact nonhuman animals too. If your dog isn't eating, that is an issue that needs to be addressed, with the counsel of a veterinarian and possibly a good dog trainer as well.

Other times, dogs are just picky. If you have a dog who's "meh" about treats, you have your work cut out for you to figure out what they're into. The grocery store could be the place to start. I have often bought a quarter pound of sliced turkey at a Manhattan corner mart on my way to a client. That's high-value stuff for many dogs and, bite for bite, cheaper than anything you'll get from Chewy.com. Possibly healthier!

Treats Forever

A common question I hear from people when they start using treats in training: Am I always going to have to use treats?

The answer is no. But also, yes.

Yes, because you should always make an effort to reinforce behaviors you like. Why? Because you're going to get what you pay for. In 1961, one of Skinner's Harvard protégés, Richard Hernstein, discovered what is now known as Matching Law: When given a choice of what to do, if there are two choices that require similar effort, an animal will do the thing that has been reinforced more. It's why you probably check your email a lot more than you check your voicemail. If you got multiple little shots of dopamine throughout the day because of new things arriving in your voicemail, you would check it more. At any given moment, the environment is rewarding lots of things your dog is doing. Or not. The world is not *always* generous: I am guessing that not every lamppost sniff is great. Sometimes, the sounds outside go away because of barking. Sometimes not. The environment isn't trying to get any specific behavior from your dog, except insofar as you arrange it. A dog choosing between doing something that might be rewarded randomly or by forces that don't have her (or your) best interests in mind, and doing something that will always be rewarded by you, will more often make the choice that has been reliably rewarded.

And no, because positive reinforcement has a cumulative effect, and you won't always be in treating "mode" or have treats on you. My dog Poppy is lying on the couch next to me as I write this, and I'm stroking her gently. There is behavior going on here—one that I like—and my light petting is likely encouraging the behavior in some small way. An hour ago, however, two plumbers were doing work in the other room. We were pretty much in the same position, and my criterion for her behavior was similarly low. But I was giving her cheese. Sometimes, life happens. You're out for a walk and you ask your dog to sit. There's a parade of squirrels going by and a gang of children on scooters and your dog…listens to you. Your dog sits. And gives you eye contact, to boot. But you're out of hot dog bits. Have you ruined your dog? Not if you've been generous in the past. Again, you can think of this in terms of currency. When your bank account is so full because you've made so many deposits, your dog, in the role of your banker, will be likely to give you a little bit of credit. She knows you're good for it.

As you and your dog get better at training, you can set higher criteria for when your dog gets a reward and what she will need to do to warrant one. There's an art and a science to this. It's actually variable rates of reinforcement—not being reinforced every time—that keep many behaviors going as we, dogs included, play the slot machine of life. I think variable reinforcement got me stuck in more than one crappy relationship for a while: If I just stick with this a little longer, the good stuff will come our way again and it'll make all the getting-peed-on times totally worth it. You know you've been there. It's why people become actors and entrepreneurs. It's why we see Adam Sandler movies. Behaviors rewarded at a variable rate are hard to put under extinction. On the other hand, a fixed reinforcement schedule can have its drawbacks: Consider the unchallenged worker who gets paid every Friday regardless of how many hours she spends on Facebook, versus the salesperson working on commission. Ultimately, we want a worker who's challenged, but not before they're ready. Most people who come to us at School For The Dogs are starting out their training journey with either a puppy or a fearful dog, animals living inches off the ground in a crowded city that they didn't choose. They don't speak the language. And they're not sure where the bathroom is.

Before we get fancy, we need these dogs to think we are the world's most reliable—most generous—employers. Imagine you start a new job, and the second week, your employer doesn't pay you. You probably wouldn't go back again. But if you got paid every week for many years before that happened, you most likely would have developed enough goodwill toward your employer to keep coming in.

Until you're sure your dog thinks you really are the world's best employer, I suggest being very liberal with your rate of reinforcement. Aim for a hundred percent. If you don't have food on you, use whatever you have.

Conditioning Reinforcers

In the 1630s, Dutchmen traded furniture and oxen, and even houses, for tulip bulbs.

In the 2020s, people all over the world are buying artificial intelligence–generated cartoons of monkeys. Or heroic renderings of Donald Trump.

The financial value of a flower or a monkey NFT is subjective, but it is real to the person who invested, thanks to classical conditioning. The pairing of these things with money turned them into reinforcers in and of themselves. Someone, somewhere is having some kind of behavior rewarded by the digital representation of a blue-eyed monkey wearing pink fur and a black leather cap. Someone like Madonna, who bought such a digital image for $570,000 and imbued it with even more reinforcement value by pairing it with Madonna. At the same time, she seriously reinforced the behavior of some AI robot. (This is why the computers are considering taking over.)

Those dollars only have value because of all the associations you and I and Madonna have made with them. These little digits that live on a screen, representing paper rectangles with signatures on them, we're nuts about these things. Money gets its meaning from being repeatedly paired with all the stuff we need. A conditioned reinforcer has value only because we've learned to associate it with other stuff.

Primary reinforcers are all the rewarding things whose value we don't need to be taught about. They're the things that you were born with an interest in, the big ones being food, water, sleep, and sex. Of those, food is the easiest to chop into bits for strategic use in training (although I've heard of male dolphins trained to work in open water being rewarded with access to their girlfriends).

Punishers can be conditioned too. After Holly the yellow Lab has been prodded by a fake arm enough times—Cesar Millan's idea of exposure therapy—she runs whenever she sees it. In a rare instance of applied behavior science on *The Dog Whisperer*, Millan tells her owners that they could get Holly to avoid their toddler by having him carry around the fake hand.

But back to reinforcers: the bottom line is that the more you reward a dog, the more your presence may become a conditioned reinforcer, at which point your attention and praise may be enough to sustain behaviors.

The Training Triad

GOOD TIMING

"Man is a biological organism, not something floating free of the physical world, and behavior is part of his biology."

—B. F. SKINNER

YEARS AGO, I had the opportunity to meet the man who had trained the original Sandy for the play and film *Annie*—a personal favorite of mine. Over coffee, he told me positive reinforcement was, in his opinion, silly at best, and possibly harmful. "Generations of dogs have been spoiled because of reward-based training," he said.

Spoiled. What did that word mean? I thought of my friend's sister who pitched a fit on her eighteenth birthday because the car her parents gave her didn't have a CD player. Was some human version of reward-based training responsible for that? And was my dog at the time, Amos, with whom I used rewards daily, spoiled? He seemed to appreciate the treats I offered, unlike Yashika when her parents gave her a seven-carat diamond on MTV's *My Super Sweet 16*'s season 6 ("There better be more," she said). And Amos was willing to work for his seven-carat noms, without any 'tude. So maybe he wasn't an entitled brat? I certainly didn't think so.

This highly esteemed trainer seemed to not know the key difference between "spoiling" an animal and training one. This chapter is about that difference. It's the third pillar of the Training Triad: timing. As you get specific about what you're reinforcing, you're going to do less of the "make it rain" type conditioning discussed earlier and more precision work. For this, you need a well-managed environment appropriate reinforcers, and you need to make sure to deliver those rewards with good timing.

Dr. Martin Levy

It's a Friday in October, and I'm in a windowless room in the Bronx, surrounded by saws and drills and rope. Across from me is a man who knows a lot about broken bones. He is saying one word to me, over and over, softly:

Good.

Good.

Good.

This is Dr. Martin Levy, an orthopedic surgeon, and he's telling me about how this one simple word has helped him transform the way he teaches hands-on skills to orthopedic residents.

But let's back up a moment.

What brought Dr. Levy and me together in this room can be directly traced back to stupid pet tricks. Or rather, Stupid Pet Tricks, the segment on the *Late Show with David Letterman*. For decades, Letterman would invite people onto his show to do funny things with animals, some of which must've involved some good training.

In 1985, Dr. Levy saw a dog catching Frisbees on the show, and he was mesmerized. "It was the coolest thing I'd ever seen. I wanted a dog who I could play Frisbee with, too!" he says.

Fast-forward a few decades, and he is now a part-time dog Frisbee instructor as well as a doctor, and he lives with four border collies.

Dr. Levy didn't enter the world of dog training with any kind of dogmatic ideals about how one should train. Or even any ideas about behavior. He was a science guy, and that stuff was in the psychology department. But the more he learned about positive reinforcement, the more it made sense to him.

He can pinpoint the exact moment when he came to see how problematic it can be to train with punishment. It was an accident, really. He was practicing agility moves with his third border collie, Penny, a dog he refers to "as the smartest dog on Earth," and she kept knocking over the pole she was supposed to be clearing. He got frustrated, grabbed one of the poles, and softly said "damn" as he banged it down on the ground. It wasn't directed at Penny, but she didn't know that. She went into a tunnel (part of the agility course) and cowered, and it took Dr. Levy an hour of cajoling to get her to even go near him again. "I thought I had broken her," he said.

The whole thing got him thinking about, of all things, his orthopedic residents.

"We would get these really bright kids coming in. Highly motivated on day one. And then six months later I'd be hearing how stupid and lazy they were. And I finally said to my group that we're taking all of these really smart, highly motivated kids, and we're breaking them."

His students were taught more or less as he was: shown the thing, told to go practice it and come back later. They often came back getting things wrong, and this would frustrate the teachers. If there was harshness, so be it. This wasn't kindergarten. He and his colleagues had long told themselves that the students could handle it. Dr. Levy thought otherwise: *Maybe they're not tough enough.*

"What am I doing to humans?" he said. "It may not be the kind of thing that leads a human to fall on the ground and stop eating, but they're still affected by it, and it doesn't improve our performance. And all I care about is improving performance. So how can I improve performance?"

What he discovered was that orthopedic surgeons do not need to be trained with peppy stickers or freeze-dried chicken bits. The reward centers of their brains are activated simply by getting it right. The problem was that they were just not getting enough information about what they were getting right—and things were further confused by all the static around them about what they were doing wrong.

Around this same time, the American Board of Orthopaedic Surgery had started programming to help improve residents' skills. "But it was all procedural: This is how to fix carpal tunnel; this is how you fix a fracture. I mean, if you're gonna teach a dog to get me a beer from the refrigerator, you don't say, 'Go get me the beer from the refrigerator.'"

The tasks had to be broken down.

Levy was using "good" with me to try and slice, with scalpel-like precision, the moments where my behavior was correct. He was showing me how to tie a surgical knot. "Good" is a conditioned reinforcer being delivered at just the right moments to reinforce each in a series of desired behaviors. For me, in this personal demonstration, I didn't need it followed by food. The joy of getting it right is enough.

But when we work with dogs, in my experience it's wise to start with the assumption that the joy of getting it right may not be enough. So, we back up the "good" with something else the dog wants. Your "good" to a dog should always, or nearly always, be backed up by something, just like how when money buys nothing, societies tend to tailspin; or when your paychecks repeatedly bounce, you start job hunting. Sometimes the "good" may be followed by bacon and other times a head scratch (if your dog is into that kind of thing). But it always needs to be followed by something.

Good Yes Training

Conditioning a word, like "good" or "yes," is stupidly easy.

Load up your hand with treats. I like to keep treats in the palm of my left (nondominant hand). If your dog is mugging your hand, put your hand in a different spot, or just wait until she loses interest, or try again when she isn't paying attention.

Now, say the word "yes."

Then use the fingers of your dominant hand to reach in and take a single treat and give it to your dog.

"Yes," treat. "Yes," treat. Do this ten times.

That's it! You've just taught your dog the value of this word.

What's handy about conditioning a word in this way is that, like money, you can use it to represent any number of different rewards. A check doesn't care if you're going to use it for groceries or weed. The word doesn't either. "Yes" can mean "I'm going to give you a little bit of hot dog" or "I'm going to toss your duck toy."

This tiny exercise is so easy. So easy! Saying "yes" and tossing a treat? Yes! That's it. And, guess what: It's not really going to get a lot harder than that. Once you have this conditioned reinforcer in place, you can use it to communicate with your dog, possibly for the first time, with meaningful currency. And with precise timing, since you can get a "yes" out of your mouth faster than you can deliver a physical treat into theirs.

You've figured out where you want your dog to work, and what you can use to pay him. Now, you have a tool with which you can slice time in order to let him know exactly what you're paying him for.

From Skinner to Sea World to Bone Saws

Dr. Levy's suspicion that his residents were experiencing some version of what Penny felt when she was cowering in the tunnel led him to the doorstep of one of the world's greatest living dolphin trainer, Karen Pryor.

In the early 1960s, Pryor was living in Hawaii with her family. One night, her husband asked a favor of her: Dear, can you please get a half-dozen newly captured dolphins to perform some tricks? You see, he had just bought Sea Life Park on the island of Oahu, and the people he'd hired weren't working out. Pryor had never trained anything aside from a Weimaraner—she'd learned how to yank the dog when he was out of line and then praise him when he obeyed. To keep the marital peace, she said she'd give it a go. Her husband handed her a short dolphin-training guide written by a student of Skinner's who had worked with the Brelands to create the world's first dolphin shows a few years earlier. Pryor was transfixed. In this twenty-page booklet, she found instructions that solved problems with solutions that were incredibly rational. "Here was an elegant set of laws, as explicit and prim as mathematics, for building behavior with what the manual called 'positive reinforcement,'" she recalls in her 2009 book, *Reaching the Animal Mind*.

She stayed up all night thinking about operant conditioning.

By the time the park opened, Pryor had created a dolphin show that featured eleven individual dolphins doing synchronized spins and coordinated jumps. The first step to getting her dolphin students to be excited about their acting job was conditioning the whistle, the dolphins' "yes." This conditioned reinforcer would be used to pinpoint the moment that the dolphins offered the behaviors she wanted to have in her show. A fish followed the whistle. The whistle was called a "bridging stimulus." A regular bridge connects two places in space; this kind of bridge connects two events in time. On one side is something the trainer wants (a certain behavior), and on the other is what the trainee wants (a primary reinforcer).

I picked up a yellowed copy of *Don't Shoot the Dog!* and read it right after enrolling in the Karen Pryor Academy for Animal Training and Behavior. It was the first time that I understood that my decision to become a dog trainer might impact other areas of my life.

"This book is about how to train anyone—human or animal, young or old, oneself or others—to do anything that can and should be done," the book's foreword announces, "all by using the principles of training with reinforcement. These principles are laws, like the laws of physics. They underlie all learning–teaching situations as surely as the law of gravity underlies the falling of an apple. Whenever we attempt to change behavior, in ourselves or in others, we are using these laws, whether we know it or not."

Capturing + Crickets + Clickers

In 1992, Pryor received an invitation to talk to a group of dog trainers in the Bay Area. At that point, Pryor had only worked with a handful of dogs herself. But she was happy to speak about the bigger principles of animal training. She arrived in California with five hundred novelty noisemaking gadgets, nearly identical to the handheld "crickets" developed during World War II for use by the 101st Airborne Division paratroopers on D-Day. They'd used a one- or two-click system to communicate with each other in the dark on the beaches of Normandy. Shortly thereafter, Skinner suggested the gadgets could be used with dogs—a more living-room-friendly marker than a whistle. The Brelands would go on to make prodigious use of them.

"For thirty years, modern operant training had been almost exclusively the province of marine mammal trainers," she remembered, in a 2014 article in the journal *Aquatic Mammals*. "In the hands of this community, the technology evolved to a very sophisticated level, but somehow it was stuck there, as if it were only useful for dolphins. Now, that changed. Clickers caught on instantly with the San Francisco dog trainers. What we did had a name now—*clicker training*. It was identified and defined by this little plastic talisman on which, handily, you could print your contact information. Every clicker became a sales pitch for clicker training."

In 2007, she started the program to train and certify dog trainers where I matriculated.

Although I had seen a clicker dangling from the occasional leash and spotted them near the checkout at the pet store, I didn't know what they were for. In 2012, Will Ferrell went on *Conan* to show off a new hobby of his: dog agility. Turns out he'd brought an agility course with him, along with a bunch of hapless dogs who have no interest in weave poles and A-frames. Instead, they scatter themselves through the theater. Ferrell is chasing them down in a tizzy. "Get back here or I'll neuter you with a spoon!" he shouts. All the while, he's got a clicker going like it's a castanet. This is, to me now, really humorous. But I think it's probably how I once thought the thing was used.

Actually, it's a conditioned reinforcer, used to pinpoint the moment that something you wanted to have happen, has happened. It's another way to say "good." But its sharp sound is more precise than a word can be. And it's more consistent than a word, in that it's going to be the same no matter who is delivering it, and no matter what the context is. My monotone "good" may never be completely emptied of emotion. And it isn't going to sound the same as my husband's, should he also want to get involved in training.

Some people love using a clicker. Some people have an aversion to it. I initially scoffed at the idea that I needed any kind of tool to train my dog, as his love of me and some treats seemed like enough. Why would I need a tool to better our relationship? Our relationship was already great! Little did I know that the technology behind this tool could at least improve *his* relationship with *me* and the world into which I'd plopped him, if not also open up my heart even wider than I thought it could go.

However, it's not always the right solution for every dog in every moment. With Poppy, I rarely use it. The main reason is that I now have little kids, and training them to not turn every spare clicker they come across into a musical instrument is just not how I want to spend my time. Every time Poppy hears a click that isn't followed by a reward of some kind, it's like I've written her a bad check.

Amos, with whom I'd done thousands of hours of clicking prior to having kids, I think was able to discern that when a little person was going crazy with a clicker, it had nothing to do with him.

There are various kinds of clickers. Some are plastic ovals with a spring-loaded push button. Others are plastic rectangles with thumb-operated bent pieces of metal. There are also plenty of clickers you can get online as an app—but more on that in a minute.

Here's how to use it: I usually keep it tucked into my left hand (I'm right-handed), my thumb on it, treats shoved into my palm. It depends on what I'm doing, but my hand is usually at my chest or in my lap. Click, reach right hand into left hand, grab treat, toss, begin again.

With this, I am communicating: I like that thing you just did.

Dog trainers call this *capturing*. And the thing that you're using to capture a behavior—a clicker or a word or whatever else—is called a *marker*.

Could you just shove the treat into your dog's face the second that he does something right? Yes. Some of the time. Maybe. But it's going to be a less precise maneuver. A quick conditioned reinforcer can be delivered much more efficiently than pretty much anything else. If you're looking to cut up time like it was a cut of beef, it's the difference between using a steak knife and just going at it with your teeth.

Capturing Good

"A student should indeed seek glory, but in such a way that it is ensured that he attains it; thus, he will be spurred on by praise and rewards."

—QUINTILIAN

Criterion: Anything Good

This is an exercise you could do today and keep doing every day for the rest of your dog's life, if you wanted to. But you don't need to commit to forever just yet: just commit, during one day, to marking your dog fifty times. That means counting out fifty treats in the morning, and you should have none left by the end of the day. If you are reading this and thinking *But that's a lot of treats!* then just lighten your dog's dinner by fifty bits of kibble.

You can keep these treats in a central spot in your home where anyone can get to them quickly (in my house, that's the dining table), you can have them on your person in a pocket or pouch, or you can load up a Treat & Train or something similar.

Kathy Sdao, dog trainer and believer in abundant grace for all creatures, developed this exercise. She calls it SMART-50. SMART is for "See Mark And Reward Training," and what I love about it is that it trains *us* to look for all the things we like about our dogs. What a nice way to be in the world! Dog training has traditionally told a story about control and power struggle. But this turns the relationship into one where you're like a suddenly very attentive and generous grandparent.

At the same time, it gives our dogs some space to figure out how to occupy their time without having to follow orders from us. We don't usually think about rewarding dogs for choices they make on their own, but a truly "good" dog is one who, in my opinion, is adept at figuring out how to exist in our world without constant instruction from us. The more time they're doing the stuff we want, the less time is left to do all the other stuff that annoys us. Maybe you'll mark your dog when he chooses to quietly lounge in his bed. Or maybe she tilts her head in a charming way when the dishwasher turns on. Maybe he just refrained from barking at the doorbell. You notice your dog chewing a bone (and not your shoe). Maybe she's simply enjoying a good butt scratch. If you see your dog engage in a behavior you'd like to see again in the future, you mark it. We will move on soon to marking behaviors that seem more active and purposeful. But this can be the starting point.

I think of "marking" as operating the shutter of a camera, highlighting a great moment. In doing so, I'm helping my dog assemble a mental album containing all those moments I've reinforced. Next time they have to choose what to do with their time, they'll have that album to reference.

You want your student to have a lot of references in those albums. This means delivering a lot of clear information about what you like in whatever form is most appropriate and easily deliverable: play, treats, attention, or the like. At School For The Dogs, we do this with both our dog and human clients. With the latter, we don't use food. But we do sometimes use stickers! I think keeping a high rate of reinforcement with lots of conditioned reinforcers ("You're wearing a treat pouch! Great!") in the beginning minutes of a class keeps people engaged. In our puppy classes, for instance, we usually have people offer a work-to-eat toy to their dog the second they get to their spot. Everyone's behaviors go down a positive reinforcement water slide from there: By asking the people to put treats in a work-to-eat toy right away, the dog is getting reinforced for engaging with the toy, and the people are getting reinforced by watching their dogs engage with this new item with their paws and noses (a puppy trying to get a treat out of a felt burrito is pretty darn rewarding to watch). On top of this, the trainer usually walks around the room, tossing extra treats to the dogs, and complimenting the people.

We want to reinforce as much good stuff relating to the subject at hand as possible. The thinner we can slice time, and the more good behaviors we can reinforce, the less likely we'll have dogs pulling to get to one another through the barriers, or people lost in their phones.

Criterion: Something Specific

It's never going to be a bad idea to just reward all the things you like. We can give pats on the back all day long to generally encourage our friends and loved ones when they do good. But sometimes, we have a more specific idea of what behaviors we want to see more—which is how you end up staring at your dog on the couch, plastic noise-maker clenched in your palm, eagerly waiting for him to stick out his tongue.

Teaching Amos to lick his nose was the first hands-on assignment given to us during our first unit at the Karen Pryor Academy. I understood that it was a human skill-building exercise, not an important end behavior. It was a great demonstration of how you get the behavior you mark, and the more you mark, the more you get. And I didn't have to do anything to make the lick happen. I just had to wait for it. This meant staring at my dog a lot, which was something I was happy to do anyway. Once the behavior gets going, licking can happen both quickly and frequently, which can result in a nice and dense training session.

You can do this with your dog. Load up with a clicker and fifty TicTac-size treats, give one to your dog, and then look for the first sign of tongue after your dog's swallow. As part of a dog's swallowing reflex, their tongue usually exits their lips for just a moment. The size of the lick is going to depend on what your dog ate, and your dog's natural anatomy. But basically, you're just looking for pink. You're clicking the pink. Then following it with a treat.

Using the simplicity of a marker to capture that super-quick frame in time, I taught Amos that there was something he could do to manipulate *me* into giving him something he wanted. And it was as simple as a lick.

Project Pigeon: Touching This to That

In 1943, Skinner and a handful of his graduate students (among them Keller and Marian Breland) spent months holed up on the top floor of a flour mill in Minneapolis with a goal that you might call lofty: they wanted to end World War II.

Their idea had to do with training pigeons.

You see, one problem faced in global warfare was the precision with which missiles could be dropped. This was long before drones and GPS. Once the weapon left the plane, it couldn't be guided. But Skinner had a thought: *What if missiles could be outfitted to house pigeons trained to steer them to hit precise points?* An army of kamikaze birds.

General Mills agreed to fund him to create a pigeon-guided-missile program. The birds would be harnessed and placed in the nose of specially equipped missiles, facing a screen on which the target would appear. By pecking when the target lined up with the one on the screen, the pigeons would send corrective signals that could move the missile's fins to keep it on target.

If the project didn't, um, "fly," it was because the army never perfected the bird-operated missiles that they'd promised. Their budget, and attention, was occupied with the Manhattan Project, which of course ended up producing the bombs dropped on Hiroshima and Nagasaki in 1945 that killed over a hundred thousand civilians. Talk about the fallout of punishment.

If I'm telling you about this curious entry into could-have-been military history eight decades after the fact, it's not because I am convinced that a handful of trained birds could've changed the course of twentieth-century warfare. Rather, it's because I think it's a prime example of the simplest bit of animal training that exists. Skinner's pigeons weren't avian prodigies. They were simply taught to do a bird version of the very first thing I have taught every single dog I've trained: touch *this* to *that*. In the case of the birds in the Minneapolis flour mill, *this* was their beak and *that* was the target.

If *this* is tongue and *that* is lip, we have a nose lick.

If *this* is dog eyes and *that* is your eyes, we have a "look at me."

If *this* is body and *that* is dog bed, we have a "go to bed."

To Sit (Or Not to Sit)

Typically, the first thing people teach a dog to do is to sit. This is certainly a touch-this-to-that situation, with the "this" being the butt and the "that" being the floor. A "sit" is somehow equated with control, I suppose, because if a dog's tush is on the ground, she isn't also jumping or running away. In any case, I think humans tend to overvalue dogs sitting. Just before Hyrum Lai leaves Holly to spend the rest of her life at the Dog Psychology Center with Cesar Millan—yes, this is how the episode ends—we see him trying, in vain, to get her to sit.

While it's smart to start out training a behavior that a dog is likely to do on their own, sometimes we start out by asking too much too soon. Lai didn't just want Holly to sit, he wanted her to do it in the context of being in a new place, with other dogs around, with a camera crew inches away. My friend Alex recently came over and asked Poppy to sit a million times until I told him to stop. He is one of her favorite people, and she wasn't containing her excitement about his arrival. "I thought if she sat, she'd be calm," he said. Maybe? But asking her to "sit" over and over didn't seem to me like it was encouraging calmness.

There are other reasons why a sit might not be a good starting place for training. There could be a physical limitation, if a sit is less comfortable than standing or lying down. It might be a position in which a dog doesn't feel comfortable in novel situations where their instincts otherwise would have them upright in case they need to flee. What's more, it takes over a dozen muscles for a dog to go from a standing position to a sitting one. Since we're always trying to set up our dog students for success, I like to start by teaching a behavior that requires almost no muscle movement at all: moving their nose to touch something.

Nose Touch

A nose touch involves, as you might expect, a dog touching her nose to an object. Sometimes we refer to this as *targeting*. In most cases, we start out teaching the nose touch to a human's hand. But if you have a dog who seems to have any reservations about people's hands, you can use a spoon or a fly swatter or a chopstick. I like to use two outstretched fingers, but you could use one finger, or your palm, or your fist—doesn't really matter as long as you're consistent.

The nose touch is a foundational exercise that can lead to many useful behaviors. But to begin with, you're just introducing your dog to the if-this-touches-that concept. It's also a simple place for a trainer to start—after all, you're learning too!—to work on training mechanics, the physical process of eliciting a behavior, marking it, and following it with a reward. Lastly, I like teaching this exercise because if someone never goes beyond this behavior, they can still do a lot, as they will have created a hand that is effectively magnetized to the dog's nose. The hand can then be used to get a dog to come to you from a distance, or to lure your dog into different positions without needing to wield a treat all the time. The dog's nose will want to go where your hand goes, and if you control where your dog's nose is, you pretty much control where the rest of the dog's body is too.

> **STEP 1:** To start out teaching the nose touch, put eight or so small treats in your nondominant hand. If you're going to use a clicker, put the clicker in the same hand as the treats, leaving your dominant hand fully free.

STEP 2: In a nondistracting environment, hold out two fingers of your empty (dominant) hand just an inch or so from your dog's nose. Most likely, your dog will use her nose to inspect your fingers. Wait for the moment that happens, and then click or use a verbal marker, like "good." Then reach your dominant hand into your nondominant hand and give your dog a single treat.

STEP 3: Repeat!

STEP 4: Refill your treats and reward for your dog making direct contact with your hand.

And that's it!

Touch Applications

There are countless ways you can use a "touch" in training from the get-go. Once your dog knows to touch your hand or a target stick, it isn't hard to get them to touch something else instead. You can start by just putting your hand or a stick on the thing you want them to touch. I taught my dog to target my thigh when I'm at my desk and she wants to go for a walk or have her dinner. It's a much more polite way for her to get my attention than barking at me. We have a lot of clients who have taught their dogs to nose touch the back wall of an elevator in order to keep them focused on something that is *not* the door that is opening, seemingly at random, sometimes with another dog behind it.

Touch is also a behavior that can be used to do something you probably do yourself all day long: poke a touchscreen. There are lots of touchscreen clicker apps that will register a little "ding" or "click" when a dog's nose touches the screen. I like using these apps with new learners, especially kids, as they take away any stress of having to "mark" the dog, as the dog is essentially marking her own behavior. I helped develop the app App For Dog, which makes a sound on nose–screen contact and registers each touch of the nose as a bit of paint on the screen. Within the app, a dog can also choose between two buttons, each of which can be programmed with a sound, like a clicker or a bell, to act as a secondary reinforcer. A company called Joipaw is currently developing a touchscreen game for dogs where the screen is built into a treat dispenser. To start, all the dog needs to know how to do is nose a screen.

Capturing versus Traditional Ways of Getting Behavior

The idea of waiting for behavior to happen on its own, then marking and rewarding it, was a revelation to me.

Like many people, I had predominantly been taught two ways of getting behavior from a dog. One was pushing or pulling the dog into whatever position I wanted him to be in. There is no shortage of footage on YouTube—both vintage and recent—of people showing exactly how to bring your foot down on a leash near a dog's collar, to force him into a down, or how to wrap your fingers around a leash for the perfect upward leash jerk to get a dog to sit if pushing his butt down doesn't work. The dog does a behavior either to make a bad thing stop or to avoid a bad thing happening.

The other (and gentler) way of getting behavior that I knew of was luring—helping a dog along the way to doing something by leading them in one direction or another with body language or, more often, visible bits of food in my hand. Although I now appreciate that lures and prompts can be helpful and used skillfully, we don't want our dogs' behavior to depend on always having treats held two inches from their noses, which is what can happen. Focusing on capturing behaviors with a marker separated in time and space from the primary reinforcer is a way to help you from getting stuck in "treat land," always having to have (or pretend to have) food in your hand to get your dog to do anything. It can be awkward, and limiting, to have a learner who only wants to work when the payment is visible. I see this with the behavior "sit" all the time. If you hold a bit of food over a dog's head, often their rear will go down. So, people raise their hand with fingers pinched as if they're holding food long after the dog needs that kind of visual prompt.

But in certain instances, in a careful way, luring can be useful—especially if the lure can be faded, which I will explain how to do. Rather than luring with food, my preference is to lure with my hand. It's one of the many reasons to teach a foundational hand touch.

Sit and Down

Sit may not be the first thing I teach most dogs I work with, but it very well may be the second. Ditto down. Which one comes first? I like to let the dog decide.

Lead your dog to a comfy spot, ideally in a quiet and familiar place, load up your nondominant hand or your treat pouch with small treats, and then just be boring. If your dog barks or jumps on you, pay as little attention as possible. Just wait. The second your dog either lies down or sits, you're going to click or say "yes" or "good" (just be consistent with your marker), and then deliver the treat just far enough away from your dog that he has to come out of the sit or down to get it. Repeat, this time waiting for the same behavior that your dog gave you before.

TIPS

If you're having trouble getting your dog to sit, try moving your position. If you've been working on it while seated, try standing. Sometimes, if a dog has to raise their head to look up at you, it'll encourage their butt to go down. You can also try experimenting with different surfaces. Some dogs prefer a rug to cold, slippery linoleum!

You can also try luring a dog into a sit with a hand touch, holding your hand a little over your dog's nose, as encouraging a nose up position may help the butt go down. After two or three lured sits in a quick succession, hold back the lure for a beat and see what happens. If your dog doesn't sit after three seconds, give some kind of very minor version of the lure you'd been offering.

Down is something that, with enough patience, you will capture eventually. Dogs don't usually sleep standing up! However, there are two ways you can help your dog get it a little faster if you want to jump-start the process.

One is to use a hand, target stick, or food lure. Start when your dog is in a sit position, luring them there if need be. Then, put your lure at the dog's nose and slowly bring it down to the ground, keeping it near their body the whole time, almost as if you were tracing all the way from their neck to their chest to their belly button. When you get close to the ground, if the nose is still following the lure, bring it slowly toward you, still keeping it on the ground. Mark and reward when your dog's body gets down to the ground. I like to deliver the reward up above their head to lure them back into a sit position, which resets them nicely for another down.

Another method is to sit on the ground with your back against the wall and your knees bent, feet flat. Use your hand lure, target stick, or treat lure to bring your dog under your knee a few times. Then, lower your knee and start to mark and reward any lowering of the body that approaches a down as your dog goes under. (NB: if you have short legs and a big dog, this might be a challenging option.)

FLIRT POLES

When working with puppies or any high-energy dog, I like to use a flirt pole when teaching stationary behaviors, like sit and down, as I find it's a nice way to teach a dog that they can ramp up excitement, and then tone it down, all the while learning. Flirt poles look like big cat teasers. They are commercially sold, but you can also make one yourself: just thread some rope or fleece through a long PVC pipe and tie a toy to the end. It's easier than training by, say, throwing a toy, as you get to hold onto it the whole time. I like to get a dog going crazy chasing after it, then I take it away and wait for a sit or a down. When they offer it, the game starts again. If they end up getting the toy, it's a good chance to practice my classically conditioned drop it.

Look

Teaching your dog where to look is a kind of "touch": you're rewarding the moment that a kind of imaginary ray beam comes out of your dog's eyes and lands on something else. In some cases, that might be another dog, or something potentially scary. You can teach this by marking the moment your dog looks at something that you worry may trigger fear or excitement, then giving the treat. What you're doing is training them that looking at whatever it is that you're marking is a way to get good things from you. You're both rewarding a behavior that is nondisruptive and creating an association that will pay dividends. *Hey, that scooter over there must not be such a scary thing because just looking at it produces good stuff from my person!*

Teaching your dog to look at you can help them focus when they're distracted or help distract them from something that might bother them if they see it.

TIPS

When teaching a dog to "look" at me with a lure, I sometimes start by holding the treat between my eyes, then marking and rewarding the moment the dog looks up at it. I'm then careful to deliver the reward right in front of the dog on the ground in front of me. While she is eating, I get my next treat ready to go between my eyes. Because I've put the treat down where she has to lower her head to get to it, I'm setting her up to have to lift her head when she is done, which puts her in the right position to look at me again.

Criteria: More

One recent afternoon I was busy tidying up the products in the shop area at School For The Dogs when an older man came in carrying a Yorkie. I heard him ask the person at the front desk what is taught in our Prep School class—an intro-level training course we offer. When she mentions that "sit" is one of the things we work on, he scoffs.

"My dog already knows how to sit."

I resist the urge to butt in, but, in my mind, I'm peppering him with questions.

Does your dog know how to sit … in a classroom full of people and dogs?

…when a new person asks?

…when you ask just once, without moving your body?

…when you ask while you're standing on a busy street corner?

…in an elevator?

…when you ask in a whisper, with your back turned, while jumping up and down?

What if you ask while you're at a distance? What is the length of time between when you ask for it and when it happens? And, once your dog is sitting, how long will she remain in that position?

It's easy to think of every behavior as just one thing. In fact, that's a vast oversimplification. Instead, we need to consider that every behavior can be endlessly perfected and proofed.

In chapter 8, we started with establishing a very low bar. Recall that Criterion Zero is about creating good feelings even when there's no behavioral contingency beyond the most basic thing you could ask for: Is your dog existing? Yes? Great. Reward your dog. If you're working with a dog who is very young, or fearful, you might spend quite a lot of time at Criterion Zero. Kate, who specializes in working with dogs who have behavior issues often stemming from fear, recently told me it amazed her how much of her work involved simply tossing food on the ground for dogs. Sometimes training actually is easy, but not simple.

Then we fixed our eyes on capturing things we wanted: First, everything. Then anything at all we like. Then a nose touch or a sit. This was a small step up from zero. We considered the behaviors we wanted to see and then waited for them to happen. We set up our dog for success by arranging the environment to up the likelihood of getting the behavior. Every complex animal behavior—be it jumping through a series of hoops or finding land mines—began with some kind of encouragement of some small behavior. If you wanted to stop here, you could still go pretty far. Reinforcing just a not-very-hard building-block behavior is no small feat. It's helped your dog clue into the fact that he can control things in his life by doing this one simple thing that you seem to like. In that way, it's like you've taught your dog to say "please." Reward every sit your dog gives you, and you will have a dog who sits to get your attention more than he jumps.

However, if you want to, next you can think about refining these behaviors. What do I mean by refining?

HAPPENING WHEN YOU WANT IT TO HAPPEN

In the beginning, we want our dogs to think they're in control. *All I have to do is put my bottom on the ground and the person gives me a treat!* But in many cases, we want to have some control over getting the behavior to happen when we want it to based on specific stimuli in the environment, and not just at random. A big part of this means bringing our dog under "stimulus" control. The stimuli that we want the behaviors to happen in the presence of or in reaction to? Those are called cues.

HAPPENING IN DESIRED SEQUENCES WITHOUT INTERRUPTION

How do dogs zip through agility courses or lead visually impaired people down busy streets without having to stop for a treat every few blocks? It's called *chaining*. As you develop your training chops, you'll put behaviors together so one behavior effectively reinforces the one before it.

RELIABLY OCCURRING IN A MULTITUDE OF SITUATIONS

Is it noisy outside? Are you using a new leash? Is this a room your dog has never been in before? This is the process of *generalizing*.

INCREMENTALLY BEING SHAPED

The most basic versions of a behavior are satisfactory at the start, but you can become selective about what you reinforce in order to get responses that are quick, precise, and possibly quite complex. This is called *shaping*.

Let's tackle cuing, chaining, generalizing, and shaping in the following chapters.

Good Cueing

> "The social organization of dogs and their behavior in the company
> of human beings depends upon the contingencies of reinforcement
> arranged by those human beings."
>
> —B. F. SKINNER

IN THE FIRST years of the 1900s, a nine-year-old stallion living in Berlin made headlines around the world because of his extraordinary abilities to tell time, do multiplication, spell out names, and more. His owner, a retired teacher, had taken on the horse's education as a pet project. Clever Hans, as he was called, would use a hoof to stamp out numbers in response to questions, or to tell someone systematically pointing at a board of letters when to stop. He was always right, even when his trainer wasn't present.

In a way, it was a brilliant early display of positive reinforcement training in action. A zoologist explained to the *New York Times* in 1904 that his owner "has succeeded in training Hans by cultivating in him a desire for delicacies. This desire is aroused by questions and finger signs, according to which the stallion acts, in order to satisfy his aroused desire, for as soon as he puts his foot down he snaps for the delicacy in the hand of his master."

Indeed, he engaged in a behavior (stamping a hoof) that was reinforced by a food reward. But, in 1907, an experimental psychologist demonstrated that the horse didn't actually understand numbers and letters: He was simply hoofing the ground until he noticed the subtle head motions of observers looking up from his foot, which they tended to do when, coincidentally, he stamped the correct number of times or someone pointed to the right letter on the board. Head lifts were a cue to stop. And he'd get an apple. A certain number of foot stomps was the people's cue to look up! Everyone involved had learned to engage in specific behaviors under very specific circumstances. They were all behaving on *cue*.

All living things are surrounded by stimuli all the time—we live in seas of information that tell us what to do next. We're constantly looking to our environment to give us clues—sometimes literal signs—that help us to understand what to do and when. What's more, animals are primed to do this when food is concerned: to learn the cues that indicate that primary reinforcement will follow certain behavior.

Strategic reinforcement is like putting frames around the behaviors we like, so we can point to them again. We're teaching our dogs that a certain behavior "works" in whatever environment it happened, with the added benefit that the more times your dog does that kind of behavior in this kind of moment, the less time she has to be doing some other behavior you don't like, and that's a win. Cues are all around your dog, and they're picking up on ones you may not notice or even perceive. For instance, sometimes when I was putzing around the kitchen, Amos would go up on his hind legs in a kind of gummy bear position that was pretty irresistible, and he'd just stay like that. I didn't ask him to do it. But he'd learned that, when I was in the same room as the treat drawer, this was a behavior that was very likely going to be noticed and reinforced. Me being in the kitchen was the cue. Was it a behavior that I cared about in that moment? Not really. But it was cute, and it beat any other number of things he could be doing. It was like he was saying "please." One friend says her dog goes and sits pertly by the door when she asks her partner, "Do you want Starbucks?" That behavior has been rewarded for her, in the form of walks, in moments following people saying "Starbucks?" (Who *hasn't* been trained by Starbucks!?)

How do you take back control and get a behavior to happen precisely after your dog perceives a cue of your choosing? I promise I'm getting there, and it's actually not a difficult process. If I'm going on a bit about all the cues a dog is perceiving unbeknownst to you, it's only because, when you're just starting out, I think it's easy to become overly focused on getting dogs to do the things you want them to do when you want them to do it, and to think that the words we use to ask them to do those things are the precipitating events—the puppet strings pulling on limbs to make whatever behavior occur. While the desire to have things happen when and where you want is understandable—you might say it's the point of a lot of dog training—people too often skip the first step of simply rewarding all the things they like as they naturally happen. You can trust that your dog is picking up on what happened—what he did— before you rewarded him, without any purposeful cues from you. This can result in a dog who, like the German stallion, seems almost telepathic in his ability to preemptively behave as you like.

However, once we have a behavior we like, we can control which stimuli lead to which behaviors. This means, among other things, putting behaviors on cue.

When I first heard the word "cue" as it relates to dog training, I figured it was just a nicer way of saying "command." I had never really stopped to consider the strange vernacular of traditional training that involves giving a dog a "command" (given by a "master," no less), but once I thought about it, it seemed weird that we "ask" things of each other but go around "commanding" our dogs. "Cue" was a word I associated with high school theater, where I had to learn not only my own lines, but also the lines that preceded them in the script, so that I would know when to speak.

It was only one day when I was checking my mail that the real difference hit me. I was holding two letters in my hand: One was my cable bill, which was overdue, and one was a friend's wedding invite. They both called for a response from me. But one was manipulating me with negative reinforcement: pay this *or else*. A command. The other was alerting me to an opportunity to engage in a behavior that could be positively reinforced: show up to this place at this time on this date, and there will be cake. The former was a command. The latter, a cue.

Could I have ended up at my friend's reception with a mouth full of fondant even if the invitation had gotten lost in the mail? Possibly. But the cue certainly helped me get there. Same goes with putting dog behaviors on cue. With cues, we give dogs the ability to clearly understand what we want, and when. Seen this way, we go from being tyrants barking orders at our furry minions to being considerate bosses, issuing clear instructions on what needs to be done to earn a bonus. We've already helped our dogs understand what behaviors are worth their while. Now we're helping them learn when it will benefit them most to offer these behaviors.

A cue can be anything that an animal can perceive. It's best, especially at the start, if it's salient and different from other things in the environment. Of course, we humans appreciate cues like this as well—there's a reason stop signs are large and red, rather than small and taupe. By the same token, words and body gestures are not always the best cues for dogs, as they hear us say things and watch us move our bodies all the time. Flashing neon or jingling bells might better grab their attention, but dogs, bless them, catch our drifts even when we use subtler signals.

The way to add a cue is to get a behavior happening reliably on its own at a nice rhythm. Then, start presenting your cue right before the behavior occurs.

So, to teach sit, I'm first going to capture a bunch of sits. Then, I simply say the word "sit" when I know my dog is about to sit. How do I know he's about to sit? Because I've just reinforced ten sits in a row. I have my money on eleven.

Cues also help teach your dog what behaviors aren't going to work. Just as you have learned that the behavior of going to vote works on voting day (cue) but not on other days.

Note that when you first add a verbal cue, you're really not asking for anything. The word is not making the behavior happen. You're just inserting the word right before you know something is going to happen. To someone observing the process, it can look like you're controlling the behavior, when really you're just announcing it.

Also note that everything that is happening in the moment right before your dog sits could be (and may be) a cue; your goal is to indicate which of all the things in their perception is important, which thing green lights the good stuff coming their way. It is usually wise to keep your body as still as possible and make your movement intentional. Your dog is likely paying attention to tiny movements you're not even aware you're making. Remember Clever Hans!

After a few trials, you can start giving your cue earlier. As soon as your dog finishes the treat, ask for another sit. If it takes a moment, that's okay. Don't repeat it. Since you've built up a nice rhythm of sits, you probably won't have to wait very long. People get impatient, at this point, if they have to wait more than two seconds for a response, and you may be tempted to repeat the cue. Be patient. Can you imagine how you'd feel if your bosses began repeating themselves if you didn't respond within two seconds? At best, repeating the cue will teach your dog that the cue is "sit sit sit." At worst, it makes you a nag, with a dog who learns that sitting is how to get you to shush.

The next step is to only reward the behavior when it happens after you give the cue. You say sit, your dog sits. Mark, reward. You say sit again, your dog sits. You mark and reward. Then, you stay mum. Your dog will probably sit. Do whatever you need to do to get your dog out of the un-cued sit, then offer the cue again right away and mark and reward when he sits. Repeat, at a similar cadence. The behavior of sitting when not cued will undergo extinction.

This is how I first learned to add a cue, and it works. There's usually a kind of "lightbulb" moment when your dog understands the salience of your cue. The more things you put on cue with a dog, the faster, in my experience, a dog gets at playing this game.

However, there's a variation of this process that I've come to like, because I think it is a kinder method, without some degree of failure baked into the game. Engaging in a behavior that is undergoing extinction is not a lot of fun—and we want our learners to be into the game! So, here is an alternative method for putting a behavior on cue:

After you've cued a few sits, you're going to hold back giving the cue, and then, right away, mark and reward your dog for not sitting. In this way, you reinforce the behavior of not sitting, which, if you haven't given the cue, is the right thing to do. Then, when your dog is done with the treat, offer the cue again. It's a true win-win situation, where you're being generous about giving the dog information about what you want, and generous with your rewards, to boot.

Often, I think dogs aren't listening to people at *all* when they say "sit." They're just guessing that's probably what you want, because humans are obsessed with sitting. In fact, I bet *you're* sitting right now! It's often the only thing a dog is expected to know how to do when asked, so they get really good at doing it on the off chance it's what you want. You can always test whether a dog is heeding your cue or just hedging his bets, by saying the word "banana" to a standing dog and seeing what he does.

Building a Cue from a Lure

The process of adding a cue can sometimes be sped up by making use of a lure or a prompt of some kind. Sometimes, the prompt has already become a cue inadvertently. While I'm sure that this has been observed by many animal trainers before me, it was something I discovered on the job, after working with hundreds of dog owners who had lured their dogs into sits and downs so many times that the beginning of the movements involved in giving the lure had become the cue.

If you already have a kind of cue that has developed out of a lure, you can add a new cue—one that is intentional, and clear. All you need to do is say the cue word, pause a beat, then give your old lure or prompt.

Mark and reward the behavior. After a few trials, pause between your cue word and your lure. Eventually, your dog will anticipate what you want before the lure and you won't need it anymore.

If your dog already has a history of paying attention to fingers that have food in them when you're asking for something, you can swim with the tide by building a hand signal out of the original luring motion. (Note that you can attach more than one cue to a behavior, but if you want your dog to heed both a hand signal and a word as a cue, it's better to teach them separately and not offer them at the same time.)

Here's what this looks like with some commonly lured behaviors:

LOOK

If you've been using a food lure held near your eyes to get your dog to look at you, you can begin giving the cue—saying "look"—and pausing before you put the treat between your eyes. After a few reps of this your dog will look before you do anything with the treat, and you can mark and reward and practice with your new cue.

SIT

You may have been getting your dog to sit by holding a treat over her head, to the point where she starts sitting as soon as you hold your fingers in the position they would be if they actually had food in them. I call this the "mamma mia" hand, as it looks like the typical Italian pinched-finger gesture of exasperation. The dogs in Italy must be so confused! But you can turn this into a different cue. First, notice which hand you tend to use when you do this. Use this hand to snap your fingers.

Pause. Then do the mamma mia with the same hand. After a few reps, pause after you snap, and mark and reward the moment your dog starts to sit. Then do more reps of you snapping and your dog sitting, and soon it won't matter where your hand is when you snap. (If you can't snap, you can make the cue a bent elbow with a fist or a pointed finger. The key is to make sure that you're using the same hand you tend to use as a lure.)

DOWN

Two common lures to get a dog to lie down are pointing to the ground in front of him or holding food in front of a dog's nose and then bringing the treat to the ground. This often results in the evolution of a cue that looks like pointing or waving downward in front of your dog's face, neither of which will work to cue this behavior at any kind of distance. Again, you can build a new hand cue by front-loading it. I like to use the cue of an open hand held palm forward at shoulder height, kind of a "taking an oath" position. Again, do this using the same hand with which you're used to luring. Hold it up for a beat, then bring it down in whatever manner you were doing before. If you have to use food, try just tucking it in between your outstretched fingers a few times before doing away with it entirely. Soon enough, you'll get a down before your hand is anywhere near the ground. Mark and reward this and repeat, and just holding up your hand becomes the cue, even from a distance.

Subtle Cues

It can be fun to make cues subtle. How subtle can you get? You can fade things down to tiny bits of information. With Amos, I faded the word "bark" to just a very soft "-k" sound that I could make that would cue a bark. It was like our own secret language.

Subtle cues can make us nicer to be around, I think. I've been reminding my daughter to say "thank you" when someone gives her a compliment or a gift. But I try to remind her as quietly as possible when she doesn't remember. I also try to wait a good few beats to see if she does the thing before I ask again. I think this is probably less annoying to her, and it also is less annoying to me to not be a deliverer of reminders that are obnoxious!

Cue Criterion Zero

The more cues you teach your dog, the faster your dog will learn to acquire cues. And the better you will get at figuring out how to find ways to use cues to get behaviors you want, and teach cues that are more and more subtle, or distinct from others.

As with Criterion Zero, however, a cue may require nothing from the dog. It is just a signal of an opportunity. Like Black Friday. It's not happening because of you, but you have learned that if you behave in a certain way on that day, you are likely to be rewarded. You have been trained to get up at 3:30 a.m. (after finishing the dishes at 11:00 p.m.) to get more cheese (or discounted TVs) than you would get if you went on a different day at 4:00 a.m. You've been trained to log into the Ticketmaster site for the Taylor Swift presale. The cue isn't necessarily being given specifically to you, and it may not even affect your behavior in a super pinpointed way—you could go to one of many Targets or book a seat at any number of venues (or so you were led to believe). With dog training, I like to think about starting out with these pretty general kinds of cues— helping dogs get these classically conditioned types of announcements about opportunities. If no behavior is required, it means there is also no getting it wrong. For instance, I say "we're going for a walk" before I take Poppy for a walk. She usually runs to the door. But sometimes she doesn't get off the couch. I don't think this is disobedience. I think she just doesn't feel like going on a walk.

You can give a Criterion Zero-type cue even if the thing that's about to happen isn't something the dog necessarily desires. If you have a small dog, using an "up" cue can be a kindness. Just say "up" before you pick up your dog. You can practice this in nonessential moments and follow the pickup with a treat. There may be times when you just have to pick your dog up, and you don't have a treat on you. You're still doing them a solid by giving them some clue about what's about to happen. With Amos, I could see him shift his weight in a certain way when I said it. He was getting ready. Who doesn't like to be given a second to get ready?

Two-Way Conversations

Once, at a conference, Amos, sitting at my feet, began knocking over my water bottle. I never taught him a cue to tell me that he wanted something, but we had often done training demos where I would shape him to do something, like knock something over with his nose. He knew that was a behavior that sometimes worked out for him in certain contexts, and I think he must've known what was in the bottle, as he'd often gotten water from such a thing. It was, to me, a moment of creative problem-solving brought about by his learning history and our mutual ability to read each other's cues. He was telling me he was thirsty.

Chances are your dog has already learned to get you to do some things, and you've done those things to get your dog to stop doing the annoying thing, like whining or barking. But, if your dog would just ask in a nice way, you could reward *that* rather than inadvertently rewarding a more annoying behavior. Communication in two directions like this can feel almost like conversations!

As I mentioned, I have trained Poppy to nose my thigh when she wants attention. My household is pretty nutso these days with two small children, and I just wanted a cue that was quick and easy to teach, and that she could give whether I was sitting or standing. Before she learned to cue my attention quietly, she would whine for it or bark at me. So, when I saw the first hints that one of these bouts was about to start (standing up, stretching, approaching me), I would have her do a nose touch at my leg at her nose height. I had her practice this sometimes too, just out of the blue. She pretty quickly got to the point of nosing my leg even without my hand there to touch, and she pretty reliably comes and noses me now when she wants something from me. I either get up and figure out what she wants right away (I want to reward polite client behavior with good customer service!) or else I turn it into a game. If I'm occupied, this may mean just loading up with some treats and then lobbing one as far as I can, or loading up my beloved Treat & Train, planting it at a distance from me, and having her touch my leg and then go run to get the treat. I've done this many times while drinking a glass of wine as I sit on the bathroom floor bathing my girls. The fact that I'm able to wash my kids and exercise my dog while also drinking makes me feel like I'm a time management genius.

Sometimes the thing we want a dog to communicate is that they don't want something. This might mean teaching an "opt-in/opt-out" behavior. For Poppy, this means putting her chin flat on the ground when she is okay being handled in any potentially uncomfortable way. As long as she has her chin down, she is telling me she is cool with me looking in her ear, for example. She gets a treat for letting me do it, but we started this by her getting a treat just for having her chin on the ground with me nearby. If at any point the treats just aren't worth it to her to let me do what I'm doing, she can always "opt out" by lifting her chin. This "game" was coined the "Bucket Game" by trainer Chirag Patel, who uses a little bucket to help a dog communicate consent. The dog learns that looking at the bucket is their cue to us that they're into the game.

Bucket Game for Cooperative Care

This exercise, which we've adapted at School For The Dogs from Patel's, is good for cooperative care, a way for a dog to give consent, or opt in, to certain handling exercises. We will not be using a verbal cue; we are simply letting the dog offer the behavior.

PART 1: Teach manners and impulse control around the bucket.

STEP 1: Start by holding a bucket filled with treats out to the side for your dog to see. Ideally, your dog should be in a stationary position like a sit or a down.

STEP 2: Mark and treat (from the bucket) for the dog looking at the bucket.

STEP 3: You can then put the bucket on the ground or a chair, and mark and treat the dog for looking at it.

STEP 4: It doesn't matter what position your dog is in (sit/down/ stand). What you are treating for is eye contact with the bucket.

STEP 5: Start treating when the dog maintains eye contact with the bucket for longer durations. Don't increase your criteria on this too quickly, as it may confuse them.

STEP 6: The dog is allowed to look around between moments of focusing on the bucket because this is a game of choice, and a conversation between you and them. There is no need to call them, shake the bucket, tug on the leash, etc. Let your dog make the choice to participate in the training program.

STEP 7: (Note: Make sure to allow access to a bed or mat and water to give your dog confidence that they can take a break as needed.)

PART 2: Choose what you want to train the dog to be able to do.

STEP 1: Wait until the dog is able to focus on the bucket. (It doesn't matter what position the dog is in; sit/down/stand are all okay.)

STEP 2: When they are looking at the bucket and able to hold their focus on it for a few seconds, start moving your hand toward their side (though not touching them).

STEP 3: At this point, they can choose to continue to look at the bucket—and if they do, mark and treat. If they look away from the bucket, they have communicated that they were uncomfortable, and you should stop. Remember, this is a game of choice (theirs).

STEP 4: Once they look back at the bucket, the game begins again. This time, don't move your hand as fast or as far. If the dog is able to maintain focus on the bucket, they are rewarded.

STEP 5: Gradually move your hand closer with each successful trial until you can mark and treat for the dog allowing you to make gentle contact with (for example) their ear.

STEP 6: This continues until the dog is able to maintain focus on the bucket while allowing their ear to be examined.

IMPORTANT: This game of choice only works if you allow the dog to communicate that they wish to begin, break, and/or stop the game. If the dog looks away from the bucket, the game breaks/stops. When they reengage with the bucket, the game resumes.

Raising Criteria

This notion of creating ways to get consent from a dog and cue us to their needs is an expanding area of dog training that I hope more and more people get excited about. It's a paradigm shift from making dogs follow commands and toward giving them the vocabulary to ask us for what they need.

Working with cues, we can refine our abilities to ask dogs to do things that may help keep them happy and safe, enhance our mutual engagement with them, and let them develop and demonstrate their cognitive abilities in ways that feel like we're running fun behavioral experiments without having to get out of our slippers.

This is where dog training can start to seem like an art, a hobby, and a humane science project (with a lab partner who licks your toes.) Ongoing experiments by people sitting on the floor of their living rooms with buttons you can get for a few bucks on Amazon, some sticky tape, and treats, is suggesting that dogs are capable of more sophisticated behaviors than we might have thought.

Here are some beginning games for teaching more complex cues, using behaviors we've covered so far: sit, down, and touch.

READING

On a screen or on paper, write two letters, one on each of two different pages, large, in black and white: X and O. Practice showing the "X" to your dog, then cueing a sit. Repeat with "O" and a down. If you find your dog is good at these kinds of discrimination games, you can experiment with using words instead of symbols, or pictures (one of a dog sitting and one of a dog lying down). While this kind of exercise can be done with paper and pencil, I like a touchscreen device that lets me swipe from one page to another and has high contrast and more uniform presentation, which help a dog differentiate what to pay attention to.

TOUCHING BUTTONS

You can teach the same type of cue differentiation with the behavior being to touch one thing versus touch another. Like different parts of an iPad screen. With Amos, I had fun sometimes developing cues that he knew but that were not obvious to everyone else. If you're Bob Bailey navigating a CIA spy cat into an office park, it's useful to have a cue that will go unnoticed by others, such as a whistle imperceptible to the human ear. In lower stakes situations, it's just fun. I could pull up two buttons in App For Dog on an iPad, and Amos knew that if I said "Which is it?" he was to touch the button on the right, and "What's the answer?" meant touch the one on the left. This made it possible to make it look like he was answering a question correctly by touching the button on the screen that I wanted him to touch.

Good Chaining, Generalizing, and Shaping

"There had been altogether too much of ME as a self-appointed knower, and not enough of Strongheart and what he might have to share as an intelligent expression of life. Without being made aware of the unfair thing I had been doing, I had mentally assigned myself to the upper part of this relationship of ours, because I happened to be a 'human,' and had mentally assigned him to the lower part, because he was 'a dog.'"

—J. ALLEN BOONE, *KINSHIP WITH ALL LIFE*

IF YOU DON'T feel like getting teary, definitely don't look up a video called "Listo and Michele in 'SMILE'" on YouTube. A woman is dressed as Charlie Chaplin, and next to her an Australian shepherd balances on three legs, then circles backward around her feet during the last notes of Michael Jackson's version of the song "Smile," ending by standing on his hind legs with his two front paws on her raised horizontal cane, ducking his head under it, then jumping, four paws off the ground, as the audience claps. At no point during the routine does Charlie Chaplin stop to give the dog a piece of chicken.

Charlie Chaplin is Michele Pouliot, one of the stars of the world of Canine Freestyle, also known as competitive dancing with dogs. Each of Listo's behaviors is rewarded by the opportunity to do the next behavior. They've been daisy chained, a series of cues and behaviors that lead to a primary reinforcer. If you do this behavior, I will give you this cue, to do that behavior, and so on, until you do a final behavior that will get you the thing. It's always a good idea to work from harder to easier behaviors, since the chance to do the most fun or easier behaviors effectively reinforces the harder behavior. This is fun stuff for Pouliot. She spent forty-two years at Guide Dogs for the Blind, where she introduced the use of positive reinforcement training with a secondary reinforcer to mark behavior. Turns out the skills needed to teach a Lab to find an empty seat on the bus at rush hour and then get off at the right stop aren't so different from the ones needed to teach a Chow Chow to cha-cha. While you may not be ready to teach your dog how to dance, seeing how behaviors can be chained together will help you build better sequences of behavior (as simple as get to curb, stop, sit) and help you break the links in undesired chains that may have developed without your awareness.

Generalization

Generalization occurs when the learner detects similarities between two or more stimuli (objects, events, situations) and forms a concept or idea based on those similarities. The learner then applies the concept or idea to new situations that share the same characteristics. This allows us to learn more quickly and efficiently, because we don't have to relearn everything each time we encounter a new situation.

The environment is constantly changing. In a sense, no moment is identical to any moment before or after it. Thank goodness we learn to generalize. Dogs too. Sometimes we overdo it, which is why a dog who has been hit with a stick may attack a person with an umbrella. Or a dog that is "bonked" may attack a person with a beach towel. But, with some guidance, dogs can learn that cues mean the same things in different environments. "Sit" means "sit" both in the kitchen and the living room.

And it means "sit" if I say it or Uncle David says it, whether it was today or yesterday.

The thing is, even Uncle David isn't totally the same yesterday as he was today. Experiences change us. Any living thing might outwardly look the same one day to the next, but that doesn't mean they haven't changed—possibly profoundly so—sometimes because of traumatic experiences we may not ever know about or be able to appreciate. I think being bonked one time by one person would forever change the way I feel about other people, even despite the fact that I have had a lot of good interactions with many people! I imagine that white dog in the bonking video walked out of that brown conference room a very different dog than he walked in.

If we allow that our behavior is a product of our environment—the consequences and antecedents contained therein—then the ability to generalize to accept each other at all is what, in his play *The Cocktail Party*, T. S. Eliot called a "convenient social convention":

What we know of other people
Is only our memory of the moments
During which we knew them. And they have changed since then.
To pretend that they and we are the same
Is a useful and convenient social convention
Which must sometimes be broken. We must also remember
That at every meeting we are meeting a stranger.

Shaping

Much of what I have talked about already in this book has had to do with a concept that I haven't officially introduced, and that is shaping. You already know about shaping, I'm sure. You've been shaped your whole life, inadvertently or not, to be who you are and do the things you do. For a while something works. Your crayon scribble is the pride of the refrigerator art gallery. But then certain responses are rewarded more than others. It is survival of the fittest happening on the level of individual behaviors, moment to moment, as we try to succeed at life.

If something doesn't work, you try some different version of what you were doing, ideally with the result of you hitting on something that works better. That behavior will then be reinforced, and the other unsuccessful attempts will undergo extinction. This is the story of learning to draw, or playing music or sports. Not every attempt will be rewarded, but if enough are rewarded to keep you going, you will likely keep trying new things. And then get better and better at building the kind of fluency you need to do those things with automaticity—the ability to do effortlessly engage in learned behaviors in new environments, with new people, under different pressures. Because adding in those kinds of factors is part of the shaping process too.

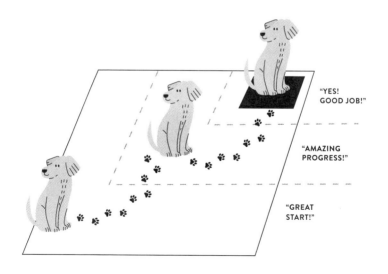

The more an animal's behaviors are shaped by positive reinforcement, the better their ability becomes to try new things with confidence, and to be resilient and creative when things don't go as planned.

Sticky Spot

This is my favorite shaping starter exercise, to give you a sense of how shaping can be about literally cutting something down to give a visual idea of what is happening when you're shaping, refining a behavior by upping your criteria inch by inch. It's essentially teaching a "go to place" or "go to your bed" cue, but I think about it more as a way to work on teaching your dog to hit a specific mark: to touch body to a spot on the ground. You can start with an old towel or inexpensive yoga mat and work your way down to a piece of paper—even a Post-it Note.

Simply toss a treat or two onto a well-defined rectangle that is a little larger than your dog (a yoga mat cut in two will do for most dogs). When your dog goes to inspect the treats, toss a treat a little ways off the mat, so that he has to get off the mat to get the treat. Try positioning the mat between yourself and where you're tossing the treat, as this will up the chances that your dog will come back toward you and will step on the mat. Mark as soon as there's even a toe on the mat. Give a treat on the mat and then toss the treats off again.

After three or four trials like this, wait a beat after your dog touches a toe, and see if they'll put her whole foot on. Yes? Practice that a few times.

Then up the criteria to two feet. How many trials you do is going to depend on your learner. Part of your development as a teacher is knowing when you can push your learner a bit, and when you need to throw them an easy one. I find that setting aside a certain number of treats for a particular training session (say twenty) and also setting a timer for a short period of time (two minutes), or even doing both, helps me make sure that I have a nicely dense training session where my learner is going to spend a lot more time getting things right than wrong. It's important to keep your speed up. (Remember, make sure your treats are small and not crumbly. Time spent scavenging for crumbs is time spent learning how to find crumbs, which is not what you're trying to teach right now.) Aim to deliver the treat in the same spot. You should be machinelike in your delivery. It shouldn't be hard to get through twenty treats in two minutes.

Once you've shaped your dog to get four feet on the mat, you can try forming a short behavior chain: cue a sit or a down when your dog gets to the mat. Most dogs quickly chunk these two things in a way that is useful, with a built-in cue: *If there is a mat on the ground, I go there and sit.*

Now, you can choose what you want to work on next.

MAT SIZE

You can try making the mat smaller. I like to do this by taking scissors to a yoga mat, inch by inch, if needed. When in doubt, always make your criteria just a little higher rather than a lot higher—that is, make the mat a little smaller rather than a lot. Most dogs, however, progress rather quickly at this game. Going from half a yoga mat to half of that usually isn't too much of a challenge. But, if you're not at that twenty-treats-in-two-minutes rate, you should make the mat larger. Usually in a single session I can get a dog to sit on a mat that is the size of one or two pieces of printer paper. At this point, it's pretty easy to transfer or generalize this behavior to get your dog to sit on any piece of paper. You can carry a small piece of yoga mat to put on the ground when you're on the go with your dog, but it can also be useful to be able to sticky spot your dog with whatever's available. I traveled all around the United States and Europe with my dog, Amos, and in a pinch it was convenient to be able to put a hotel lobby brochure or takeout menu on the ground near me to let him know exactly what I needed him to do and where. Would he occasionally find some piece of paper on the sidewalk, go lie down on it, and look at me expectantly? Yes, and it was very cute.

DURATION

Once you have your sticky spot, you can start shaping how long your dog will stay on it for a reward without moving. Teaching a "stay" is about shaping the number of seconds, or even minutes, that a dog remains in a position. So if your dog can keep butt to ground on the sticky spot for one second for four or so trials, up it to three seconds. If that is too hard, try two seconds. You don't have to add a verbal "stay" cue here. You can if you want, but the sticky spot itself can be the cue.

DISTRACTION

You want your dog to remain on the spot without you having to be staring at him the whole time, flat palm facing the dog like you're shooting him with some magic invisible laser beam coming from your hand while walking backward. And without the room having to be perfectly silent. So, you can start shaping the ability to remain put while you walk around, or in a new space. When you're adding distraction, you will probably want to lower the other criteria. Better to make just one thing hard at a time. If you can get a ten-second stay in your kitchen on a small sticky spot, when you practice in the lobby of your building you might try a larger sticky spot and lower your duration criteria.

CUE DISCRIMINATION

Teaching a dog actor for a movie or TV show to go to a mark is really just a version of sticky spot. Think postage-stamp-size sticky spot, which cues them about what to do next.

❖

So far, we've had just one sticky spot, which could be shaped down to something the size of a little piece of tape, like you might see on a stage or set for an actor. If there is more than one possible thing you would want them to do when they get to a spot, you can bake that into training, where a piece of tape that's a line means go there and lie down, but if the tape is crossed, go there and sit.

To start this process, develop two sticky spots, each one with a different meaning and way to tell them apart, such as an "X" on one and an "O" on the other. Or pieces of black and white yoga mats. One means sit and one means lie down. While the applications for this are endless, it's also just another fun learning game for a dog, and a chance for a trainer to experiment with the process of teaching. You can impress people with a dog who will "sit" on the piece of paper that says "sit" and lie down on the one that says "down." (While you can train this kind of visual discrimination between two words—see the section in the previous chapter on reading—I have found that Amos going and lying down on a piece of paper I wrote "DOWN" on was a good enough party trick for most occasions.)

The Bowling Pigeon

One day in 1943 in a pigeon-filled Minneapolis flour mill, B. F. Skinner and his graduate students took a break from their bird-bomb work to see what else they could train a pigeon to do. Sounds like a good time to me! Let Skinner describe what happened next:

> One day we decided to teach a pigeon to bowl. The pigeon was to send a wooden ball down a miniature alley toward a set of toy pins

by swiping the ball with a sharp sideward movement of the beak. To condition the response, we put the ball on the floor of an experimental box and prepared to operate the food-magazine as soon as the first swipe occurred. But nothing happened. Though we had all the time in the world, we grew tired of waiting. We decided to reinforce any response which had the slightest resemblance to a swipe—perhaps, at first, merely the behavior of looking at the ball—and then to select responses which more closely approximated the final form. The result amazed us. In a few minutes, the ball was caroming off the walls of the box as if the pigeon had been a champion squash player.

Skinner would later recall it was a "day of great illumination."

I think I know a bit of Skinner's thrill that day. I can guess that it is the same sort of joy tinged with magic that I felt on so many Friday evenings at School For The Dogs sitting on a folding chair training Amos to play a kid's toy boom box that I'd found the toy on the street. It had various big buttons that would make a sound when pressed. Could I get him to reliably hit a button twice? Or more buttons in a certain order? I started by rewarding any interaction with the thing, then waited to see if he would try using his paw, then only when the paw was on the blue button…

Other nights, he'd play a clanky orange toddler's plastic piano. He'd go from hitting any key to begin with to using only his right paw to play the green key on the left.

Or maybe just knock over a cup.

I wouldn't be alone at this game. I'd be with as many as a dozen dog owners who had come (for this class, without their dogs) to learn as much as I could impart about dog training in ninety minutes. Amos's demonstrations were always a highlight. I'd start by coming up with a few ideas of things we could get him to do that he hadn't done ever or much: nose open a book, pick up a pencil with his mouth, jump over a broomstick, kick a ball with his right paw. Whatever. I'd get someone to pick one of my ideas. Everyone would get a clicker and five treats. First, they'd each practice doing a nose-to-hand touch with him. One go at it with a "yes" and one with a clicker, just to practice. This was, after all, not Amos's first time at the rodeo, and the people were the intended students. Then we'd go around again, and each person would get three opportunities to reward a certain criterion that I'd assign—if Amos had succeeded with the previous person, I'd make it a little different—to do the thing a little longer, or a little harder. If he didn't seem to be getting it, I'd keep the criterion the same or lower it. But usually, it got raised with each person and he was engaging in the "terminal" behavior we'd decided on by the time we got to the fifth or six person, three treats each. If there was time, we'd go around again with each person choosing their own criterion.

There was another game we'd play at these sessions: the human shaping game. I'd learned about this in *Don't Shoot the Dog!* One person volunteers to be the "animal" and someone the "trainer." The trainer would click for some close approximation of the final behavior that we all had secretly decided on while the animal waited outside the room—usually something like getting a cup of water from the cooler or picking up a book from the table. It's a simple game, much like "hot and cold," but with no speaking, no pointing. I'd instruct the trainers to try to not go more than ten or fifteen seconds without a click. After watching people play this game over and over, I saw that the more people click, the faster their partner seems to learn, if only because it gives them less time to wander and waste time and energy trying wrong things.

You build empathy for your dog when you take a turn as the animal in training (even though, don't forget, you are really always an animal in training).

❦

Amos loved shaping games. It was only in training Amos that I began
to see how it was possible to skillfully, incrementally change criteria to
get behaviors that wouldn't otherwise occur and then to refine them.
It's important to never raise criteria so high that your learner gives up.
As you select for certain behaviors, others will undergo extinction, and
that can be frustrating for a dog who doesn't already have a bank account
filled to the top. You have to know your learner.

Amos was a resilient learner: Quick to try new things. A born entre-
preneur. I could sometimes get pretty lofty with my criteria—stingy,
almost. But he'd stick in there for a good while trying new things. It's only
as I've become a bit more mature as a trainer that I've grown to appreciate
how important it can be to not rush the process. Poppy isn't Amos. She
likes to bring every treat to her bed to savor it, which can slow us down
if we're training anywhere other than on her bed. She also needs to clock
more reinforcements at any one level before I can push her to another
one. And that usually involves starting at the equivalent of Skinner's flour
mill pigeon just looking in the vague direction of the ball.

We can always, and I think often should, start any shaping process at
this kind of Criterion Zero and then build up reps like coils on a gently
curved pot.

Let's take a look at some situations where you can shape better
behaviors.

Loose Leash Walking

You can start teaching loose leash walking by rewarding at your dog's head
height at some very frequent intervals. I like to be very thoughtful about
treat delivery outside, being consistent about giving the food in a specific

spot on my leg, near where the dog can reach it. With clients I've sometimes gone so far as having them put a chip clip on their jeans so they have a specific magic zone "spot" to give the good stuff.

Pick a measure, like every one step, or every crack on the sidewalk. Whatever your dog is doing doesn't matter: he's going to get a treat on that one spot in the magic zone by your leg after the step or at every crack. When you're competing with the exciting world outside your home, you want to use something really good. Cheese is my go-to. You want your dog to be so interested in what's happening in the magic zone that everything else pales in comparison, even for a moment.

You can then raise the criterion to two steps, or every two cracks. What is the criterion? Walking. You should be marking and rewarding progressively at longer intervals but frequently enough to keep your dog from pulling.

You can raise the criterion: raise it to walking-while-not-pulling, and you can get there with very little or even no pulling to begin with. Sometimes, this can be accomplished by simply getting a longer leash! It may seem counterintuitive, but a longer leash will get to its taut spot slower, giving you more time to reward for walking that is happening near you, and may make everyone's walk more comfortable. I like to suggest that my clients think of a leash like a seatbelt: there in case there is a parade of skateboarding squirrels eating chicken wing bones across a busy street, not as a tool to control your dog. If you have a save place to practice, you can even teach your dog to walk nicely near you, and then you can add in the tether.

By skillfully setting up the schedule and knowing where you're going to deliver the reinforcers, it's possible to slice the behavior into small enough bits so that pulling is not going to happen to begin with. You can also begin following your marker signal with a reinforcing little sprint—sometimes running in an unexpected direction, as it both changes the position of an in-front-of-you dog (*Who's in front now, chump!*) and keeps a dog interested in paying attention to you for direction cues rather than just bolting in front and waiting for you, the lagger. You can also sometimes swap out the treat, instead bringing out a toy for a bit of on-the-go tug. Be prepared so that you're proactively figuring out how to get the slack-leashed behavior of your dreams rather than worry about yanking your shoulder out of its socket.

Being Alone

The ability to be alone is just another thing that can be shaped. For dogs who have anxiety related to being left or when a certain person leaves, the training remedy, broadly speaking, will likely involve building the dog's ability to be alone at very, *very* small intervals: seconds, even. But, when starting out with a dog who is new to the idea of people coming and going, it's possible to shape the ability to exist without people present in baby steps, a minute at a time, with difficulty introduced incrementally. Can you be in the other room while I take a shower? Yes? Okay. What about a slightly longer shower? What about if I go to the laundry room? All the way up to being cool while I go for dinner and a movie.

To start, begin by teaching your dog to relax and settle in a comfortable spot, such as a bed or a crate. Gradually increase the duration of time that your dog spends in their designated spot, rewarding them for longer periods of calm behavior. Once your dog is comfortable relaxing in his spot while you're in the room, you can gradually start to introduce separation. Begin by taking a step or two away from him, still within his line of sight, and reward him for staying calm and relaxed. Slowly increase the distance never pushing your dog beyond their comfort level.

Shaping Rules

To truly excel at shaping, I think it helps to be the kind of person who takes notes, draws up plans, and charts performance. I struggle with this kind of stuff. I like to think on my feet. Under duress, I can keep a beat and read music, but I prefer living my life as a kind of jazz performance. That is why I think I probably will never shape a bomb-detection dog or work at Guiding Eyes for the Blind. I have great respect for those who do work like that.

I also have huge admiration for the trainers who work for me who work with dogs who are dealing with fear or aggression-based issues that can lead to someone getting hurt. These are the kinds of cases where it is crucial to craft a training plan, shaping both the client and the dog, figuring out how to create situations where success is likely, and rewarding successful successive approximations. New good behaviors need to be shaped, while the length of time an unwanted behavior isn't happening is also being stretched step by step. And the behaviors need to be generalized in new places, with new people. Criteria are being raised in small enough steps that everyone is pretty much guaranteed something like a B+ at worst. This isn't because the students are necessarily geniuses. It's because if students are flunking, the teacher is the failure. It also doesn't make for very good business.

But training can still be rewarding if you are, like me, a little more casually about shaping. Manhattanites usually aren't seeking out professional dog training because it's a hobby, but I have seen many a client take it on as one—people get really excited when they start to see how fun it can be to shape their dogs to do things. Shaping your dog to roll over or do a handstand is really fun and can be done in the space between the couch and the coffee table. While drinking a beer and possibly watching *The Crown*.

You can use a little bit of shaping to teach something fun or to train a dog to not bark when you leave. You can use it to choreograph a two-step with your collie or to get a dog to do search-and-rescue work. Or you can do gamelike versions of these things at home: a spin around your legs and then go find the glove that smells like Mom.

Whatever your level of passion and commitment, you'll find that you get better at shaping the more you do it, and you also will get to know your learner better and better. Your shaping successes will shape your ability to shape!

The only "rules" I've ever been taught about shaping are Karen Pryor's "Ten Laws of Shaping"—training knowledge gleaned mostly from her Sea Life Park work with dolphins. These "laws" definitely informed how I approached shaping from the start. Here is how, over the years, I have distilled her dolphin-training wisdom for people with goldendoodles in East Village studio apartments—people for whom it might be a stretch, at least on first meeting, to hear me go on about what they can learn from dolphin training when they're just trying to get their dog to not pull on the leash.

BE CLEAR ABOUT WHERE YOU'RE GIVING THE TREAT

Delivery should be machinelike. After watching me train Amos with an iPad one afternoon, a *Times* reporter once described me as a treat munition dispenser. Damn straight! You want your dog to know exactly where to find the treat and to not waste any time about it. Think about where you're giving the reward as you may be able to use where you're placing it to get the behavior you want to be more likely to happen, or more likely to help you get more reps faster. For instance, if you're shaping a dog to go into a crate, initially you might want to reward inside the crate, to solidify interest in going into the crate. But, as you begin to shape the behavior of running into the crate, with the criterion being the speed with which your dog runs into it, you might be better off resetting by tossing the treat outside the crate.

ADJUST THE ENVIRONMENT TO ENCOURAGE THE BEHAVIORS YOU WANT

As much as you can, arrange the nonedible parts of the environment as needed to encourage the chances of getting the behavior you want. If you're shaping a dog to go to a mat in a room, you can make sure it is the most comfortable thing to sit on in the room. You can use gates or arrange the furniture so that there aren't a lot of interesting things to do other than go check out the mat. If you're working on loose leash walking, start out in the hallway or find the quietest possible route outside. I like training with a dog in a crate when it's possible, as it limits the opportunities to do other things, upping the chances I'm going to get a sit, or a touch, or whatever. It also can help her build good associations with her crate. Ditto something like a slightly raised platform like the plastic KLIMBs we use at School For The Dogs. It defines, and limits, the space where behaviors are going to be reinforced. They're not so high a dog can't jump off of them, but enough so that it's maybe calorically less expensive to see what might be reinforced without getting off it.

START AT CRITERION ZERO

Don't be afraid to start at Criterion Zero. You can build up from there. Consider loose leash walking. What is the lowest criterion you can think of? Often, people start training their dog to walk outside by bringing them outside and then introducing them to their new leash. It may be their first time outside, and their first time being tethered. That's a lot of criteria you're adding all at once. A better place to start may be to have the criterion be simply walking next to you. You could do this at home.

Or in the hallway. Adding new equipment is a new criterion. And even that might be sliced into smaller and smaller asks. It depends on the dog. It's crucial to raise criteria only in increments that are small enough so that there's a good chance your learner will get it right. The criterion should be achievable enough that you're in that twenty-treats-in-two-minutes zone.

GO BACK TO THE BEGINNING

Never hesitate to go back to Criterion Zero if you need to. Karen Pryor calls this "going back to kindergarten." If you hit a training plateau or rut, you can just train the whole thing up again from the beginning. I've found you can do this even if there isn't a problem, almost like a warm-up—one that's kind of fun, because you've done this stuff already. But also, could it ever be a bad idea to sometimes work at the easiest level of a behavior you're mastering? What do pro musicians do when they sit down at their instrument? Scales.

It can be important to be able to shift criteria on the fly, since you may find yourself sometimes working in environments where we can't control everything. You're shaping some beautiful loose leash walking and then suddenly there's a gaggle of kids on scooters and you're between them and the ice cream truck. This wasn't part of your shaping plan. You better lower your criteria, and do it quick.

START WITH A BASELINE

If you're using shaping to work on changing a problem behavior, make sure you have a baseline of the behavior you are trying to change. How many times is the behavior happening to begin with? What exactly does the behavior look like? You need to know this if you're going to start trying to get more or less of that behavior.

ESTABLISH CLEAR GOALS

Know what your goal is. You want to be able to celebrate your shaping wins and see them in relation to where you started. This will help you track and gauge success. For the drinking-and-watching-Netflix variety of shaping, this isn't so important. If the journey is the goal and the whole thing is an interspecies game, I give you permission to make up your criteria as you go.

If you are goal oriented with what you're doing, you also want to have some idea about what the goals after that are going to be so that you're prepared if your dog jumps ahead. For these reasons, it might be good to write a plan and plot where you are. A lot of people have a hard time doing this. It's why, if you're trying to shape a behavior that is truly important—a behavior that is for your dog's safety, or your own, say—it can be smart to work with a professional.

SPEED THINGS UP WHEN YOUR DOG IS READY

Consider speeding things up by smartly using targets and sticky spots as interim steps to build behaviors. Then shape those behaviors. For example, you can teach a dog to target a target stick, then shape the dog to touch the target stick on your leg while you're walking, and then shape that down to just touching your leg at the back of the knee. This can help shape the dog to be in the stationing position someone might want to send their dog into, right next to them. You can then raise your criteria to rewarding the dog when he is in that position, with body facing in the same direction as you, while moving, and so on. If you want to train a dog to rest under a chair, you can shape that by waiting for the dog to try to go under the chair, or you can use a sticky spot under the chair to help speed up the chances that he is going to try that behavior. Then you can begin to shape that behavior: Will he go under the chair if the chair is outside? What about on the bus? How long will he stay under a chair? Will he do it when I cue it and refrain from doing it when I don't?

DON'T MAKE TWO THINGS HARD AT ONCE

If you're shaping for distance (how far of a "come" can you get your dog to do), don't also shape for distraction (will he do it off-leash in a new place). If you're shaping for latency (how quickly will your dog sit after you ask for it?) don't also shape for discrimination (can she differentiate between "sit" and "pit"?).

BE FLEXIBLE

You can always change the plan. I like the way Julie Vargas, Skinner's eldest daughter, describes working on one's own ability to adjust "according to Moment to Moment Progress" in her book *Behavior Analysis for Effective Teaching*:

Steps in shaping are ephemeral because shaping requires constantly moving to new levels. If one level is not mastered in a few minutes to be replaced by a new level, you need to find out why. Are the steps too large? Is the click still a conditioned reinforcer? Has a particular student overworked particular muscles or reached a physiological limit? No one should be stuck at a fixed level. If performance does not improve at least in rate, change your strategy. Work on a different behavior or a different property of the same behavior. You can come back to a former level later. Or if a student seems to be having a bad day, you can change to an activity where he or she will be successful. Extra practice on an already mastered skill never hurts, but failure does.

PART FOUR

Good Going Forward

The Least We Can Do

*"The Good Life is waiting for us—here and now!… At this very
moment, we have the necessary techniques, both material and
psychological, to create a full and satisfying life for everyone."*

—B. F. SKINNER, *WALDEN TWO*

TEN YEARS AGO, I was living alone, and playing training games with my
dog was literally my job. We would do shaping demos throughout the week
both at School For The Dogs and at office events for continuing education
luncheons. Sometimes I'd drop my dog at home, go train with a client or
two or three, then come back home, and we'd train some more, just because
it was fun. It was what we did. I often had no end goal in mind. Shaping was
just a way we passed the time. It was a kind of love language. The more he
learned, the better he got at trying things, trying *different* things.

For fun, I'd let him take "selfies" with his nose on my phone, or draw
Christmas cards with his paws on the iPad, or perfect how long he could
hold a "play dead" position after I said "bang bang." Could he hold it in
the living room? What about…on a Paris sidewalk (where a street artist
had conveniently painted a bed on the sidewalk)? Life was a big shaping
experiment. One where he got lots of hot dogs and lamb lung. The result

was a dog I think had an above-average canine understanding of how the world works and, because of that, got to enjoy a lot of time with me without me getting worried about his stress level. It meant we literally traveled the world together—me and my buddy. But he also had a social life of his own, because he knew how things worked. On the beach in Greece, when I got tired of tossing his toy to him, he'd bring it to strangers, drop it at their feet, then sit quietly and stare at them until they got the idea.

When I worked at *Too Cute!*, Amos came with me to the office every day, by bike or subway. When I taught playtimes at School For The Dogs, I put him on top of a bunch of stacked platforms to separate him from the puppies—as he got older he had little patience for puppies—so we could still hang while I led the class. Dogs have short lives; a life of constant shaping games made Amos a dog I spent as much time as possible alongside for as long as I could. It was not a relationship of equals. But it was a wonderful relationship. I treasured every moment. I think he had a good time, too.

Today, however, I have a different relationship to training. Amos was in great shape until age fifteen. He died at fifteen and a half. When he was nearly twelve, I met my husband, who runs a student travel business based in Italy. This meant Amos spent his last years swimming in Roman fountains and fetching his favorite rubber toy off the coast of Capri. My older daughter got to spend her first two years with him, and I'm so glad they crossed paths in the world—he'll always be her first dog. I wear his ashes in a locket.

Poppy, a brown chihuahua mix with a black muzzle, came to us a month later at five months old, driven up from Alabama with her sisters. She is the most affectionate dog I have ever encountered, with a desire to touch and be touched like I've rarely seen in any living thing before. Once, when I returned after a week away and was lying on the bed, she put her front elbows on top of me, butt in the air, draped her head over my shoulder and held that position for twenty minutes, moving occasionally only to lick my cheek.

When we play shaping games, she will usually retire to her crate for a nap if I withhold even one click/treat. I interpret this as a doggie version of sulking.

When I got her, I was pregnant and had a toddler, while running a business, while starting this book, while navigating a pandemic. I didn't have the time or mobility to give her anything like the kind of life experiences Amos had. But I also don't know if that would've ever been right for her. Given our current lifestyle, that is okay! Because the fact is that I do not have the kind of time and space and flexibility I used to have to train my dog just because it was a fun thing to do. We are both okay with her couch-potato tendencies.

This leaves me thinking about others in my position who might be asking themselves: *Given the limited amount of time and energy I have available to devote to training my dog, how can I use the principles of good dog training to make sure to have a dog who can fit into my life?*

The first step is to set everyone up for success. To some extent, this means considering the animal you're getting. I hesitate to make breedist distinctions, because the "average" behavior of a certain breed may not reflect the behavior of the individual in front of you. But, I'm willing to make some broad suggestions. Like: If you don't have an active lifestyle, maybe don't get a border collie. If you want a running companion, don't get a corgi. If you're hoping to be able to leave a dog alone for ten hours at a time, get a cat.

If you're getting a dog from a shelter, ask if they work with any rescues or fosters who've had dogs in home settings; they might be able to help you figure out if a particular dog is going to be a good match for you. If you're going to a breeder, see if you can meet your potential puppy's parents, and speak to other people who have had dogs from the same parents or breeder, so that you can get a sense of what to expect, ballpark.

Then: Work on a hand-to-nose or nose-to-object target. Perfect your treat delivery and your marking. These skills are going to be applicable to everything else.

Next: Be prepared to reward behaviors throughout the day, à la Kathy Sdao's SMART-50. Capture behaviors that you like. Count out treats for each day in advance and make sure they are either on your person or in a place where you can reach them. You get what you pay for, and by having fifty "dollars" on you at the start of each day, you can pay for some good behaviors that you'll see happen more because of the reinforcement.

Then, think about three categories of activities:

✦ Stuff I have to do to my dog

✦ Activities that will help my dog be happier

✦ Relaxation techniques

Stuff I Have to Do to My Dog

One of the major reasons clicker training is used in zoos is to train animals to comply with husbandry-related activities. Gorillas have teeth that need to be brushed, and orcas need to go onto scales to be weighed. Using secondary reinforcers and food or tactile rewards—nothing like a good tongue scratch!—trainers work at teaching animals to literally cooperate so as to get good care.

Likewise, we can train dogs to give us their paws for inspection, let us look into their ears, open their mouth for tooth brushing, or take pills without having them forced down their throat. If you have a dog who will need to go into a bag and be carried on public transportation, that's an exercise you can work on from day one, before you ever go anywhere. Each of these behaviors can begin with Criterion Zero and be shaped. If this feels like an overwhelming list, pick one thing to focus on at a time. With Poppy, for me, that is nail care. If she wants attention, I can take out a plastic cutting board onto which I have put some stair tread tape. It was easy to get her to use this from the start as a large emery board. I shaped her to put one foot on it, just like I shaped her to put a foot on a mat. I then began lifting it at an angle and eventually rewarding every second or third scratch to get her doing it with some verve. This has turned into something I can do with my four-year-old: she can hold the board while I give the treat and vice versa.

Activities That Will Help My Dog Be Happier

Dogs need exercise! Pick at least one thing you can do that will help your dog get out more or use indoor space more. Again, you can get there by targeting and shaping, starting at Criterion Zero if need be.

For the client who taught their dog to target the back wall of the elevator instead of lunging at incoming dogs, that made it possible for her to take him out more.

For another client, that might mean getting clever about using cueing and conditioning in other ways. Turn the smallest bit of leash pressure into a secondary reinforcer by pairing the smallest bit of pressure with a reward at your leg; hitting the end of the leash can become information to your dog that it's worth checking back with you.

For still other clients, it has meant teaching their dog to run on an indoor treadmill: acclimating them to being on it, then being on it with it moving, incrementally, until they get to the point of enjoying the chance to jog.

For Poppy, our "exercise" routine involves indoor calisthenics. At night when she gets antsy, I'll sit on the couch, foot on the coffee table in front of me, knee slightly bent, and I'll get her to jump over it or go under it. It's as easy as targeting her on one side or the other. Last night I found myself doing this while watching *Frozen* with my daughters, using a plastic Elsa wand as a target stick. Sometimes after she jumps my leg or limbos under, it, I'll trigger the Treat & Train on the other side of the apartment, to add a little bit of extra cardio to the routine.

Relaxation Techniques

You can shape a dog to be okay on a mat with a focus on rewarding your dog for showing increasingly relaxed behaviors in that place. This is sometimes referred to as Relaxation Protocol: a step-by-step process of systematically increasing the criteria for your dog to be on the mat for extended periods. One criterion you can begin selecting for is the signs of relaxation: a shift of weight; a deep sigh. You can underscore these moments by marking and rewarding them to up the chances that next time that special relaxation mat comes out, the behavior isn't just lying there, it's lying there like you're ready to watch a three-hour Belgian feminist art film. Part of the shaping process is building the dog's ability to…do nothing. To not act on every impulsive whim. To, at least some of the time, be able to chillax a bit between reinforcers. This ability to relax even when reinforcers aren't coming at a steady stream, and then to be able to do that in novel environments, is always something you can work on shaping to the stars.

Here is the School For The Dogs Relaxation Protocol:

PART 1: Down with Duration on Mat

STEP 1: Select a designated mat, towel, or bed for your dog to lie on, which you will only bring out when you practice this exercise.

STEP 2: Place the mat on the floor and sit next to it.

STEP 3: Lure your dog into a down position on the mat using a closed handful of treats.

STEP 4: Keeping your hand relatively still, slowly release one treat at a time on the mat in between their front paws for thirty seconds. (Think PEZ dispenser.)

STEP 5: During this thirty seconds, your dog should be able to remain in the down position, since the treats are being delivered without pause.

STEP 6: After thirty seconds of slow but steady treating, remove your hand, rest it on your knee, and wait for one second. If your dog remains in down position as you count to one silently, return your closed hand to the mat and release another treat in between their front paws.

STEP 7: Repeat this five times, pausing for one-second durations.

STEP 8: If five of those repetitions are successful (that is, your dog remains down), increase the duration of your hand on your knee to two seconds. Mix in longer durations by varying the amount of time that you pause feeding. Avoid making the duration too long too soon; instead, pick your dog's max duration (e.g., five seconds) and have them wait for four-, three-, two-, and one-second durations randomly in addition to five seconds.

STEP 9: If your dog stands up at any point, give them several seconds to decide to come back to the mat and/or lie down again. If they choose to do either of these behaviors on their own, reward heavily in between their paws; if they haven't lain down again after several seconds, lure them back into position on the mat.

STEP 10: Once your dog can consistently stay down on the mat for periods of at least five seconds in between treats, you can move on to part 2.

PART 2: Adding Disengagement

STEP 1: Set up the mat and give your dog several seconds to lie down on it. If they don't, lure them into a down on the mat.

STEP 2: Once your dog is down on the mat, begin treating every few seconds in between their paws. Deliver at least five treats this way as a warm-up for this next step.

STEP 3: After the warm-up, raise your criteria: begin to treat the dog only when they are NOT looking at your handful of treats or at you.

STEP 4: To help make this happen, avoid facing the dog directly. You can turn your head slightly to one side. Avoid making eye contact, and instead use your peripheral vision to keep tabs on where your dog's eyes are directed.

STEP 5: As soon as you see your dog's eyes looking elsewhere (anywhere else!), treat between their front paws. After they eat it, the most likely scenario is that the dog will dip their nose downward to the mat to sniff for leftover treats in the spot you've been placing them. If they do, reinforce with another treat, but if they don't, you can just wait to reinforce when the dog looks elsewhere again.

STEP 6: Repeat five times.

STEP 7: Once your dog is consistently able to lie down on the mat without staring at your hand or your face for at least one second, you can move on to part 3.

PART 3: Adding Duration to Disengagement

STEP 1: Set up the mat and wait for your dog to lie down on it. (Note: if you still have to lure your dog onto the mat, go back to part 2.)

STEP 2: Once the dog is in a down position on the mat, treat between their front paws once they disengage from you. Do this at least five times as a warm-up for the next step.

STEP 3: After the warm-up, raise your criteria for treating further: begin to reinforce your dog only when they are not looking at you or your handful of treats for a count of three seconds.

STEP 4: In addition to increasing the length of time the dog is not looking at you, this level also allows you to begin selecting for behaviors that indicate a deeper relaxed state, such as hip shifts and head rests.

STEP 5: Increase the duration of these disengaged and "restful" behaviors at the dog's pace, again making sure to vary the durations you reinforce for as you increase them (i.e., four seconds, five seconds, two seconds, four seconds, one second, three seconds...).

STEP 6: Once the dog is not staring at your hand or your face for at least five seconds and has begun to offer restful behaviors, you can move on to part 4.

PART 4: Changing Your Position

STEP 1: Set up the mat and wait for your dog to lie down on it. Have a chair nearby to sit on. You'll begin this session by sitting on the floor; later you'll move to the chair, and then to a standing position.

STEP 2: Once your dog is in a down position on the mat, treat between their paws when they disengage from you for five seconds. Do this at least twice as a warm-up for the next step.

STEP 3: After the warm-up, deliver a treat and then gently slide yourself up into the chair, preemptively treating them from the chair before they have a chance to get up.

STEP 4: From the chair, rebuild the behavior by treating every couple seconds for up to thirty seconds. From there, begin to select for disengagement and longer durations than a couple seconds.

STEP 5: If the dog gets up when you move into the chair, stay in the chair and reset them on the mat, lowering your criteria on duration and disengagement to help them succeed.

STEP 6: Once they're able to remain down on the mat while you're in the chair, stand up. Reinforce the dog frequently and heavily for staying down on the mat when you first make this positional change.

STEP 7: Sit back down and repeat until you can easily stand up and change positions with the dog noticing but remaining in a relaxed down.

PART 5: Adding Distractions

STEP 1: If you have been practicing in the same environment thus far, take your mat elsewhere to practice. Select a different room or some other mildly distracting environment to practice in.

STEP 2: If your dog is staying put but there are things your dog can notice in this environment, begin by reinforcing the dog just for engaging with the stimuli (Do they look at it? Deliver a treat between their paws!).

STEP 3: Select one new distraction at a time—your movement, other stimuli, etc.

STEP 4: Important reminder: Any time you increase criteria for one aspect, you should decrease for others. For example, if you change the environment you're working in, you might need to reduce duration back to that of step 2.

Good Dog Trainers

Sitting at a diner one recent afternoon, an aunt made a tearful confession. She had two regrets in her life. One was the way her family treated their dog when she was growing up. She never hit the dog herself, but she watched her father do it and didn't intervene. She got an early lesson in classical conditioning when she realized the dog would flinch when she merely raised her hand.

I too was shown how to use coercion and punishment-based training methods on my childhood dog—mousetraps on the bed to keep the dog off it, leash pops for pulling, shock collars to stave off barking, deep-voice admonitions for all infractions. I didn't know it at the time, but I was, essentially, learning a method of teaching.

Her second regret: The frequency with which she lost her temper with her kids when they were small.

She didn't seem to see any connection between these two things. But I did. While using coercion and pain to get the family dog to behave as he wanted, I believe my grandfather was also giving his kids an early lesson about how we take care of those in our care—especially when they don't behave as we think they should. Dog training changed how I think about learning, even broadening how I think about what "teaching" is. It's not just about disseminating information or building skills; it's doing so in a way that can help those in our care thrive. Good dog training is more about the *how* than the *what*.

If you get the how right, the what should follow: a dog that seems well trained. But, if you get the how wrong, sometimes you can also get...a dog that seems well trained. Sometimes I wonder if many dogs are living in a state of depression that people misinterpret as good behavior. Fear and anxiety in dogs can lead to bad behaviors. But here's a funny thing about dog depression: It can turn a dog into some people's platonic ideal. A dog who is "calm" and "submissive" may be roughly equivalent to someone who has decided to stay in bed all day in total surrender.

It's what happens when there are no good choices to be made. Or any choices at all. Escape is futile.

Early in my dog training career, I learned the term "learned helplessness," and it made sense in a kind of "oh duh" way. We've all had times where it feels like any effort is futile, so why try at all. I'm pretty sure it's why I slept in the nurse's office during most of high school. Funny that I had to become a dog trainer to become familiar with the concept as studied in laboratory settings with a variety of animals and scientifically codified, when it's something most of us have either experienced firsthand or can at least recognize.

In the late 1960s as a graduate student, now world-famous psychologist Martin E. P. Seligman, put dogs in restraints and shocked them to study the effects, if any, of an animal's control over aversive consequences. Some of the dogs were given a switch to flip with their heads to turn off the shock. Others had no control over whether they got shocked.

When both groups of dogs were subsequently placed in a box and given shocks and all had the means to escape it by going to the other side of the box, the dogs who'd had no choice before were significantly less likely to figure out there was a way to avoid the pain.

Seligman attempted several methods to encourage the dogs to jump the barrier, including placing food on the other side and calling out to them, but the dogs remained unmotivated and resigned to their fate. As a last resort, he used ropes tied around their necks to forcefully pull them over the barrier. It often took more than thirty sessions of pulling before the dogs realized they could avoid the shock by voluntarily jumping over the barrier.

Everyone appreciates being able to make choices. That is a gift that training can give a dog, a gift *you* can give.

You might give choice in the form of a training game. How many sits can we get in a minute? Can he run laps from this mat to the treats I'm delivering on the other side of the room?

You might offer the apartment dwelling dog the choice to do a more apartment-appropriate version of stalking elk through the damp canyon forests: getting the chance to go at a bully stick, or dislodging a biscuit from a puzzle toy.

Or it may just need I turn around and go home when my dog stops and sits near our door rather than making her come with me for another turn around the block. Or taking the cues that she doesn't want to be petted by someone new.

But, at the very least, I think it means not forcing her down on her back until she cries uncle.

We assume that dogs know what they're being punished for. They may. Or they may not. If they are repeatedly being punished, they likely don't know what they're being punished for or they've become inured to whatever the punishment is.

Either way, punishment elevates cortisol, a hormone released in response to stress. It can have many effects on the body, including the disintegration of dendritic spines—the small protrusions on the surface of neurons that play a role in memory formation and storage. When they disintegrate, it can impede the ability of synapses to collect and store memories. This can have a negative impact on learning.

Seligman tried to undo the misery he'd caused the dogs. What he found was that it was possible, but not easy, to undo all the bad stuff. He realized that he had essentially caused depression in a mammals—ones he loved. The issue didn't seem to be the strength of the shocks. It was their inevitability. Later, in partnership with his longtime partner Steve Maier, who went on to be a pioneer in the field of neuropharmacology of stress, he discovered that what they had called "learned helplessness" is not actually learned. It's depression as a natural, *unlearned* reaction, to something unavoidable. Seligman went on to devote his life to helping people be happier: fight depression or, better yet, never get depressed. He is the founder of the Positive Psychology Center at the University of Pennsylvania and is credited with starting the scientific study of what makes people thrive.

What makes animals feel like life is worth living? One thing is having agency to opt out of or into a situation, in order to build their ability to not just throw up their hands in difficult situations that really cannot be escaped. Resilience, Seligman calls this.

In his own life, he quickly learned that punishment was dangerous: He had seen too many depressed dogs. On the first page of his memoir, *The Hope Circuit*, he explained how the universality of these principles hit him like a lightning bolt after his daughter Nikki, just five, accused him of being a grouch. "It occurred to me for the very first time that maybe any success I'd had was not because I could see every flaw—because of my 'critical intelligence'—but in spite of it," he writes. "My 'remedial' view of raising my children was wrong. If I could correct all my kid's errors…I would somehow end up with an exemplary child. What nonsense. Instead, I had to identify what Nikki was really good at… reward it, and help her to lead her life around her strengths, not waste her time thanklessly correcting her weaknesses."

Sounds like good dog training.

Today on YouTube, TikTok, and Instagram, people who train dogs argue with other people who train dogs. There are a lot of interesting conversations going on there, and some points of view I agree with wholeheartedly. But there are also plenty of people using collars that are meant to control with punishment and negative reinforcement and commenters thanking a certain trainer for showing them how to properly smack their dogs with a rolled-up towel. How can this be happening? Why were misguided psychologists' and punishing dog trainers' methods not resoundingly shunned from the start? I think it's because, as anyone who has ever been depressed knows, you're likely to take the path of least resistance and not fight back even though you're dragged with a rope thirty times. Depression can make an animal docile. And docile

Prisoners are easier to manage than rowdy ones. "Calm submissive dogs always pay attention to their pack leader's instructions," says Cesar Millan.

If compulsion-based trainers are doing a brisk business, I think it's also because they coat their approaches in an appealing veneer. Trainers who use methods that I think can skew in the direction of abuse tend to describe their work with buzzwords that sound good—"communication" and "relationship," for instance.

In these ways, torturing behaviors are reinforced, and maybe become enjoyable to humans as the end result is a creature who is pleasantly "calm submissive."

Too often, the message broadcast to dog owners is all about embracing the power of imposed will and believing in your ability to at least fake a commanding presence and project the correct energy. "Think Oprah! Think Cleopatra! Think John Wayne," writes Cesar Millan. "Straighten your posture. Lift your shoulders high and stick your chest forward. Do what it takes to really own that calm assertive energy and project it through the leash and to your dog."

Many people, like myself when I got my first dog as an adult, don't know what they don't know about training. I went to the place closest to me. If someone had explained it to me in such a way that I saw how much choosing your approach to dog training matters, it may have been hard for me to find a trainer using what I now consider "good dog training." This is because it is not a well-regulated field and truly anything goes.

Anamarie Johnson, School For The Dogs' third employee, is now getting a PhD in behavioral neuroscience and recently published a research paper about how confusing it is to tell what methods trainers use based on their websites. She surveyed one hundred top United States–based trainers, trying to identify their methods based on what she could find about them online. What she discovered was that it was frequently difficult to parse whether trainers used, or rejected, force or punishment-based methods of training. Only about half were explicit about identifying what training methods they used. "I admit that I hoped that there would be some kind of clear word-use case that I'd be able to offer up as a kind of litmus test," she told me, "but nothing was that clear cut."

Electronic or shock collars, Anamarie says, were the only dead giveaway. Not many training operations did refer to them, but when they did, 100 percent of the time the trainers Anamarie had identified as using aversive methods opted for the euphemistic term "electronic collars," since even people who don't know what they don't know about dog training tend to recoil at the prospect of shocking their dog. Whereas all the positive reinforcement trainers who mentioned these aversive tools used the word "shock."

Even if you have strong ideas about the kind of trainer you're looking for, you have your work cut out for you.

If professionals aren't clearer about what kind of training they're offering, one reason may be that they don't think their potential clients care. As if dog training were like dog grooming: the groomer doesn't expect the owner to ask what kind of clippers are used.

If owners don't care, I think that it's not because they're callous. It's only because it doesn't occur to most people—at least, until there is a major problem—that whether or how we train our dogs really matters, no less than it matters how we treat living beings and how we see the world we share.

But Isn't There a Place for Punishment?

Most people can agree that children and violence don't mix. The United Nations Committee on the Rights of the Child issued a directive in 2006 calling physical punishment "legalized violence against children" that should be eliminated in all settings through "legislative, administrative, social and educational measures."

In 2012, the American Psychological Association quoted Sandra Graham-Bermann, PhD, a psychology professor and principal investigator for the Child Resilience and Trauma Laboratory at the University of Michigan: "It's a very controversial area even though the research is extremely telling and very clear and consistent about the negative effects on children. People get frustrated and hit their kids. Maybe they don't see there are other options." Later in the article, on the topic of spanking, Dr. Alan Kazdin, a former American Psychological Association president and head of the Yale Parenting Center, said, "We are not giving up an effective technique. We are saying this is a horrible thing that does not work."

Are there cases where dogs are better off being shocked or smacked as the only alternative is euthanasia? Possibly. But if the goal is to save dogs from euthanasia, we can start with good dog training. I would put money on there being a lot more dogs euthanized because they've been the subject of coercive or punishment-based training, than there are bonked dogs thanking their lucky stars.

Here in the US, there is no federal regulation of the use of shock collars or physical force in dog training. But at least we have the American Veterinary Society of Animal Behavior's recommendation: "Punishment should not be used as a first-line or early-use treatment for behavior problems. This is due to the potential adverse effects which include but are not limited to: inhibition of learning, increased fear-related and aggressive behaviors, and injury to animals and people interacting with animals."

I agree. I'm with science and I believe how we care for the vulnerable among us has a huge impact on the kind of world we live in. I don't think we should be so lighthearted about the behavior experiments we are inadvertently running when we have someone in our care, human or dog, who isn't there by their own choice, and may be poorly matched for the environment. Alas, given a field that isn't regulated, it's too easy to follow the advice of whoever's methods *seem* to work first.

Ethics: Don't Be a Dick to Your Dog

Dog trainers I know think a lot about the ethics of training methods, especially for treating dogs who have problems that are leading them to be a danger to themselves, or to others. These can be tough, emotional situations. Good dog trainers try to find the right balance of unobtrusiveness and efficacy. The closest thing we have to a Hippocratic oath is probably position statements that outline a Least Invasive Minimally Aversive (LIMA) approach. Together, these comprise an ethical standard that is proactive, progressive, and radically different from traditional dog training. I think of LIMA as a set of questions everyone working with a dog should ask themselves, especially when approaching any kind of problem: How can I tread as lightly as possible here? How can I make as few assumptions as possible? How can I arrange the antecedents and the consequences to better the chances of getting the behaviors I want, lowering the chances of getting behaviors I don't want, and do it all in a way that keeps me from being a dick to my dog?

LIMA makes us first ask ourselves if changing a dog's behavior can be done with some kind of environmental makeover. We need to figure this out on a case-by-case basis. Because each dog is its own case, just like us. Our genes set us apart from each other, but possibly less so than the different and ever-changing environments that shape us from day one.

By adhering to LIMA, we focus on setting up animals (including ourselves!) for success in incremental steps, making success reachable every step of the way. We do this on a schedule that our learners can handle, using rewards that are meaningful to them.

LIMA truly is radical—fundamentally different from traditional, aversive, and myth-based approaches. It's a whole different paradigm for learning and care. It's also radical in the sense that we look at the root of a behavior, rather than approaching it from the top down—an approach that necessitates a light touch, even if that means a training plan that is longitudinal and holistic, not quick-results oriented.

Science for the Win

Is it possible to change the world through dog training?

Seeing the spark of excitement in my clients' eyes when they realize how rewarding dog training can be leaves me optimistic. Our ability to keenly understand how animal behavior works may benefit both dogs and humans in meaningful ways. At its best, good dog training can result in a kind of nurturing dog–human loop.

It's easy to swallow misinformation about the dog–human bond. Myths about power structure can seem reasonable. It's not hard to point to some kind of invisible and ineffable energy as the cause for manipulation and coercion that can seem like magic. But the real magic is science.

Even before behavior was codified as a science, technologies of science were helping us bring dogs into our homes. Laboratory-made advancements, such as vaccines, tick and flea preventatives, and surgical interventions like sterilizations are now facts we take for granted, but these developments have made our snuggling-on-the-couch-together interspecies friendships possible.

Operant conditioning is just another lab-born science that holds keys that can help us exist with dogs in our homes, urban or otherwise. The principles of good dog training have been there all along. The more humans who develop an understanding of the basic applications of this area of science—the basics! You don't have to get a PhD!—the more enjoyable and humane our relationships with dogs will become.

The Future of Good Dog Training

"In light of what we know about differential contingencies of reinforcement, the world of the young child is shamefully impoverished. And only machines will remedy this, for the required frequency and subtlety of reinforcement cannot otherwise be arranged."

—B. F. SKINNER

I BECAME A dog trainer because I was looking for a fun, new vocation. What I found was a window into a whole new way of seeing the world. My interspecies and intraspecies relationships shone in a new light. I fell in love with how much sense it made—this natural science that is behind puppy socialization and loose leash walking, and somehow had larger implications about my own ways of existing in the environment, being impacted by consequences, controlling consequences to encourage or discourage certain behaviors of myself, and sometimes others too. Simple stuff, but not easy.

One thing that makes it all "not easy" is that good dog training does not always net speedy change. The fact that positive reinforcement–based training that respects LIMA principles cannot always provide instantaneous solutions is many people's mark against it. But I stand by the assertion that it's eas*ier* than alternatives. Eas*ier* than dealing with inadvertent fallout. Eas*ier* than getting to the bottom of how to improve your energy and make it "calm assertive." In my investigations of the Millan oeuvre looking for the most concrete explanation of how to achieve this, the best recipe I found was probably in his book *Cesar's Way*: "Fake it till you make it," he writes. But "faking it," he advises, is far from easy: It may involve practicing "biofeedback, meditation, along with other relaxation techniques [that] are excellent for learning about how to better control the energy you project." Also, doing eight years of judo training (like he did). I'm getting tired just thinking about it. If that doesn't work, he suggests reading books about philosophy, psychology, and the work of Dr. Phil McGraw and motivational speaker Tony Robbins, *and* studying acting techniques by Konstantin Stanislavski and Lee Strasberg. If you have the time.

He goes on to implore us to be like Oprah with our dogs, because she is someone who "doesn't need to prove she's important; it simply radiates out of her being."

I'll be honest: Trying to be Oprah sounds really hard. And, truth is, even she can't get this stuff right. Just a few pages later, we find Millan in Oprah's home, accusing her of being insufficiently "calm assertive," not living "in the moment," and "nurturing" her "insecure-dominant" cocker spaniels.

I guess that's a bit of a relief, since I don't think I will ever be very much like Oprah. But, I have had a few pretty great dogs, and learning how to train them has made me a better person in the world. In that way, I guess you could say that I sort of *feel* like Oprah. Actually, maybe I am like Oprah. I'm my dog's Oprah. Does that mean that the right kind of dog training energy radiates out of my being? I guess! I mean, based on the dogs I've known and loved, I'm pretty awesome. So, color me calm assertive. Also like Oprah, I'm crazy generous. I can't give away Pontiacs, but when it comes to freeze-dried meat products, my pockets are deep. You get a treat! And you get a treat!

We don't have to be better people to be good dog trainers, but good dog training *will make us better people*. And there's this added benefit: You get to hang out with a dog who thinks you're Oprah.

Teaching Machines

If there is a future for good dog training, I think it can be summed up in one word: technology. The twentieth century brought us the formidable technology of the conditioned reinforcer used as a bridging stimulus. B. F. Skinner stood on the shoulders of giants and tossed us life-changing, potentially world-changing, knowledge and applications, no battery needed.

When his younger daughter of box-fame was in the fourth grade in Cambridge, Massachusetts, Skinner came to school on a parent observation day and saw that, if the goal was to get Deborah's class to willingly and efficiently learn math, the environment needed to be altered.

Many of the problems he saw had to do with the timing of reinforcers. There was behavior happening: kids sitting at desks, doing math problems. But each child's behavior was not being positively reinforced immediately or certainly. They'd maybe get a grade the next day. If only, Skinner thought to himself, every teacher could have the opportunity to train a pigeon.

He went to his basement and began tinkering with the beginnings of what would become his "teaching machine," a device designed to prompt a student to try an achievable task and immediately reward success with, in the case of math, confirmation of the right answer and the chance to move onto the next, harder step. It wound up looking like the love child of an electric typewriter and a Rolodex. It worked by shaping the learner incrementally toward more difficult levels of instruction.

You could find teaching machines going up to quite advanced levels in schools in the 1950s and '60s, but people largely recoiled at the idea of them, complaining that they were an insult to the students' humanity and would result in social isolation. Teachers feared they'd lose their jobs to the machines. *Time* called teaching machines "Orwellian." *Parents* magazine asked, "Is it 1984 already?" Skinner's lifework was to create environments and societal structures that help people function well with more encouragement, or "reinforcement," and less punishment. But popular media missed the whole point.

Skinner died in 1990, a decade shy of seeing the century that has given us digital technology in our pockets, on our wrists, and walls, and everywhere else. This has led to conditioning experiments on a mass scale. Not all of them with good results for us, for sure. Our screens and social media and the humans behind them have already taken us to some frightening places. We're in this technology for the quick rewards. After a stint in Italy with our family for a few months, I asked our American babysitter if she could imagine living abroad. "No," she said. "I'd miss two-day Prime shipping."

In 1993, the *New Yorker* ran a cartoon by Peter Steiner in which a dog sitting at a desk in front of a computer tells another dog, "On the Internet, nobody knows you're a dog." Thirty years on, I'm starting to think that the Internet really could be for dogs, because of its potential as a teaching tool, a potential that is dying to be harnessed by people who see how exciting and effective operant conditioning can be. In the scheme of things, online learning has only just been invented.

After the discovery of operant conditioning but before the iPhone, the Treat & Train was invented. It was developed by Dr. Sophia Yin, a veterinarian and applied animal behaviorist who pioneered teaching "Low Stress Handling" to pet professionals, training dogs using positive reinforcement to give consent and to use good dog training principles to make necessary handling be as pain free as possible.

In 2003, while she was doing research on her master's thesis on barking at University of California, Davis, The home electronics brand Sharper Image called her to ask if she would help them develop a machine that could translate barks. She thought about it and basically replied, "That's silly." It would make more sense to just help people learn how to decipher their dog's barking directly, no gadget needed. On her website in 2012, she explained what happened next:

> Unable to resist the idea of working with a company that could probably make any animal training device I conjured up, I went on, "But, how about these ideas instead?" Their product idea had to do with barking, since excessive barking is a huge problem for dog owners. The products available to deal with excessive barking all focused on punishment and, thus, came with a number of pitfalls or unwanted behavioral side effects. So, I suggested, "How about making a device that addresses the barking issue by rewarding quiet behavior and that's backed up by research to prove that it works?"

They said yes, and Yin did the research to set up a protocol on how to use a Treat & Train to reduce a dog's barking at the door, and the result is this funny beige device that I use every single day in my home. I was using it years before I realized there is a direct line from Skinner to this automated, remote-treat-delivery system, via Bob Bailey, who taught Yin chicken training, and to Karen Pryor, who consulted with her on the project.

I joke that I'm outsourcing some amount of a dog's love to this little robot. I may not always be around to feed you, Poppy, but this thing will.

I have rolled my eyes at a lot of gadgets geared to pet owners looking to part with their money: a "Smart Bed" that tracks weight, collars that count steps, and several Bluetooth treat-dispensing Treat & Train competitors. I've tested many of them, and most weren't effective for training. One spit out treats like a drive-by, freaking out both me and the dog. Another showed your face on a screen and spit out a single rice-cake–sized biscuit. Not useful if you're trying to reward a behavior more than once.

Doing something once isn't good practice.

That's important, because the key to getting better at anything is practice. It is so obvious as to seem almost not worth saying, but when you start thinking in terms of truly shaping a behavior, you see that you need to have behaviors happening a lot, and rewarded a lot, to really kick learning into gear. You want the hard stuff to be easy just because you've done it so many times.

If people give up on positive reinforcement–based methods, it's often because they're not getting in the kinds of reps good dog training needs. They're losing opportunities to teach their dogs, letting the dogs learn from whatever the environment has to offer to teach them instead. Using the kinds of cameras we now have available in our homes, and the creativity of countless people, I expect we are at the beginning of a dog training revolution. I think the ability to train dogs effectively at a distance using screens and AI is going to help people get the kind of drills they need to make training "stick," to speed up training and both enable and motivate dog owners to try more new and fun training things.

The web is also bringing dog owners into people's homes virtually. By making it possible for people to train with professionals without having to leave their homes, we are actually helping dogs learn in environments that may be a lot easier for them to handle, and we can also help them work on issues that would be situationally significantly different if a trainer were physically present.

In the last year, I've been excited to see others warming to the potential in this market. What if you could train your dog at home from your office during your work breaks? Or have your niece train your dog from another state? Or work remotely with an expert trainer who could give treats to your dog from the other side of the ocean? Or record yourself giving cues to lead your dog through a training session to play back to your dog when you're not there? Some companies are building gamelike elements into dog training apps, and sharing, to keep people motivated. Others are putting twenty-first-century teaching machines into shelters, with movement detectors that can reward the dog for, say, sitting. It's all coming, and this is a great thing.

Will trainers lose their jobs? No, in fact, trainers will be among the beneficiaries of these technologies. Skinner saw the potential for teaching machines to free teachers from overseeing rote drills, supporting them as big-picture shapers who bring creativity to the classroom, and outsourcing the drudgery. I think dog trainers can be brought in in the same way, creating training plans for students who will use the apps and machines to practice.

Maybe I'm overly optimistic. But if there's a hair of hope that the devices in our lives can do something good for us, I think one may be in the way they can help us help our dogs.

A Friend like Me

The other day I opened up the mail to find a yellowed 1971 issue of *Time* magazine I'd ordered. Its cover was by Don Punchatz, an illustrator best known for drawing science-fiction monsters—he's most famous for doing the cover art for the video game *Doom*. Here, his monster was Skinner. Punchatz painted him completely blue.

The story inside says that Skinner argues that man's behavior is already controlled by external influences, just too often the control is haphazard or not in people's best interest. "Skinner hopes for a society in which men of good will can work, love and live in security and in harmony," the article states. "Observing that society is already using such ineffective means of behavioral control as persuasion and conventional education, he insists that men of good will must adopt more effective techniques using them for 'good' purposes to keep despots from using them for 'bad' ones."

They weren't talking about dog training. But they could've been.

We can look inward to find ways to help the dogs in our lives, but not in the kind of made-for-reality-TV way that involves a cleansing of past demons leading to self-revelation. Rather, we can look at how we learn in order to try to understand how our dogs learn. And vice versa.

In the world we are governing for our dogs, we control most of the resources. This means we can do a lot to arrange their lives to help them succeed in our worlds. We can work to create environments where they can be offering behaviors that can be positively reinforced. You can build that world. There, you can live together in the sunshine of positive reinforcement. It might not be easy to do, but it's simple. That's good dog training. If you need help finding someone to help you structure this kind of world, you can always get some help from a teacher. At our school, we call them good dog trainers.

That same day that blue Skinner arrived in the mail, I took a nap and woke up to the sound of a familiar song coming from the living room, where the kids were watching TV. Someone singing about how he has magic that he's going to give to his "boss" or "master." He is dying to know if he can get his master anything. *Anything.* Baklava? I went into the living room to see Will Smith, shirtless and periwinkle. Two blue people in one day!

The Genie is bigger than Aladdin who he is serenading. We see him dressing Aladdin, feeding him, desperately trying to figure out what this human wants. The Genie is the servant, forced to live in a lamp. But he also has magic powers. Like we feel dogs have. Like they must think we have (see: can openers).

If some people prefer to live in the fog of canine mind reading and nonobjectifiable measurements of ill-defined things like "energy" rather than practice techniques backed with evidence and rooted in what we know about how learning works, maybe it is from a fear that these techniques can also be "used" on us. That fact would threaten our stature as the smartest beings on the planet! Boss! King! Shah! But wait, I thought I was the Genie. And the Genie is the one who *isn't* free.

If the Genie/Aladdin relationship feels familiar to me, maybe it's because of a confusion I see echoed in questions surrounding pet ownership in general. Who is serving whom? Dominates whom? Rescues whom?

I think questions like this tend to come up in situations governed by coercive forces.

When we are prioritizing the use of positive reinforcement, we don't need to ask them.

Control is reinforcing, which is why I think, when we get too involved in the quadrants that aren't positive reinforcement, we can get stuck there. Because punishment and negative reinforcement can still get results, especially if you're looking for a quick fix in a crisis.

But dogs come into our lives from a place of surplus. Pets are animals we don't eat. If my life is good enough to accommodate that, I want my dog and me to spend as much time as possible basking on the beaches of the warm and lovely positive reinforcement quadrant. Together.

The more time I spend thinking about our relationship with dogs, the more I see the fluidity of who is controlling whom, and how control can be graceful and good. But people still misunderstand how we can use a technology of behavior, even while they're being impacted by it. How many times have you looked at your phone today?

The Genie is all-powerful. He can both control and serve. When things are working well, we all get to be the Genie. There's no need to think about who is dominating or submitting, winning or losing. It feels like being in love.

A few years ago, a local artist I know who does mosaics on East Village lampposts made one on Saint Mark's Place, near School For The Dogs, that includes a picture of my beloved Amos, next to my favorite quote from Skinner: "What is love except another name for the use of positive reinforcement? Or vice versa."

I pass by it every time I walk to work. I never had a friend like him. Or vice versa.

Let's be friends with our dogs. Let's treat them with love. There's science in that lamp.

Rub rub.

Take the Good Dog Training Pledge

WHEN TRAINING A DOG, I PLEDGE TO DO ALL I CAN TO

✦ Consider what behaviors I can encourage using positive reinforcement and to help the dog in front of me live as comfortably and healthfully as possible in the human realm.

✦ Continually build my abilities to understand canine body language and do what I can to help dogs when they show signs of discomfort, before they feel the need to flee or become aggressive.

✦ Resist labels and untestable hypotheses about motivations when trying to address issues and instead be cognizant of antecedents and consequences that may be impacting behaviors.

✦ Create reinforcement-rich learning environments conducive to helping dogs learn without having to resort to force or coercion.

✦ Enrich dogs' lives by providing safe and appropriate exercise to maintain or improve their mental and physical health.

✦ Work to change problem behaviors using the least invasive procedures possible, considering possible adverse side effects, not just efficacy.

✦ Educate others about the existence of minimally intrusive, dog-friendly training methods, approaching all dog owners, like dogs, with empathy and patience.

SIGNED: _____ **DATE:** _____

JOIN THE MOVEMENT:
Submit your pledge at SchoolForTheDogs.com/Pledge.

Products

All the products listed below can be purchased at storeforthedogs.com.

FLIRT POLES

My favorite one is made by a company called SquishyFace. It has a replaceable lure that has a squeaker and comes in a couple sizes.

CRATES

The only crate we have ever sold at School For The Dogs is the Revol, which is made by NYC-based company Diggs. A winner of the Good Design Award, it folds easily and quietly and opens on multiple sides at once. I think it's the nicest crate on the market right now.

SINGLE INGREDIENT TREATS

Our go-to treat at School For The Dogs is freeze-dried lamb lung. It breaks up easily into very small pieces and isn't slimy or greasy. It's also made of just one thing—"single-ingredient" treats are a good idea for dogs who have sensitivities. We also often recommend Crumps Natural Mini Trainers—perfectly tiny cubes of beef liver.

LICKABLE TREATS

Treats that can be licked can go a long way toward acclimating dogs to new things and also to delivering treats without getting your hands dirty! We like using tubes like our Liquid Treat Dispensers with peanut butter, liverwurst or cream cheese or the prepackaged tubed treats by Bark Pouch.

KIBBLE BALLS

The Bob-a-Lot, the Wobbler, Twist-n-Treat, the Orbee, and the Gnawt-a-rock are all great toys.

KONG-STYLE TOYS

My favorite KONG-style toy is the Toppl. Made by Montana-based company West Paw, it is shaped like a large thimble with a wide-enough mouth to provide access to all the food in it. It also has a hole in the side, through which you can poke a bully stick or thread a zip tie and attach it to a crate.

SNUFFLE TOYS

Kay Rhee's beautiful mats, which she makes under the label DogNmat, are available at our shop and in our online shop. We also often recommend the Wooly, a bath mat–like toy that holds up well in the washing machine, and the equally sturdy Snuffle Bowl. Mats are a subcategory of snuffle toys. There are also nosework toys, which are plush toys that have spots in them that are meant to be hiding spots for treats.

PUZZLE TOYS

Thirty years ago, a Swedish dog owner named Nina Ottosson began crafting toys to keep her Bouvier des Flanders occupied while she was tending to her small children. She basically invented this category of toy. There are still only a handful of other companies making hard plastic or wood toys designed to have parts pushed or pulled in order to reveal food. Most of these toys can be modified so that they're easy for newbies or can be made more challenging for pros.

LICK MATS

Give your dog's tongue a fun time with products meant to be licked. It can be super soothing for them, and they're usable with wet food, peanut butter, and more. SodaPup and LickiMat are two companies that make these kinds of silicone plates with grooves, making them extra slurpable.

TRAINING POUCHES

A good training pouch is essential. The two I like to use most are silicone ones that will clip to my belt, or the handmade custom waist pouches we sell by California-based company Give A Dog A Home, which are made of sturdy Sunbrella fabric—like what awnings are made from—and have a French hinge that stays open and also easily pops closed.

LEASHES

I have found that a five-foot-long thin nylon leash works fine for most dogs in most situations. You want the leash to have a bend in it and not be something that is getting tugged on a lot or super heavy feeling for you or the dog. We carry the Mendota line of braided and woven nylon leashes at School For The Dogs. They make very thin ones that are great as drag lines for puppies to wear around the house, and also very long leads that are useful when hiking or in a field. But mostly we sell their five- or six-foot braided leashes with a sturdy snap clip at the end.

I also like wearing a leash around my waist, which leaves me with two hands for delivering treats. My go-to hands-free leash is a double-ended nylon rope leash by Found My Animal.

HARNESSES AND COLLARS

We sell a lot of front-clip harnesses at School For The Dogs, mostly made by the company 2 Hounds Design. They also have a back clip, and you can attach the leash to one or both spots. A front-clip harness can reduce a dog's pulling. If you don't have a pulling dog, a back-clip harness can be fine, or a flat collar. Amos often wore a simple nylon back-clip harness, and Poppy usually wears a martingale collar, which has a nylon loop that allows it a little give and will tighten enough so as not to go over her head if she was trying to pull herself out of it (but that has never been a concern!).

TRAINING SPOTS

The KLIMB is a nice raised platform, just high enough off the ground to designate it as its own spot. It can be adjusted to be higher or lower with removable legs, and you can also stack them. If you are handy and have some wood and PVC pipe, you could probably make such a thing, and I've told myself I would do so many times, but in the end I just end up using a KLIMB. They're plastic so they're easy to wipe off and lightweight enough to toss into the back of a car.

CLICKERS

There are pretty much three types of clickers I've worked with. Box clickers are plastic and rectangular with a piece of metal that you press down with your thumb, button clickers (sometimes called iClickers) have just a button you click that makes a noise thanks to some mysterious inner element, and "cricket" clickers are made of tin and make a sound that is softer than the others. I mostly use box clickers, but the cricket ones are nice because they slide into a pocket, and their gentle *click-clack* is better for dogs who are sound sensitive. The button ones are easier for some people to use—kids tend to prefer them. Occasions sometimes arise where it's not convenient for an animal trainer to use their hand in a training session, and, in those situations, the iClicker is there for you: it can be clicked with a toe or your chin or even your teeth.

TREAT DISPENSERS

We carry the Treat & Train at School For The Dogs. Alternatives that I like for some purposes include the Pet Tutor, which has some great features, like you can operate it with the sound of a clicker or with your voice, or you can put the remote in a toy and when the dog bangs the toy around, the device spits out treats. It also has a mode where it can shape your dog for not barking. And it can work with a larger variety of treat types and texture than the Treat & Train can. But the Treat & Train tends to be my preferred device as it's less expensive and easier to use out of the box. The same company that makes the Pet Tutor is now also making the Uno, which is a small 3D-printed device that can be attached to a crate and triggered from your phone. It's pretty cool.

Books

I've mentioned many books that have shaped me in this book, but they are not necessarily all good starting places when you have a new puppy or you are dealing with a specific problem with a dog. Here are some good reads if you fall into one of those categories.

PUPPY OWNERS

✦ *Perfect Pup in 7 Days* by Sophia Yin
✦ *The Puppy Primer* by Patricia McConnell
✦ *Puppy Start Right* by Debbie Martin and Kenneth Martin

SEPARATION ANXIETY

✦ *Separation Anxiety in Dogs* by Malena DeMartini

FEARFUL/REACTIVE

✦ *Click to Calm* by Emma Parsons
✦ *A Guide to Living With and Training a Fearful Dog* by Debbie Jacobs

Acknowledgments

It was more than six years ago when a client asked me, "Have you ever thought about writing a book?" Little did she know it was the *only* thing I thought about. I am hugely grateful to that client, Stephanie Higgs, for working closely with me on the proposal that led to this project and holding my hand ever since. Thank you so much, Stephanie, for helping me make this happen.

I am stupidly lucky to have such fantastic agents: David Halpern and Janet Oshiro. The best. I am sure I'm the luckiest wedding-announcement-writer-turned-dog-trainer in the world.

Erin McClary at Sourcebooks has a dog named Cheddar, and that right there makes her good people. Her enthusiasm about this book, and gentle touch with the red pen, make her *great* people. The opportunity to write for that kind of editor was a true gift.

School For The Dogs is a place where there are lots of wonderful dogs, but I think that's really because of all the wonderful humans on the other end of the leashes. Thank you to my cofounder, Kate Senisi, and to all the dog owners who have helped make it such a special place over the last decade-plus. Getting to know so many special people as they work to improve their dogs' lives has been a life-enriching experience. There's definitely not enough room here to give a shout-out to even a fraction of our amazing clients, but I'll mention three: Alix Kriss, a client-turned-employee who (among other things!) encouraged me to start a podcast; and Davide Balula and Elise Mac Adam, both of whom have become good dog trainers themselves, and also were kind enough to read early drafts of this book and give feedback. My longtime friend Maria Skorobogatov also gave the book a much appreciated early read.

I can never give enough thanks to our staff: Erin Whelan, Adam Davis, Anna Ostroff, Em Beauprey, Sandra Griffith, and Doris Guzman have all been with us since before the pandemic, and they make School For The Dogs the place it is. I wish I could mention all of our incredible employees past and present, but I need to go walk the dog. So I'm going to pick just three, who happen to have been our first, second, and third employees: Libby Sills, Ilana Alderman, and Anamarie Johnson. I'm thrilled to call these bright people my friends. They all have tolerated me texting them random things regarding the book for years, and I hope to have the opportunity to bother them in some kind of way for the rest of my life.

Abie Sussman and Lucy Goetz are the best neighbors ever: They let me write this book in their apartment! My patrons!

Jesus Diaz suggested the book's title. I knew long ago that his impact on my life would be indelible in some way. It just took me a while to realize that his mark would literally be on the cover of my book.

Thanks to my best friend, Alex Pasternack, and to my family, in particular Vicki Morgan, Ralph Erenzo, Julie Hoffman, and David Fensterheim, who have done so many things through the years to help me and to help School For The Dogs become what it is. Thanks also to my uncle, David Grossman, for showing me early on in my life what it meant to love dogs like family.

I happen to have the world's best in-laws, Holly Pedicone and Alex Pedicone. Nana and Nono did lots of extra grandparenting—in four countries!—over a period of six months so I could write. Their generosity is extreme and inspiring. Rosario Hernandez, Aniger Manrique, Cristin Biscotto, Molly Jewett, and Cathleen Dullahan helped take care of my girls so I could write, and I'm grateful for how much love they brought to the job.

Lastly, thanks to my husband, Jason Pedicone, a true partner to me in so many ways. He has helped me build a life full of positive reinforcement: another word for love, indeed.

Notes

Preface

"I think at some level": John Cleese, *So Anyway* (London: Arrow Books, 2015), 67.

Introduction: Aliens Among Us

Two life forms: *Seinfeld*, "The Dog," Castle Rock Entertainment, 1991.

Euthanized dogs: Anna Protopopova and Linda M. Gunter, "Adoption and Relinquishment Interventions at the Animal Shelter: A Review," *Animal Welfare* 26, no. 1 (2017): 35–48.

Chapter 1: People Are Weird with Dogs

"We were making the future": H. G. Wells, *The Sleeper Awakes* (New York: Penguin Classics, 2005), 137.

"To make a dog sit": "BBC—I Love 1980—Barbara Woodhouse 'Training Dogs,'" nuttysteve80, October 10, 2013, Youtube video, 14:57, https://www.youtube.com/watch?v=K-Di2COwNT8.

"Throwing a verbal rock": Monks of New Skete, *How to Be Your Dog's Best Friend* (Boston: Brown, Little, 1978), 48.

Chapter 2: Let's Stop Whispering

"We live in a society": Carl Sagan, *Broca's Brain: Reflections on the Romance of Science* (New York: Random House, 1979), 12.

Bureau of Labor Statistics estimated: Henry Kasper, phone interview with the author, December 2007.

Part of my story: Anna Jane Grossman, "A Chorus of Dog Whisperers," *New York Times*, December 27, 2007, https://www.nytimes.com/2007 /12/27/fashion/27DOGS.html.

"You are putting the legitimate": Parvene Farhoody, email interview with the author, December 2007.

Episode One of *The Dog Whisperer*: *Dog Whisperer with Cesar Millan*, "Power of the Pack," video, National Geographic Channel, aired September 13, 2004, on Disney Plus.

"Hand as Mouth" in 57 percent of episodes: Cesar Millan, *Cesar's Rules: Your Way to Train a Well-Behaved Dog* (New York: Three Rivers Press, 2010), 98.

Allegory of the cave: Plato, *Republic*, trans. G. R. F. Ferrari, ed. Tom Griffith (Cambridge University Press, 2000), Book VII, b. 510a–520a.

Luescher's letter to *National Geographic*: Email correspondence with the author, April 4, 2023.

Ken's trained butterflies: Ken Ramirez, "The Butterfly Project," Karen Pryor Clicker Training, May 27, 2015, https://www.clickertraining.com /the-butterfly-project.

Ilana's trained fish: Born to Behave, "Erasmus the Clicker-Trained Fish," YouTube video, 1:24, May 10, 2013, https://www.youtube.com /watch?v=d-qwM5E6n5Q.

Chapter 3: Dog Training Science Deniers

"The amount of totally unnecessary interference": J. R. Ackerley, *My Dog Tulip* (New York: New York Review of Books, 1999), 174.

Swiss Zoo wolf studies: R. Schenkel, "Expression Studies on Wolves: Captivity Observations," 1946, accessed March 28, 2023, https://archive .org/details/SchenkelCaptiveWolfStudy.compressed.

Book that perpetuated "alpha" label: L. David Mech, *The Wolf: Ecology and Behavior of an Endangered Species* (Minneapolis: University of Minnesota Press, 2007), 69.

"Much is outdated": David Mech, "Wolf News and Information," accessed March 22, 2023, https://davemech.org/wolf-news-and-information/.

Twenty-three million dogs: ASPCA, "New ASPCA Survey Shows Overwhelming Majority of Dogs and Cats Acquired During Pandemic Will Stay in Their Forever Homes," May 26, 2021, https://www.aspca.org/about-us/press-releases/new-aspca-survey-shows-overwhelming-majority-dogs-and-cats-acquired-during.

Chapter 4: What We Have in Common

"The difference in mind": Charles Darwin, *The Descent of Man* (New York: Penguin Classics, 2004), 98.

Nearly 99 percent of all species: L. Scott Mills, *Conservation of Wildlife Populations: Demography, Genetics, and Management* (Malden, MA: Blackwell Publishing, 2007), 11.

Natural selection of those least fearful of humans: Lee Alan Dugatkin and Lyudmila Trut, *How to Tame a Fox (and Build a Dog)* (Chicago: University of Chicago Press, 2017), 14.

Natural selection of those who came near our garbage: Raymond Coppinger and Lorna Coppinger, *Dogs* (Chicago: University of Chicago Press, 2001), 291, 61.

750 million dogs not in homes: Raymond Coppinger and Mark Feinstein, *How Dogs Work* (Chicago: University of Chicawgo Press, 2019), 25.

Breeding to change motor patterns: K. Lord, R. A. Schneider, and R. Coppinger, "Evolution of Working Dogs," in *The Domestic Dog: Its Evolution, Behavior and Interactions with People*, vol. 4 (Chicago: University of Chicago Press, 2016), 42–66.

On Descartes and the water machines: Psy vs. Psy, "René Descartes: Dualism, Reflexes, and Living Machines," YouTube video, 9:48, December 2, 2020, https://www.youtube.com/watch?v=f_Y4U0rHofc&t=.

Descartes on pain: René Descartes, "To Mesernne 11 June 1640," *The Philosophical Writings of Descartes*, vol. 3, trans. John Cottingham et al. (Cambridge: Cambridge University Press, 1991), 148.

Pavlov on Descartes: Ivan Petrovich Pavlov, *Conditioned Reflexes: An Investigation of the Physiological Activity of the Cerebral Cortex* (Oxford: Oxford University Press, 1927), 7.

"Why don't we make what we can observe": John B. Watson, *Behaviorism*, revised edition (Chicago: University of Chicago Press, 1930), 6, 111–112.

Chapter 5: Learning by Association

"That which I see in dogs": Daniel P. Todes, *Ivan Pavlov: A Russian Life in Science* (Oxford: Oxford University Press, 2014), 6.

Pavlov's work: Duane P. Schultz, *A History of Modern Psychology*, 10th ed. (Boston: Cengage Learning, 2012), 203.

Pavlov on "psychic secretions": I. P. Pavlov, *Conditioned Reflexes: An Investigation of the Activity of the Cerebral Cortex*, trans. G. V. Anrep (New York: Dover, 1960), 6.

Pavlov didn't use a bell: Daniel P. Todes and Ivan Pavlov, *A Russian Life in Science* (Oxford: Oxford University Press, 2014), 1.

On anticipatory behavior: B. M. Spruijt, R. Van den Bos, and F. T. Pijlman, "A Concept of Welfare Based on Reward Evaluating Mechanisms in the Brain: Anticipatory Behaviour as an Indicator for the State of Reward Systems," *Applied Animal Behaviour Science* 72, no. 2 (2001): 145–171.

Puppy development and receptivity: T. J. Howell, T. King, and P. C.

Bennett, "Puppy Development and Receptivity: Puppy Parties and Beyond: The Role of Early Age Socialization Practices on Adult Dog Behavior," *Veterinary Medicine: Research and Reports* 6 (2015): 143–153.

Chapter 6: Fear and Counterconditioning

"I think that if you whipped a dog": René Descartes to Marin Mersenne, March 18, 1630, in *Selected Correspondence of Descartes*, ed. Jonathan Bennett (Indianapolis: Hackett Publishing Company, 1988), 34.

The Little Albert study: John B. Watson and Rosalie Rayner, "Conditioned Emotional Reactions," *Journal of Experimental Psychology* 3, no. 1 (1920).

Archival footage of the experiment: "Little Albert Experiment," Wikipedia, June 20, 2023, https://en.wikipedia.org/wiki/Little _Albert_experiment.

"The behavior of man": John B. Watson, "Psychology as the Behaviorist Views It," *Psychological Review* 20 (1913): 158.

"The bad beep beeps": Psy vs. Psy, "What Is Sensitization?" YouTube video, 5:44, January 31, 2020. https://www.youtube.com /watch?v=Ns3U6nFka9c.

Chapter 7: Come and Drop It

"Machines that love:" Roger Grenier, *The Difficulty of Being a Dog* (Chicago: University of Chicago Press, 2011), 65.

The Parable of the Prodigal Son: *The Holy Bible, New International Version* (Grand Rapids, MI: Zondervan, 2011), Luke 15:11–32.

Leslie Hawke's wedding announcement: Anna Jane Grossman, "Leslie Hawke and David Weiss Vows," *New York Times*, January 20, 2012, https://www.nytimes.com/2012/01/22/fashion/weddings/leslie -hawke-and-david-weiss-vows.html.

On Hawke's success in Romania: Kit Gillet, "Leslie Hawke Helps Roma Children Get an Education," *Christian Science Monitor*, January 10, 2014, https://www.csmonitor.com/World/Making-a-difference/2014/0110/Leslie-Hawke-helps-Roma-children-get-an-education.

Chapter 8: If This, Then That

"Learning is connecting": Edward Thorndike, *Human Learning* (New York: Appleton, 1931), 122.

On Thorndike's work with cats: Duane P. Schultz, *A History of Modern Psychology*, 10th ed. (Boston: Cengage Learning, 2012), 197–200.

The Law of Effect: Edward Thorndike, *Animal Intelligence: Experimental Studies* (New York: Macmillan, 1898), 244.

On phrenology and other branches of psychology: Schultz, *History of Modern Psychology*, 50, 166.

On reading H.G. Wells writing about Pavlov: B. F. Skinner, *Particulars of My Life* (New York: Knopf, 1976), 300.

"At first one throws things": Skinner, *Particulars*, 300.

"At first one throws things": B. F. Skinner, *The Shaping of a Behaviorist* (New York: Knopf, 1979), 95.

Chapter 9: Negative Reinforcement

"Admitting the need": Murray Sidman, *Coercion and Its Fallout* (Boston: Authors Cooperative, 1989), 209.

Darwin and planaria: Charles Darwin, "Brief Descriptions of Several Terrestrial Planariae and of Some Remarkable Marine Species, with an Account of Their Habits," *Annals and Magazine of Natural History*, vol. 14 (1844).

"Share your affection": Cesar Millan, *Cesar's Way: The Natural, Everyday Guide to Understanding and Correcting Common Dog Problems* (New York: Three Rivers Press, 2006), 234.

Three shock levels: education, interrupter, reinforcement: Marc Goldberg and The Monks of New Skete, *The Art of Training Your Dog: How to Gently Teach Good Behavior Using an E-Collar* (Countryman Press, 2020), 133–134.

Chapter 10: Punishment

"From the time of Plutarch…": B. F. Skinner, *Notebooks* (New York: Harper & Row, 1980), 154.

"It could be something they love": R. Ruddell Weatherwax, *Training Your Dog the Weatherwax Way: The Complete Guide to Selecting, Raising, and Caring for Your Canine* (New York: Skyhorse, 2021), 83.

"I never saw anybody…": Jon Provost, Zoom interview with the author, June 2020.

"Bang open the door…": Rudd Weatherwax, *The Lassie Method: Raising & Training Your Dog with Patience, Firmness & Love* (Racine, WI: Western Publishing Company, 1971), 90.

Beth Berkobien anecdote: Beth Berkobien, Zoom interview with the author, June 2022.

Chapter 11: Positive Reinforcement

"To people schooled": Karen Pryor, *Don't Shoot the Dog!: The New Art of Teaching and Training* (New York: Bantam Books, 1985), 14.

"Those were Bob's": Parvene Farhoody, in-person conversation with the author, July 2016.

"Simple but not easy": Bob Bailey, "Suggestions for Better Training." Behavior1.com, accessed March 30, 2023, http://www.behavior1.com /page9.html.

Bob Bailey quotes: Bob Bailey, Zoom interview with the author, May 2021.

"Our biggest contribution…": CAAWT, "Marian Breland Bailey | The Bailey Interviews," YouTube video, 1:53, 2021, https://www.youtube.com/watch?v=0KHC8zZPeCE.

History of Animal Behavior Enterprises: Robert E. Bailey and J. Arthur Gillaspy Jr., "Operant Psychology Goes to the Fair: Marian and Keller Breland in the Popular Press, 1947–1966," *Behavior Analyst*, 28, no. 2 (2005): 143–159, https://doi.org/10.1007/BF03392110.

National Humane Review: National Humane Review, "Marian Breland Bailey: A Pioneer in the History of Applied Animal Psychology," Animal Behavioral Enterprise (Arkansas: Henderson State University, n.d.), https://www.hsu.edu/uploads/pages/199-0afmarian_breland_bailey.pdf.

Misbehavior of Organisms: Keller Breland and Marian Breland Bailey, "The Misbehavior of Organisms," *American Psychologist*, no. 16 (1961): 681–684.

"I think trainers philosophically…": Cesar Millan, *Cesar's Rules: Your Way to Train a Well-Behaved Dog* (New York: Three Rivers Press, 2010), 107.

Chapter 12: Getting Rid of Behaviors without Using Punishment

"Nothing happens…": Samuel Beckett, *Waiting for Godot* (New York: Grove Press, 1954), 5.

Clean Car Program: Maryalice Sloan-Howitt and George L. Kelling, "Subway Graffiti in New York City: 'Gettin' Up' vs. 'Meanin' It and Cleanin' It," *Security Journal* 1, no. 3 (1990): 131.

"He would jump over and over…": Jason Pedicone, conversation with the author, November 2018.

"The only way to eliminate…": Murray Sidman, *Coercion and Its Fallout* (Boston: Authors Cooperative, 1989), 251.

Karen Pryor's punishment alternatives: Karen Pryor, *Don't Shoot the*

Dog!: The New Art of Teaching and Training (New York: Bantam Books, 1985), 107–158.

Chapter 13: Dog Language, Part One

"The dog has seldom…": James Thurber, *Writings and Drawings* (New York: Library of America, 1996), 801.

Dog bite statistics: American Veterinary Medical Association, "Dog Bite Prevention," 2023, https://www.avma.org/resources-tools/pet-owners /dog-bite-prevention.

"The Sound Machine": Roald Dahl, "The Sound Machine," *New Yorker*, September 17, 1949, 32–41.

"You start to see these little moments of misery": Kiki Yablon, Zoom call with the author, July 2021.

The Holly episode: *Dog Whisperer with Cesar Millan*, "Cesar's Worst Bite," video, National Geographic Channel, aired September 15, 2012, on Disney Plus.

YouTube clip of Holly episode: "Showdown with Holly," YouTube video, 3:00, September 13, 2012, https://www.youtube.com/watch?v =9ihXq_WwiWM.

Chapter 14: Dog Language, Part Two

"A dog teaches a boy": Robert Benchley, *Chips off the Old Benchley* (New York: Doubleday and Company, 1949), 94.

Play and morality research: Lee Dugatkin and Marc Bekoff, "Play and the Evolution of Fairness: A Game Theory Model." *Behavioural Processes* 60, no. 3 (February 1, 2003): 209–214, https://doi.org/ 10.1016 /S0376–6357(02)00120–1.

Surplus Resource Theory: Jeremy David Auerbach, Andrew R. Kanarek, and Gordon M. Burghardt, "To Play or Not to Play? That's a Resource

Abundance Question," *Faculty Publications and Other Works—Ecology and Evolutionary Biology* (2015), https://trace.tennessee.edu/utk_ecolpubs/69.

Research on "rapid mimicry": Elisabetta Palagi, Velia Nicotra, and Giada Cordoni. "Rapid Mimicry and Emotional Contagion in Domestic Dogs," *Royal Society Open Science* 4, no. 12 (December 2015): 150–155, https://doi.org/10.1098/rsos.150505.

In 2015, a company called TailTalk: Ellie Zolfagharifard, "What Does Your Dog's Tail Wag Mean? Emotional Sensor Could Help Owners Understand Their Pet's Feelings," *Daily Mail*, October 6, 2015, https://www.dailymail.co.uk/sciencetech/article-3262311/What-dog-s-tail-wags-mean-Emotional-sensor-help-owners-understand-pet-s-feelings.html.

On tail-wag studies: Rebecca Morelle, "Scientists Decipher Dog-Tail Wags," BBC News, October 31, 2013, https://www.bbc.com/news/science-environment-24746107.

Chapter 15: The Training Triad: Good Management

"No punishment": Hannah Arendt, *Reflections on Violence* (New York: Harcourt, Brace & World, 1969), 51.

"I have come across people": Annie Grossman, "Being the Baby in the Box: B.F. Skinner's Daughter Dispels the Myths," School For The Dogs. April 20, 2018, https://www.schoolforthedogs.com/being-the-baby-in-the-box-bf-skinners-daughter-dispels-the-myths/.

Ladies' Home Journal: B.F. Skinner, "Baby in a Box; The Mechanical Baby-Tender," *Ladies' Home Journal* 62 (1945): 30–31, 135–136, 138.

Economists on retirement: Bapu Jena, "How Does Retirement Affect Your Brain?" *Freakonomics*, December 23, 2021https://freakonomics.com/podcast/how-does-retirement-affect-your-brain/.

"Cutting-edge behavioral therapy": Tad Friend, "It's a Jungle in Here," *New York* magazine, April 24, 1995.

"We gave him puzzles": Ferdie Yau, in-person interview with author, February 2020.

History of the KONG: KONG Company, "The KONG Story: Necessity and Love," 2023, https://www.kongcompany.com/company/.

Fifty million KONGs sold: Dun & Bradstreet, "The Kong Company LLC," accessed March 31, 2023, https://www.dnb.com/business -directory/company-profiles.the_kong_company_llc.071bd2d06e d9fa2e17671149e813e1d2.html.

Our best seller: School For The Dogs Podcast, "How to Make Sure Your Dog Never Swallows a Bully Stick: Expert Advice from Vaso Karras, the Inventor of the Bully Grip," episode 116, podcast audio, 52:32, October 14, 2021, https://www.schoolforthedogs .com/podcasts/episode-116-how-to-make-sure-your-dog-never -swallows-a-bully-stick-expert-advice-from-vaso-karras-the -inventor-of-the-bully-grip/.

Nancy Kearns's rawhide tips: Nancy Kearns, "Finding the Right Rawhide Chew for Your Dog," *Whole Dog Journal*, April 17, 2009, https://www.whole-dog-journal.com/care/finding-the-right-rawhide -chew-for-your-dog/.

"The child's parents": Desmond Morris, *The Human Zoo* (New York: Dell Publishing, 1969), 181.

Chapter 16: The Training Triad: Good Rewards

"Does the employee": B. B. Nelson, *1501 Ways to Reward Employees* (New York: Workman Publishing Company, 2012), 25.

Mary Poppins: *Mary Poppins*, directed by Robert Stevenson (1964; Burbank, CA: Walt Disney Productions, 2000), DVD.

The Sound of Music: *The Sound of Music*, directed by Robert Wise (1965; Los Angeles, CA: Twentieth Century Fox, 2000), DVD.

"I've come to believe": Kathy Sdao, *Plenty in Life Is Free* (Wenatchee, WA: Dogwise Publishing, 2012), 8.

"Ordinary days": P. L. Travers, *Mary Poppins* (New York: Harcourt, Brace and Company, 1997), 124.

The late great dog trainer: Sophia Yin, *How to Behave So Your Dog Behaves* (Neptune City, NJ: TFH Publications, 2004), 112.

"Hernstein's 1961 research": R. J. Herrnstein, "Relative and Absolute Strength of Response as a Function of Frequency of Reinforcement," *Journal of the Experimental Analysis of Behavior* 4 (1961): 267–272.

Madonna's NFT: Misyrlena Egkolfopoulou, "Madonna Jumps into NFTs with $570,000 Digital Monkey Image," Bloomberg, March 25, 2022, https://www.bloomberg.com/news/articles/2022-03-25/madonna-jumps-into-nfts-with-570–000-digital-monkey-image.

Chapter 17: The Training Triad: Good Timing

"Man is a biological organism": B. F. Skinner, *Beyond Freedom and Dignity* (New York: Knopf, 1971), 10.

"There better be more": *My Super Sweet 16*, "Superstitious Sweet Sixteen," MTV, March 8, 2009.

"Good, good": Dr. Martin Levy, in-person interview with author, October 28, 2022.

"Here was an elegant set": Karen Pryor, *Reaching the Animal Mind: Clicker Training and What It Teaches Us About All Animals* (New York: Scribner, 2010), 21.

"This book is about how to…": Karen Pryor, *Don't Shoot the Dog!: The New Art of Teaching and Training* (New York: Bantam, 1985), 11.

"For 30 years": Karen Pryor, "Historical Perspectives: A Dolphin Journey," *Aquatic Mammals* 40, no. 1 (2014): 104–115, https://doi.org/10.1578/AM.40.1.2014.104.

Will Ferrell on *Conan*: Team Coco, "Will Ferrell's Amazing Canine Obstacle Course Demo | CONAN on TBS," YouTube video, 3:45, March 22, 2012, https://www.youtube.com/watch?v=FuKa07Hsmu4.

Chapter 18: Capturing Good

"A student should indeed...": Quintilian, *Institutio Oratoria*, first century CE.

Smart-50: Kathy Sdao, *Plenty in Life Is Free* (Wenatchee, WA: Dogwise Publishing, 2012), 48.

A company called Joipaw: Haje Jan Kamps, "Joipaw Raises $2M for Video Games for Dogs," *TechCrunch*, November 3, 2022, https://techcrunch.com/2022/11/03/joipaw-video-games-for-dogs/.

Chapter 19: Good Cueing

"The social organization of dogs...": B.F. Skinner, *About Behaviorism* (New York: Knopf, 1974), 116.

"Has succeeded in training...": Edward T. Heyn, "Berlin's Wonderful Horse," *New York Times*, September 4, 1904.

Debunking Clever Hans: Oskar Pfunst, *Clever Hans (The Horse of Mr. Von Osten)* (New York: Henry Holtand Company, 1911), 88–101.

The Bucket Game: Chirag Patel, "The Bucket Game Introduction Part 1 720p," YouTube video, 2:36, December 4, 2015, https://www.youtube.com/watch?v=GJSs9eqi2r8.

Chapter 20: Good Chaining, Generalizing, and Shaping

"There had been altogether too much of ME...": J. Allen Boone, *Kinship with All Life* (New York: HarperOne, 1976), 53.

Michele Pouliot and Listo: keikocdf, "Listo and Michele in 'SMILE,'" YouTube video, 4:34, July 14, 2014, https://www.youtube.com /watch?v=iUt2OKnmfjI.

Michele Pouliot biography: Michele Pouliot, "Michele Pouliot Bio," accessed April 1, 2023, https://www.michelepouliot.com/.

"What we know of other people": T. S. Eliot, *The Cocktail Party* (New York: Harcourt, Brace and Company, 1950), 71–72.

"One day we decided...": Gail B. Peterson, "A Day of Great Illumination: B.F. Skinner's Discovery of Shaping," *Journal of the Experimental Analysis of Behavior* 82, no. 3 (November 2004): 317–328.

The human shaping game: Karen Pryor, *Don't Shoot the Dog!: The New Art of Teaching and Training* (New York: Bantam Books, 1985), 66–71.

Ten Laws of Shaping: Pryor, *Don't Shoot the Dog*, 54–55.

"Rounds of munitions": David Hochman, "You'll Go Far, My Pet," *New York Times*, August 20, 2015, https://www.nytimes.com/2015/08/23 /fashion/pet-care-the-power-of-training-cats-and-dogs.html.

Karen Pryor calls this: Pryor, *Don't Shoot the Dog*, 64.

"Steps in shaping": Julie S. Vargas, *Behavior Analysis for Effective Teaching* (New York: Routledge, 2009), 184.

Chapter 21: The Least We Can Do

"The Good Life": B. F. Skinner, *Walden Two* (Indianapolis: Hackett Publishing Company, Inc., 2005), 259.

Seligman's studies: M. E. Seligman and S. F. Maier, "Failure to Escape Traumatic Shock," *Journal of Experimental Psychology* 74, no. 1 (1967): 1–9, https://doi.org/10.1037/h0024514.

Punishment's impact on dendritic spines: Ying Chen, Catherine M. Dubé, Cory J. Rice, and Tallie Z. Baram, "Rapid Loss of Dendritic Spines after Stress Involves Derangement of Spine Dynamics by

Corticotropin-Releasing Hormone," *Journal of Neuroscience* 28, no. 11 (2008): 2903–2911.

Seligman tried to undo the misery: Steven F. Maier and Martin E. P. Seligman, "Learned Helplessness at Fifty: Insights from Neuroscience," *Psychological Review* 123, no. 4 (2016): 349.

The Hope Circuit: Martin E. P. Seligman, *The Hope Circuit: A Psychologist's Journey from Helplessness to Optimism* (New York: PublicAffairs, 2018), 4–5.

"Think Oprah…": Cesar Millan, *Cesar's Way: The Natural, Everyday Guide to Understanding and Correcting Common Dog Problems* (New York: Three Rivers Press, 2006), 234.

Anamarie's study: Anamarie C. Johnson and Clive D. L. Wynne, "Training Dogs with Science or with Nature? An Exploration of Trainers' Word Use, Gender, and Certification Across Dog-Training Methods," *Anthrozoös* 36, no. 1 (2023): 35–51, https://doi.org/10.1080/08927936.2022.2062869.

Committee on the Rights of the Child: Committee on the Rights of the Child, UN, "General Comment No. 8 (2006): The Right of the Child to Protection from Corporal Punishment and or Cruel or Degrading Forms of Punishment (Articles 1, 28(2), and 37, inter alia) (CRC/C/GC/8)" (Geneva: United Nations, 2006).

APA article on spanking: Brendan L. Smith, "Spanking and Child Development: We Know Enough Now to Stop Hitting Our Children," *Monitor on Psychology* 43, no. 4 (April 2012): 60.

APA article on spanking: Smith, "Spanking," 60.

Chapter 22: The Future of Good Dog Training

"In light of what we know": B.F. Skinner, *Cumulative Record* (New York: Appleton-Century-Crofts, 1959), 182.

"Fake it till you make it": Cesar Millan, *Cesar's Way: The Natural, Everyday Guide to Understanding and Correcting Common Dog Problems* (New York: Three Rivers Press, 2006), 82.

Oprah and her cocker spaniels: Millan, *Cesar's Way*, 121–130.

On Skinner visiting daughter's school: Daniel W. Bjork, *B.F. Skinner: A Life* (Washington, DC: American Psychological Association, 1997), 171.

"Is it 1984…" and "Orwellian": M. B. Kreig, "What about Teaching Machines?" *Parents*, February 1961, 44–45, 76, 78, 80; Alexandra Rutherford, "B. F. Skinner's Technology of Behavior in American Life: From Consumer Culture to Counterculture," *Journal of the History of the Behavioral Sciences* 39, no. 1 (February 1, 2003): 1–23, https://doi.org/10.1002/jhbs.10090.

***New Yorker* cartoon:** Peter Steiner, "On the Internet No One Knows You're a Dog," *New Yorker*, July 5, 1993, 61.

"Unable to resist the idea": Sophia Yin, "The Research that Lead to the Treat & Train (aka Manners Minder)," June 28, 2012, https://web.archive.org/web/20160414132414/https://drsophiayin.com/blog/entry/the-research-that-lead-to-the-treattrain-aka-manners-minder/.

"Skinner hopes…": "Beyond Freedom and Dignity," *Time*, September 20, 1971.

Index

Index

Index

Index

About the Author

Photo © Blair Greene

Annie Grossman is the owner of School For The Dogs, which has been offering group classes and private lessons both virtually and in Manhattan's East Village since 2011. She also hosts the *How To Train Your Dog With Love + Science* podcast and runs the online store, storeforthedogs.com. She is the co-founder of Petcademy, a platform that provides affordable training to families rescuing shelter animals in order to reduce the likelihood of post-adoption returns.

Prior to becoming a professional dog person, she was a staff reporter at both the *New York Observer* and *New York Post*, an associate producer for Animal Planet's *Too Cute!*, and was nominated for an Emmy for her work as a writer for the game show *Cash Cab*. Annie is a graduate of the Karen Pryor Academy of Animal Training and Behavior and one of just six thousand dog trainers certified by the Certification Council of Professional Dog Trainers. She has been quoted as an expert in the field by the *New York Times*, the *New Yorker*, *New York* magazine, and the *Wall Street Journal*, among other publications.